CONTESTED

TASTES

PRINCETON STUDIES IN CULTURAL SOCIOLOGY
Paul J. DiMaggio, Michèle Lamont,
Robert J. Wuthnow, and Viviana A. Zelizer,
Series Editors

A list of titles in this series appears at the back of the book.

CONTESTED

TASTES

FOIE GRAS
and the
POLITICS OF FOOD

MICHAELA DESOUCEY

PRINCETON UNIVERSITY PRESS

PRINCETON AND OXFORD

Copyright © 2016 by Princeton University Press
Published by Princeton University Press, 41 William Street, Princeton, New Jersey 08540
In the United Kingdom: Princeton University Press, 6 Oxford Street, Woodstock, Oxfordshire OX20 1TW

press.princeton.edu
Jacket images courtesy of Shutterstock

ISBN 978-0-691-15493-0

Library of Congress Control Number: 2015956952

British Library Cataloging-in-Publication Data is available

This book has been composed in Adobe Caslon Pro and Berthold Akzidenz Grotesk

Printed on acid-free paper. ∞

Printed in the United States of America

1 3 5 7 9 10 8 6 4 2

CONTENTS

ACKNOWLEDGMENTS

I have many people to thank for their contributions to this book, and none deserve more credit than those who participated in my research in both France and the United States. A thousand thanks to the chefs, activists, farmers, politicians, journalists, and others who let me into their worlds and shared their knowledge, stories, and perspectives. While each might find some place to object to my analysis, I hope that the picture I have painted of the past decade's fights over foie gras is seen as a fair one and that my respect for all the players involved is clear.

Northwestern University's Department of Sociology was where this project was born and took shape, and where I began to grow as a sociologist. Gary Alan Fine has inspired and pushed my analytic abilities to new levels. His dedication and work ethic continue to be inspirational, if inimitable. I am also grateful to Wendy Griswold, Bruce Carruthers, Nicola Beisel, and Laura Beth Nielsen for constructive criticism and encouragement through the dissertation process and since. The late Allan Schnaiberg deserves a heartfelt thank-you for teaching me to be a compassionate and engaged scholar and educator. The Culture Workshop, the Ethnography Workshop, the Management and Organizations Department, and the Center for Legal Studies were all intellectual homes at Northwestern that merit particular acknowledgment.

Fellow graduate students at Northwestern created an exciting intellectual environment and have continued to provide the camaraderie needed to get through a process like this. Gratitude is due to Heather Schoenfeld, Gabrielle Ferrales, Lynn Gazley, Corey Fields, Kerry Dobransky, Erin McDonnell, Terry McDonnell, Jo-Ellen Pozner, Elisabeth Anderson, Berit Vannebo, Geoff Harkness, Ashlee Humphreys, Michelle Naffziger, Simona Giorgi, Marina Zaloznaya, Sara Soderstrom, and Nicole Van Cleve. Special thanks to Ellen Berrey, who has been a superb book-buddy these last few years and helped guide this project to completion. Elise Lipkowitz also deserves a particular note of my sincere appreciation and indebtedness here. Elise has been a travel partner, dining companion, sounding board, reader, copyeditor, analyst, and pillar of moral support. I could not have written this book without her.

In the two great years I spent as a postdoc at Princeton University in the Department of Sociology and the Center for the Study of Social Organization, this project benefited from the mentorship and advice of numerous scholars. Paul DiMaggio's interest in and encouragement of my work has been ongoing. Conversations with Viviana Zelizer, Martin Ruef, Bob Wuthnow, Kim Scheppele, Mitch Duneier, Miguel Centeno, Amin Ghaziani, and Sophie Meunier shaped this project in a host of positive ways. I lucked out in sharing an office with Sarah Thébaud and Adam Slez, who read and commented on proposals, memos, and early chapter drafts, as well as became great friends. I also benefited from insights and support from Miranda Waggoner, Liz Chiarello, and my writing group of Janet Vertesi, Grace Yukich, Kathryn Gin Lum, Manu Radhakrishnan, and Annie Blazer. Sarah and Miranda, especially, have been ongoing sounding boards after we each went our separate ways.

I wrote the final version of this manuscript at North Carolina State University, where smart and wonderful colleagues have offered fresh perspectives that allowed me to see beyond the boundaries of my initial work. Special thanks are due to Michael Schwalbe and Sarah Bowen for helping me, with their constructively critical eyes, to revise the final manuscript after receiving my reviewer comments.

A number of other friends and colleagues have also given me invaluable advice and feedback along the way. Writing is a truly collaborative enterprise. This book is better because of what I have learned from (in no particular order): Kim Ebert, Sinikka Elliott, Jeff Leiter, Tom Shriver, David Schleifer, Liz Cherry, Colter Ellis, Isabelle Téchoueyres, Rich

Ocejo, Brendan Nyhan, Lauren Rivera, Christopher Bail, David Meyer, Daphne Demetry, Jordan Colosi, Alice Julier, Krishnendu Ray, Rachel Laudan, Anne McBride, Christy Shields-Argèles, Robin Wagner-Pacifici, Andy Perrin, Josée Johnston, Joslyn Brenton, Diana Mincyte, Rhys Williams, Ken Albala, Warren Belasco, Cathy Kaufman, Robin Dodsworth, Kate Keleman, Klaus Weber, Kate Heinze, Paul Hirsch, Brayden King, and many others. I hope the final result is a tribute to their work on my behalf.

Some of the research for this book would have not happened without Mark Caro. Mark and I met at a food conference in 2007 and, as perhaps the two most foie-obsessed writers in Chicago, quickly realized we would benefit by working together. He was a delightful research partner, both in Chicago and France, and his research for his own book (*The Foie Gras Wars*) was enormously useful to me. He is also great at pushing stuck Volvos out of country-road ditches.

I could not have found a better home for this book than with Princeton University Press. I am lucky to have had not one, but two excellent editors there. Eric Schwartz saw the book's potential and guided me through the process of constructing the first draft, and became a friend as well as an editor during the process. Eric secured two incredible reviewers for the manuscript, both of whom read carefully and thoughtfully, and my book is better for their detailed comments and inquiries. When he left the Press, I was apprehensive, but Meagan Levinson quickly took away any fears. She is the editor that first-time authors dream about, for her intelligence and good humor, her sharp insights, the time she has spent with my manuscript, and her genuine ability to see both details and the big picture at the same time. Ryan Mulligan has similarly been a pleasure to work with. I am also the beneficiary of wonderful production management by Ellen Foos, copyediting by Katherine Harper, and indexing by Jan Williams.

Heartfelt and loving thanks are also due to the family and close friends who supported me through this long project. First are my mom and dad—Carolyn and Bob DeSoucey—and my brother, David, and sister, Arielle. My late grandparents, Milton and Matilda Block, provided inspiration and made things possible. Anya Freiman Goldey and Valerie Lisner Smith have long been like my sisters; I am grateful for their true friendship, and I consider their families my own. I also thank Abby and Bob Millhauser for welcoming me into their family, and for clipping articles and taking photos of menus on their travels to add to my collection. My adopted family at Kinnikinnick Farm—David and Susan Cleverdon, Erin and Kevin Grace, and Staci and Tim Oien—has long provided me a special, nourishing, and safe haven.

Lastly, this book would not have been possible if not for John Millhauser, my most favorite collaborator and partner in all things. He has been an unwavering source of encouragement, smarts, advice, inspiration, and love. His influence is evident on every single page. Our son, Jasper Millhauser, is the light of my life. He is hilarious, smart, beautiful, and brings me more joy than I could have ever fathomed. He is also excited to know that I am writing a book that has his name in it. It is to these two Millhauser boys that I am most grateful.

My fascination with foie gras began as a bystander. In March 2005, a front-page article appeared in the *Chicago Tribune*, detailing harsh words exchanged between two of Chicago's star chefs, Charlie Trotter and Rick Tramonto. The chefs were wrangling over Trotter's earlier decision to stop serving foie gras at his eponymous restaurant after having done so for years, ostensibly because of the way it is produced. Foie gras is the liver of a duck or goose that has been specially fattened by force-feeding, and it is simultaneously considered a distinctive and delicious ingredient in gourmet cuisine and the product of a cruel and unethical practice. In the article, Tramonto called Trotter's decision hypocritical, because he still served other animal products, while Trotter derided Tramonto as "not the smartest guy on the block" and suggested cooking his "fat enough" liver. The exchange quickly became a lightning rod in the city's politics of food.

At the time, I was volunteering on Saturday mornings at a Chicago-area farmers market, hawking produce for a local organic farm. This market was a popular venue for area chefs to socialize while shopping for their restaurants' weekend offerings. Some were aghast at the spat, saying that chef-friends from around the country were calling them and asking, "What's up with Chicago?" Others found it somewhat humorous because they knew Trotter and Tramonto personally or had worked in their kitchens at some point. A few bristled defensively when I asked about their opinions on foie gras. Some were aware of the animal rights campaign that had led to a legal ban on foie gras's production and sale in California the previous year.

While I was personally and professionally interested in the culture and politics of food, I barely knew what foie gras was. If I had ever tried it, I did not remember. My graduate student budget did not allow me to eat at upscale restaurants, where foie gras is most commonly served, and it was not available at most American grocery stores. The following week (unrelated to the article's timing), I visited my sister, at the time a college student studying abroad in France. In different cities around the country, I noted foie gras's almost ubiquitous presence at restaurants and shops small and large. I asked my sister's French friends about it, and I brought several small cans back as gifts. While I was there, the *Tribune* was inundated with letters and online comments on the Trotter-Tramonto quarrel. The newspaper published a follow-up article by the same journalist, preventing the story from fading into the ether. Frenzied debates over foie gras's ethics dominated online culinary and chef-related discussion-boards such as eGullet and Chowhound. Upon my return, I gave one of the cans to my advisor at Northwestern University, Gary Alan Fine, with whom I'd been discussing the article. Gary took the can in his hand, looked at it and then at me, and said, "You know, this would make a fabulous project."

As is often the case, he was right.

I quickly began to see that debates over foie gras are so much more fierce and complex—and sociologically compelling—than a war of words between two hot-tempered chefs. A bit of digging revealed impassioned battles erupting in the United States, France, and elsewhere. These clashes exemplify what I am calling *gastropolitics*—conflicts over food that are located at the intersections of social movements, cultural markets, and state regulation. The term purposefully evokes "gastronomy"—a word that itself doubly refers to the study and practice of culinary excellence as well as to cooking styles that are specific to places, cultural backgrounds, or groups of people. Gastronomy is about identity, and it is about food or cuisine that is socially distinct in some way—in other words, it is about tastes for foods that people venerate or, alternatively, vilify. Gastropolitics permeates the spaces, rhetorics, trends, and social institutions that anchor episodes of contestation over food objects and culinary practices. Such episodes are situated in time and place, which can lead to very different outcomes in different social contexts. Gastropolitics can also be quite divisive: as I have found, food consumption can quite literally create bonds or erect barriers between people.

I was not the only person inspired by the *Tribune* article. A few weeks after the story first appeared, a populist Chicago alderman introduced a bill in the City Council calling for a ban on selling foie gras in the city's restaurants. As I detail in chapter 4, the ban passed in 2006 but was repealed two years later following sustained lobbying from activists on both sides, the filing of several lawsuits, resistance from some chefs and diners, and amused derision from local and national media outlets. This ban's trajectory offers a prime example of the multivocal interests behind competing ideas of "good" food, as well as how different parties identified their "allies" and "enemies" and acted to promote what they deemed to be in the public interest.

Foie gras has sparked consternation and activism around the country and the world. In the United States, even though it is a niche industry (worth a relatively small $25 million), few issues within today's world of food politics have proven more fraught. California passed its 2004 production and sale ban on foie gras after a few animal rights groups put it in their crosshairs. (The ban took effect in July 2012, shutting down the state's only producer, Sonoma Foie Gras, and was rescinded by a federal district court in January 2015.) At that time, a similar law was being discussed in New York State, where the country's other two foie gras farms, Hudson Valley Foie Gras and LaBelle Farms, are located. Legislators in a few other states had recently passed production bans, even though those states did not have any producers within their borders. Other cities were considering restaurant bans. Letters to the editor, celebrity testimonials, and the texts of the different legislative bills opposing foie gras production were filled with the language of morality and ethics: "human values," "civilized values," "American values." Several other countries—including Israel, Australia, and Britain—saw bans proposed, as well as protests, vandalism, and the harassment of chefs and shopkeepers. Ducks were tugging at heartstrings in polarizing ways.

I was hooked. What was so significant about foie gras that people were protesting in the street, writing hate mail, contacting politicians, and even willing to break laws over it? How and why did duck liver, which seemed like such a marginal issue, turn into such a hotly contested and emotion-laden political symbol? I also wanted to know how the vilification of such a small but symbolically rich industry would affect the broader goals of animal rights and welfare movements. And how were people in France—by far the world's largest producer and consumer of foie gras—responding to these accusations of egregious cruelty?

Over the course of almost a decade, I've sought out answers to these questions, using the lenses of the sociology of culture and organizational theory, to study how and why certain foods become touchstones of moral and political contention, and how the outcomes of those processes can differ. Early on, I made the methodological choice to follow foie gras as a "cultural object" from its historicized origins to its modern industry and debated ethical status.[1] At the beginning, however, even basic information about foie gras was not easy to obtain. There were no books about it available at my university library, and academic journal articles were limited to veterinary reports on waterfowl liver chemistry. On Amazon.com, the only available English-language book on foie gras that offered more than recipes was *Foie Gras: A Passion*, published in 1999 and cowritten by one of the owners of Hudson Valley Foie Gras in New York State.

Searching for information on the Internet led to similarly limited results. Today, while there is more information online due to growing awareness of the controversies,[2] most of what is available still comes in the form of public relations materials from staunch advocates or opponents. Tourism and French producers' websites call foie gras a "traditional" and "authentic" food and depict ducks and geese residing in grassy fields or old-fashioned barns. The birds' lives are described as idyllic and the farmers as artisanal caretakers of a cherished, historic, and delicious tradition. These geese and ducks, the websites explain, are raised with care on small farms and will even run up to the farmers at feeding time. Photos of the feeding process depict kindly looking older women and men with weathered faces and callused hands, sometimes wearing berets, holding the birds firmly but tenderly between their legs as they feed them with a metal tube. Culinary and foodie websites, then and now, expound on foie gras's sought-after taste and creamy, unctuous texture, and typically feature photographs of beautifully prepared dishes on well-set dining tables.

Animal rights websites, on the other hand, pronounce foie gras farms to be torture factories. Photos on these sites show forlorn looking, filthy white ducks, some dead and others injured, stuck in lines of individually sized metal cages in dark, cavernous rooms. The few photos of feeders tend to show glowering, swarthy men huddling in pens of birds or leering at the camera. "Undercover" videos show human hands grabbing ducks' heads and thrusting metal tubes at their heads and in their beaks, or people literally throwing ducks around and slamming them on the ground. Somber voiceovers describe the lives of the ducks as unbearably horrific, using aggressive terminology such as "jamming," "shoving," and "torturing" to describe the feeding process. These sites also link foie gras with hardhearted elite consumption, calling it a "diseased" object of "gourmet cruelty" and a "delicacy of despair."

The gulf between these two polarized portrayals is a great one. It forced me to reflect on not just my own eating preferences, but what food choices others make that I am willing to tolerate. By virtue of the conflicts and critiques surrounding foie gras, I began to see it as a microcosm of the competing and layered social concerns that we have with food more generally. Each side in the debates over its production ethics offered morally potent, yet wholly incompatible, interpretations of the empirical "proof" of the process, all of which were laden with strident moral overtones. Of significance, I also found that most vocal defenders and detractors of foie gras do not set markets and morality in stark opposition to each other. Instead, they appeal to market actors in order to legitimize their moral arguments, and they seek legal and political strategies to turn those arguments into reality.

How, then, does one reconcile the disparate moral stances that have been taken in regard to foie gras? This question raises the issue of how we recognize, name, and interpret social problems, especially those related to the textures of consumer culture. To properly answer questions about a food's cultural value, we are necessarily challenged to consider the complexities of the social relations and spaces in which various groups struggle and compete to imprint their own particular tastes as legitimate. Thus, I had to go to the places where people were willing and eager to fight about it.

A combination of luck, persistence, social networks, and helpful strangers made it possible for me to collect data for this book. I knew I could not understand the interplay among culture, politics, and the market for foie gras without going to France, which I did in 2006 and 2007. I collected data in the United States primarily between 2005 and 2010 and continued to monitor developments and conduct additional interviews through 2015. Across the two countries, I spent time at more than a dozen farms and production facilities, at retail outlets, in restaurant kitchens and dining rooms, at activists' protests and meetings, and in the suit-filled antechambers of the Chicago City Council. I amassed news articles, press releases, ads, tourism guides, animal rights literature, court and legislative hearing transcripts, veterinary reports, photographs, and ephemera such as stickers, magnets, keychains, and even a small box of foie gras–flavored bubble gum. I spent time in the Bibliothèque Nationale in Paris researching the industry's history. Across both countries, I conducted eighty interviews and had many informal discussions with people working to produce, promote, defend, cook, oppose, or report on foie gras. (I also encountered a lot of ducks and geese.) From these myriad sources, I worked to tease out the nuances of different streams of action, resources, and motives.

I attempted to approach people on both sides of the issue, in both countries, in order to present them to the reader evenhandedly with equal vividness. Yet this proved challenging, for two key reasons. First, a number of people in the United States I wanted to interview—including Chef Charlie Trotter, the owner of LaBelle Farms, and the head of the Animal Protection and Rescue League—did not respond to my multiple requests. I was also unable to secure a visit to the now-defunct Sonoma Foie Gras. A number of chefs across the country replied (often via public relations managers) that they did not have time, or refused outright. As one told me by email, "Unfortunately, the topic of foie gras is so polarized, that anyone who goes on record does so at some risk." Others were instructed by their bosses or parent companies to withhold comments, even after I told them I would not use their names.

Luckily, I was not the only one interested in exploring the issue in greater depth. At a culinary conference in Chicago in the spring of 2007, I met Mark Caro, the journalist who had written the *Chicago Tribune* article that ignited the foie gras fracas there. It turned out that Mark was working on a book of his own (*The Foie Gras Wars*, published in 2009 by Simon & Schuster). Mark and I decided to team up, and we even conducted a joint research trip to France that fall. Through his position as a staff reporter for a major newspaper, Mark had terrific access to people I wished to know more about—not limited to the individuals mentioned above—and he shared some of his transcripts and notes with me. When attending events, visiting farms, and interviewing people together, he was "reporting" and I was "collecting data." We asked different types of questions and noticed different aspects of the same setting or event, and we fact-checked and idea-checked each other along the way. My work is better because of him.

Additionally, people in both countries wanted to embroil me more deeply in their own goals. I didn't realize the extent to which I would be questioned or tested by just about everyone I encountered. At restaurant protests in Chicago, for example, both restaurant employees and animal activists admonished me to "pick a side" and accused me of "fraternizing with the enemy." In one surprising moment, a person working in the gourmet food business asked me to give up my academic research and "go underground and infiltrate PETA" to figure out "what they were really up to." My field notes show that I spent a good deal of time bothered by moments like this, especially in the beginning.

It also became clear that my own consumption choices mattered for access to potential interviewees and what they would be willing to share with me. Many activists asked if I was a vegetarian and, when I said no, resisted my prepared questions and instead tried to convert me to veganism. Unfortunately, this happened often enough that I decided conducting further sit-down interviews with them would not be a fruitful use of my, or their, time. Instead, my analysis additionally relies on notes from Mark Caro, field notes from protests I observed, and their organizations' literature. One Chicago-based activist kept me abreast of related events and discussions on her group's electronic mailing list. I also gathered comments from key activists in the campaign that were published by other journalists and academic researchers, and on social media and online discussion boards.[3] As a consequence, the limits of my access to activists bounds my analysis of their candid voices.

Some French foie gras producers were also hesitant to meet or talk with me, or even tested me based on my identity. My status of "American" made more than a few people uneasy with my presence. One French woman I saw as a potential expert informant told our mutual acquaintance she would only meet with me if I "enjoyed eating foie gras." In several other instances, I had to eat meat or foie gras in front of people before they would speak openly with me. On two different occasions in on-site abattoirs at small farms in Southwest France, I was even given morsels of raw liver—"like raw cookie dough!"—nicked from freshly killed and butchered ducks to eat then and there in front of my informant. My realization that a committed vegetarian could not have done this research was confirmed by incidents like these. Foie gras was indubitably a sensitive and boundary-verifying issue.

Importantly, however, my goal from the get-go has not been to prove or refute foie gras's cruelty, or to adjudicate between its most strident challengers and defenders about who is in the right. Qualitative sociological methods are excellent for finding out why people perceive things as they do and give the accounts that they do, but they are not particularly well suited to answering normative questions about what we should or should not eat. I say this up front because the ways that foie gras's friends and foes utilize contradictory evidence and accuse each other of duplicitousness plausibly raises the question of who is right, or at least who is more accurate. To be honest, at the start I thought that if my sympathies fell anywhere, it would be on the side of the activists, based on the initial information I had gathered from news reports and websites. However, while I continue to value these groups' commitments to the animals that become food, and have succeeded in better understanding the philosophical bases of their movement, I found the overall issue to be more complicated than they have claimed it to be.

To reiterate, this book does not aim to make a normative argument about moral choices in the food system. It neither chronicles nor pro-scribes what people should or should not eat. Instead, it offers a socio-logical analysis of moral sentiments, talk, and tastes as they interact with rich and divisive symbolic politics. It brings the reader along on my journey into the world of foie gras in France and the United States, foregrounding the cultural contrasts of foie gras's gastropolitics. While I use the terms "American" and "French" and discuss how fights about cultural tastes are structured in part by national context, I also recognize the need to avoid essentialist categorizing. In both countries, foie gras has defenders and opponents, connoisseurs and critics. While this book is concerned with national differences, it is also concerned with varia-tions on cultural processes found within both nations. Still, to say that foie gras is a culinary rarity is true in the case of the United States but not in France, making the contrast a valuable one. The chapters that follow the introduction bring localized and detailed emphases to the study of how conflicts over symbols can create material outcomes, as well as unintended consequences. I aim to help readers understand who has been involved in these fights and what they feel is at stake, how polarizing moral sentiments influence culinary trends, and what hap-pens when cultural veneration and contempt collide.

Fueled by growing attention throughout popular culture, food pro-duction and consumption have become hot topics for scholars. People are passionate about food, both personally and professionally, and our food choices are evermore imbued with moral undertones. There are debates worth having about the ways our food system treats animals and what related practices should or should not be sanctioned by law. While I recognize that foie gras is a somewhat precarious place upon which to focus this much larger debate, it is also an especially rich case because of the ways it is constitutive of the contemporary world of food politics. By showing how this works in contrasting contexts, my study of foie gras contributes to a larger conversation.

As such, the questions this book addresses are not just about foodie delight, factory farm cruelty, or the proper place of tradition in the mod-ern world. They are also about the configurations of our social identities and the institutions that shape our consumption choices. How do we engage with each other over what signifies who we are? I hope that this book provides a compelling case of qualitative sociology—warts and all—that is interesting on its own merits and highlights the significance of food politics as a topic for sociological inquiry. I also hope it is one that expands our theories of symbolic politics to encompass how people come to understand what is, or is not, moral. As we learn from the case of foie gras, in both our culinary tastes and our political controversies over food, moralism is what makes one group's pleasure another's poison. Moral politics are at the basis of what we decide to eat, of the political economy of food production, of government regulation of food, and of civil society's efforts to influence the food system. Our preferences for some types of food and our disgust at others might seem like a matter of personal proclivities, but in fact they are often guided by our moral sentiments of right and wrong.

CONTESTED

TASTES

CHAPTER 1

What Can We Learn from Liver?

*I*n the summer of 2003, animal rights activists targeted the Santa Rosa, California home of Didier Jaubert, a French-born lawyer and entrepreneur, and his American wife, Leslie. Their house was splashed with red paint, the locks on the house and garage doors filled with glue, and "murderer" and "stop or be stopped" spray-painted on the house and car. Jaubert was a partner in a soon-to-open business venture called Sonoma Saveurs, a specialty shop and café, located in a historic adobe building on the plaza in downtown Sonoma. The café would feature a variety of locally made artisan food items, including foie gras. The day after the vandalism, an anonymous poster on an animal rights website called BiteBack wrote, "We cannot let this restaurant open . . . Jaubert needs to hear that people will not tolerate this atrocity."

Jaubert's business partners were Laurent Manrique, the French-born corporate executive chef of the Aqua Restaurant Group in San Francisco, and Guillermo and Junny Gonzalez, the owners of Sonoma Foie Gras. Two nights after the attack on Jaubert's home, Manrique's Marin County home was vandalized in a similar way by "concerned citizens," as they were called on BiteBack, which also posted the two men's home addresses. Red paint was thrown at his house, paint thinner splashed on his car, the garage door and car locks sealed with glue, and the words "murderer," "torturer," and "go back to France" spray-painted on his property. The next day, Manrique found a videotape in his mailbox. The video was shot from the bushes in his front yard and showed him in his living room playing with his toddler son. An unsigned note was taped to the video. It read that that his family was being watched and demanded "stop the foie gras, or you will be stopped."

Two weeks later, activists broke into Sonoma Saveurs and caused an estimated $50,000 worth of damage to the historic building. They covered walls, appliances, and fixtures with red paint and graffiti ("foie gras = death," "end animal torture," "shame," "go home," and "misery"). They poured concrete down the drains where sinks and toilets were going to be installed. Then they turned on the water, flooding the building as well as its neighbors, a jewelry store housed in another historic nineteenth-century building and a women's clothing store. A gloating account of the attack was posted soon afterward on BiteBack. The tactic of pouring concrete represented "the forcing of high density feed down the throats of ducks. The damage this will do to the plumbing symbolizes the damage done to the ducks' digestive systems by force feeding them." Additionally, the flooding would "punish" Guillermo Gonzalez for "depriving the ducks he tortures to make foie gras of water in which to preen and bathe." The post continued, "Now Guillermo will be sure to have a swim when he opens the door."[1]

No one directly claimed responsibility for these acts, and no arrests were made. After adjusting the business plan and menu and forsaking the original logo of a smiling duck, Sonoma Saveurs opened later that year,[2] but closed soon after.[3] The Sonoma County police chief described the attacks to reporters as a "sophisticated campaign of domestic terrorism." Upon the advice of local law enforcement, Manrique installed a security system at his home. "I came to America because it is the land of free speech," he told a reporter for the *Los Angeles Times*. "But all of this, involving my family like this, is going way too far."[4] Manrique left the venture soon after receiving the videotape, citing obligations to his restaurants in San Francisco. Jaubert, too, called foie gras part of his cultural tradition and pleaded for more reasonable forms of protest than vigilantism. As he told the *Sonoma News*:

> If you don't like foie gras, I can understand. If you don't want foie gras to be sold, you can demonstrate in front of the store, you can write letters to the editor. But to destroy a historical building, to

attack a family's home, to do this at night and to be proud of your actions—this is very difficult for me to understand.[5]

Who Cares About Foie Gras?

This event, and those that followed elsewhere in California and around the country, centered on a particularly contentious food item—foie gras (pronounced fwah-grah). This specially enlarged "fat liver" of a goose or duck is a popular food in French cuisine and one that animal rights supporters find morally repugnant. The debate centers on how foie gras is made. To enlarge and fatten the liver, the goose or duck is fed measured and increasing amounts of grain (typically corn and/or a mash of corn and soy) through a specialized tube or pipe during its last weeks of life. This process is called *gavage* in French, which most easily translates into English as force-feeding, and the person doing the feeding is the *gaveur* (if a man) or *gaveuse* (if a woman). During the gavage period, which ranges between twelve and twenty-one days depending on the farm, the bird's liver grows six to ten times in size and increases from approximately eighteen percent to up to sixty percent fat by weight. A duck foie gras averages about 1.5 to 2 pounds (compared to about four ounces for a non-force-fed liver). Gavage and its product, foie gras, are alternatively acclaimed and reviled by different parties.

Renowned culinary historian Silvano Serventi writes that foie gras is "synonymous with pleasure of the senses."[6] As a dish, it is typically served as a small-portioned first course. It can be eaten hot as a quickly seared preparation, often accompanied by a sweet fruit garnish. More traditionally, it is slowly cooked over low heat and then served cold as a pâté or terrine. It is silky in texture and rich and unique in flavor. Celebrity chef Anthony Bourdain once called foie gras "one of the most delicious things on the planet, and one of the ten most important flavors in gastronomy."[7]

While a fairly new delicacy in the United States, foie gras is a food of global origins and has long been considered a symbol of luxury and prestige. Ancient historians have traced practices of domesticating and fattening waterfowl for their livers back to ancient Egypt; papyrus scrolls and stone reliefs, including two that hang in the Louvre museum in Paris, depict the process of moistening grain to feed to geese through hollow reeds.[8] These practices traveled throughout eastern and southern Europe (where sizable foie gras industries still exist in Hungary and Bulgaria) and took hold in France, where foie gras has played a leading role in the country's world-famous culinary canon for over two hundred years.[9] There, until the mid-twentieth century, foie gras—made mostly from geese, but also from ducks—was primarily a seasonal food (harvested in autumn) that was reserved for fine dining restaurants and families' special occasions, especially at Christmas and for celebrating the New Year.

Following World War II and with state-financed support, French foie gras production (like that of other types of food and agricultural products across Western Europe and North America) became industrialized, enabling year-round production, lowering costs, and encouraging new consumer demand. Alongside foie gras's industrialization came substantive changes to the product itself. Most notably, the industry switched from using primarily geese to ducks due to the latter's better ability to cope with new mechanized (and more cost-effective) feeding methods. Today, while foie gras is a small piece of the panoply of French agriculture, it is a €1.9 billion industry (about $2.2 billion in 2014 dollars). Eighty percent of the world's foie gras production and ninety percent of world consumption occur in France. According to national estimates, the total industry includes around fifteen thousand farms and six hundred processing facilities, ranging from small family-run businesses to national commercial firms. The French foie gras industry employs about thirty thousand people and indirectly affects about one hundred thousand other jobs in areas such as veterinary practice, retail sales, marketing, and tourism.

For consumers, foie gras is a mainstay of France's culinary landscape, always available at specialty shops, supermarkets, prepared food *traiteurs*, chain stores, and outdoor markets, as well as online. Restaurants from nondescript corner bistros to Michelin-starred gastronomic temples feature it on their menus. Yet, despite the widespread use of language and imagery proclaiming its authentic ties to tradition and history, these days most foie gras in France comes from a modern and industrial production model that is largely hidden in plain sight. Several firms control the large majority of the market, sell under different brand names, and take pains to downplay their commercial motives to the public.

In the late twentieth century, parallel to its industry's modernization, foie gras became increasingly viewed as an endangered asset in France's cultural treasury. In the late 1990s, duck foie gras from Southwest France was added to the country's array of specialty food products that have a European Union–designated label of "protected geographical indication."[10] In 2005, the French National Assembly and Senate voted to protect foie gras legally as part of the country's "official gastronomic heritage." This was done ostensibly in response to concerns from other EU member states about its production ethics. This decision embedded foie gras materially and symbolically within the idea of the nation in a country whose international legacy of culinary excellence is several centuries old and a key point of national pride.

Today, the rural landscapes and small-scale proprietors of French foie gras production are identified as national treasures, and these reverential sentiments have helped transform them into a magnet for tourists. An artisanal foie gras sector is thriving in the Southwestern regions, where local governments and tourism associations promote foie gras as a unique element of cultural patrimony, gastronomy, and *terroir* (the taste of place). Several towns proclaim themselves the "capital" of foie gras, marketing themselves as attractive, authentic, and delicious places to visit. Visitors are introduced to foie gras as a special and artisanal, and not an industrial, product that needs to be protected. The larger industry's production conditions are omitted from these more marketable national myths and masked by sentimentalized narratives of shared history and invocations of collective memory. But how foie gras assumed this status of imperiled tradition—making it mostly (but not fully) unavailable for contestation—was not an inevitable process. Importantly, this occurred because international affairs can and do have consequences for local settings when the political climate is right.

In the United States, commercial foie gras production did not exist until the 1980s, with the establishment of two independent business ventures, one on each coast. Sonoma Foie Gras was founded in California by the aforementioned Guillermo Gonzalez, an El Salvador native who had learned to produce foie gras at a small goose farm in Southwest France. Hudson Valley Foie Gras was established by Michael Ginor, an ex–bond trader turned chef, and Izzy Yanay, an Israeli-born duck breeder, who bought and converted a rundown chicken farm in upstate New York. Before the 1980s, fresh foie gras was nearly impossible to obtain in the United States, namely because of federal government restrictions on importing fresh poultry products from Europe.[11] Close proximity to the culinary epicenters of New York and San Francisco aided business for each farm. In the 1990s, foie gras dishes became a hot culinary trend at elite urban restaurants in conjunction with Americans' expanding tastes for gourmet cuisine.[12] Mentions of foie gras in the *New York Times* peaked in the late 1990s.[13] Hudson Valley's marketing director during that time period told me that it "was on everybody's menus. The restaurant reviewer for the *New York Times* would use the words 'ubiquitous foie gras dish.' So it went from this weird thing to part of the vernacular." As foie gras came into the language of prestigious restaurants, leading chefs, and affluent diners, she said, "We saw our sales go up, and everybody just wanted it. We were mostly worried that people would get bored and move on, as they always do, to some other ingredient. Not about legislation."

By the mid-2000s, Hudson Valley employed two hundred people and was producing about three hundred and fifty thousand ducks a year, distributing its products through gourmet food purveyors across the country. Sonoma Foie Gras, later rebranded as Sonoma Artisan Foie Gras, was producing about seventy-five thousand ducks a year before was it shut down by California's ban on foie gras's production and sale in July 2012. In the late 1990s, ex–Hudson Valley employees started raising foie gras ducks at nearby LaBelle Farms, which produces about one hundred and thirty thousand ducks a year. A fourth operation, Au Bon Canard—a two-person farm outside of Minneapolis that produces around two thousand ducks per year—was founded in the early 2000s. While multiple economic interests are indubitably involved in its operations, the US foie gras market was worth about twenty-three to twenty-five million dollars in the late 2000s—1/100th the size of the French industry.[14]

For US consumers, foie gras is a curiosity. Calling it an industry (five hundred thousand ducks out of the ten *billion* animals that traverse the American food system each year) is almost laughable.[15] A typical modern chicken plant in the United States processes more birds in a single day than Sonoma Foie Gras did in an entire year.[16] Foie gras's price point puts it out of most Americans' reach: its retail cost is around seventy dollars a pound, and it is available to consumers primarily at upscale restaurants and gourmet food stores.[17] Most people in the United States don't know what it is; even fewer have ever tried it. Where foie gras *has* made a mark is among an influential group of restaurateurs and chefs, many of whom have entered the realm of celebrity as cultural taste-makers.[18] Foie gras dishes have graced the menus of some of the country's most celebrated restaurants. And foie gras found a fan base among a crop of "omnivorous" and "adventurous" food lovers who seek out unusual, exotic, and exciting eating experiences and take food very seriously[19]—people who are often and sometimes pejoratively called "foodies."[20]

Foie gras, however, is not just a symbol of gourmet cuisine; it is also a matter of moral politics and contention for people who believe abstention is not enough. In the United States and elsewhere, foie gras production is heavily criticized on ethical grounds. Detractors argue that the practice of force-feeding ducks and geese with a twenty-to-thirty-centimeter-long tube—typically made of metal[21]—to enlarge and fatten their livers is an obvious case of animal cruelty.[22] Though activists attempted to raise public awareness of foie gras's existence in the 1990s, beginning with a 1991 "investigation" by People for the Ethical Treatment of Animals (PETA) of Hudson Valley Foie Gras (then called Commonwealth Enterprises), their impact was limited. In 1999, after receiving letters from animal rights organizations and concerned celebrities, the Smithsonian Institution cancelled a panel discussion and tasting organized to promote *Foie Gras: A Passion*, a newly published book by Michael Ginor of Hudson Valley Foie Gras.[23] These and a few other actions received little notice beyond animal rights circles and a few brief newspaper articles.

Then, at the turn of the twenty-first century, the stars aligned for foie gras's opponents. A month after the vandalism to Sonoma Saveurs, San

Francisco ABC television affiliate KGO aired clips on its evening newscast from a short film called *Delicacy of Despair*, produced by a group called GourmetCruelty.com.[24] The film (which remains available on the Internet) showed the group's "undercover investigations" and "open rescues"—a common direct action tactic where activists remove animals from farms or animal operations for "rehabilitation" while documenting the conditions in which they were found—of ducks at Sonoma Foie Gras and Hudson Valley Foie Gras.[25] Immediately after the broadcast, the *Los Angeles Times* reporter who had earlier reported on the Sonoma Saveurs vandalism contacted the head of the Animal Protection and Rescue League (APRL), a law student turned animal-rights activist named Bryan Pease, who had collaborated with the GourmetCruelty.com team in trespassing onto and secretly videotaping operations at foie gras farms for the previous three years. Pease invited him to sneak onto Sonoma Foie Gras's grounds with him and three other APRL activists and a video camera the following night. The *Los Angeles Times* story—which detailed how the group squeezed into the barn through a gap in the wall and took four ducks with them (out of the fifteen hundred there)—ran the next day.[26] Guillermo Gonzalez sued Pease in civil court for trespassing and theft; Pease and In Defense of Animals, a legally oriented animal rights group, countersued Gonzalez for breaking anticruelty laws.

Then the state of California got involved. In February 2004, John Burton, a Democratic California state senator and then–president pro tempore, introduced a bill in the state legislature—the first of its kind in the country—to "prohibit force feeding a bird for the purpose of enlarging the bird's liver beyond normal size and the sale of products that are a result of this process." Burton proposed this legislation, co-sponsored by a number of animal rights organizations, because he felt, as he explained, that foie gras "is not only unnecessary, it's inhumane."[27] That September, the bill passed in a 21–14 vote and was signed into law by then-governor Arnold Schwarzenegger.[28] Importantly, the new law's text included an almost eight-year implementation delay, professedly to give Sonoma Foie Gras time to develop "a humane way for a duck to consume grain to increase the size of its liver through natural processes." This allowed the state to balance the right of somebody to have a legitimate business with that of the thing to be ostensibly protected, namely the humane treatment of the ducks. In exchange for withdrawing his opposition, Guillermo Gonzalez was granted legal immunity from the anticruelty suits filed against him by APRL and In Defense of Animals (which he told writer Mark Caro had cost him $400,000), as well as from any other lawsuits filed over the extended period. The law took effect—putting Sonoma Foie Gras out of business—on July 1, 2012.

Thereafter, foie gras became not only a prime and energizing issue for a number of animal rights and animal welfare activists, who were loosely connected through online communities and preexisting networks, but also one that received enormous media attention.[29] Events in California provided a clarion call for animal rights activists in different cities across the country to create anti–foie gras campaigns. National media outlets—from the *New York Times* to *Time Magazine* to Fox News to *Wine Spectator*—began to take notice of these self-proclaimed "duck freedom fighters."[30] Food writers and restaurant critics published think pieces about their own divided views. Foie gras was becoming a new hot-button issue in the politics of food.

As a target, foie gras offered animal rights activists something relatively incomparable within the multi-trillion-dollar food industry. Any number of arguments or issues could be made regarding cruelty to animals in the contemporary industrial food system, yet few of them become *causes célèbres*.[31] Foie gras production appeared shockingly inhumane and, along with having a foreign-sounding name, lacked cultural or affective connections for "regular folks." It also lacked institutional resources. None of the four farms in the United States has had strong ties to national poultry or meat industry lobbies. This meant that activists could ostensibly own the issue. They anticipated that they could harness enough public indignation to make foie gras disappear completely. They could be the moralistic voices that would convince restaurants to stop serving it, people to stop eating it, and politicians to outlaw it. And while legal bans on foie gras would be mostly symbolic victories—in that they would not actually affect most American eaters—ostensibly they could be footholds into these groups' larger battles against animal agriculture. The opportunity was golden, and the stakes were high.

Claims to Moral Authority

The realities of the last decade's disputes show that the cases for *and* against foie gras are much more about moral imperatives than objective ones. Most people and groups involved in the fights—both opponents and supporters—profess to care deeply about the contemporary food system. Yet how all of these people categorize foie gras on a spectrum of serious social problems, food-based and otherwise, is particularly relative. The stories recounted in this book are about the actions of social actors who all truly believe that they are doing the right thing—even working to promote a more just and better world. Yet, these people and groups have fundamentally different priorities, motives, and base moral convictions. Additionally, each argument for or against the production and consumption of foie gras is conceptually incomplete unless one also appreciates its political and economic contexts; more specifically, we cannot disentangle the moral politics of food from the practical politics of state regulation and the logistics of market forces.

The people fighting against foie gras are activists in a global social movement—that of animal rights. Animal activists of many stripes argue that they are following in the footsteps of earlier moral reformers who challenged society's dominant cultural codes and focused on the societal injuriousness of racism and sexism. Animals, too, deserve respect, compassion, and rights.[32] The animal rights movement is largely nonviolent, yet, like most large and diverse social movements, it has factions that believe in different courses of action that use force, lawbreaking, coercion, or intimidation to fight what they believe to be moral injustice to animals. When selecting a particular target, social movement activists often have many goals in mind, including heightening people's awareness, fundraising, increasing and shaping media coverage, and fomenting behavioral and legal changes. For those eager to combat animal cruelty, the very notion of force-feeding ducks with a metal tube seems to demand public outrage. In the United States, this is only exacerbated by the fact that the process results in an unpronounceable and expensive luxury food. The activists' other main allegation is that the fattened liver's metabolic changes are not the result of a normal physiological process, as producers claim, but instead a painful one of induced pathological disease.[33] As one activist told me, alluding to societal consensus on what Americans care about, there is too high an ethical price for an "entire industry that just revolves around cruelty" to continue to exist.

Symbols, words, and vivid images have played crucial roles in conjuring collective disgust over foie gras in the US court of public opinion. In my interviews with animal rights activists, as well as in their media interviews and press releases, on their websites and at their protests, they repeatedly used the terms "jamming," "shoving," and "forcing" to describe a process they consider to be "traumatic," "abhorrent," "torture," and "inherently cruel" and causing the birds "unmitigated pain and suffering."[34] Veterinarian and anti–foie gras activist Holly Cheever described the force-feeding process in testimony before the Chicago City Council as

[a] rough inflexible metal tube ... jammed down their esophagus three times a day while they are being forcibly restrained. . . . Once they can no longer walk, because they are so crippled by their swollen abdomens, they are seen pathetically dragging themselves on their wings to try to escape the humans who are feeding them.[35]

Hard-hitting and grisly as such accusations can be, they have proved more persuasive to some than to others. A number of restaurants and prominent chefs have sworn off foie gras. Elected officials in some states that did not have foie gras production introduced bills to prevent farms from setting up shop. A number of local anti–foie gras campaigns in cities around the country received national press coverage—a social movement achievement.

Yet activists have also encountered resistance to their depictions of foie gras as the epitome of evil. Attitudes toward food tastes—and the overall ethics of eating animals—are, of course, diverse. Many diners and chefs consider foie gras a legitimate culinary choice that should remain just that, a choice. Moreover, a number of journalists, academics, and opinion leaders who have visited foie gras farms themselves have raised questions about the veracity of animal rights activists' claims of cruelty and their depictions of the production process.

Foie gras's champions maintain that while the force-feeding process might look harmful to an untrained human eye, it does not necessarily cause the birds to suffer. Most Americans, even many agricultural scientists, know little about waterfowl biology.[36] The problem that foie gras's proponents face is that people are anthropomorphizing the birds—ascribing to them human attributes and qualities. Of course ducks *can* feel pain and stress, foie gras producers concur, but what would hurt humans and ducks is not the same. As industry members repeatedly told me, waterfowl and human digestive tracts are physiologically different. Waterfowl esophagi are keratinous and do not have nerve endings; they swallow rocks for their gizzards to grind food as part of their digestion. Additionally, the birds have separate passages for ingesting food and air, unlike humans, and do not have gag reflexes, as we do. At one farm in France with an on-site slaughterhouse, I asked to see and touch the esophagi of geese that had just been butchered. The insides felt smooth and rubbery, and they bent like fingernails after a hot shower. Additionally, producers and concurring scientists assert that the fattening process takes advantage of a natural physiological feature of migratory birds, which gorge and store excess fat in their livers for energy for migrating. They claim that the process is reversible if it is ceased (unlike liver disease in humans, which is not). You could not do the same to chickens, because their livers would not transform as migratory waterfowl livers would.

In France, I found that producers responded to charges of torture and cruelty by dismissing, or even gently mocking, the idea that they and their work were causing pain. Many claimed to "adore" their birds; yet, as one told me, "It is their job, their destiny, to give us livers. They are farm animals, not pets." They pointed to waterfowl's biological uniqueness as well as to the relatively small-scale and intimate, hands-on nature of foie gras production. They declared unapologetically that great care is taken with the birds on "good" farms—that "a duck that is treated poorly will not produce a good foie gras." "There is an enormous complicity between the goose and the feeder, a respect, an affective link," says Ariane Daguin of D'Artagnan, a French-born gourmet food purveyor in the New York City area (and daughter of an esteemed chef) who was among the first to introduce fresh foie gras to Manhattan restaurants.

Similarly, in trying to occlude controversy, foie gras's US defenders in the culinary realm suggest that its production is no morally worse than our modern system of giant factory farms, and because of its relatively small-scale and precise production methods could even be considered more humane. Every time we choose to eat meat, we balance our desire to do so with an animal's discomfort and/or death. From this perspective, if a person or society believes it morally acceptable to raise and kill animals for their meat, they should have no objection to foie gras that comes from "good" farms. (Of course, not all foie gras farms are well-run.) The larger issue, these defenders assert, is people's general disconnectedness from the unromantic realities of farming. Although surveys show that rising numbers of people are concerned about the well-being of farm animals in intensive modern agriculture,[37] for many, seeing any type of animal operation that does not resemble a child's storybook is jarring. Significantly, an influential segment of people involved in contemporary food politics in both countries—chefs, critics, food writers, sustainable-agriculture proponents, and others—declare that the fight against foie gras is a red herring, that it diverts attention away from "real" and "more serious" social problems found in, and caused by, the modern industrial food system.

It is important to reiterate that the "problem" of foie gras cannot be easily resolved by an appeal to scientific study, in this case to objective research on waterfowl physiology, independent of biases. Both sides of the debate claim empirical certainty and each has recruited sympathetic scientific experts to lend authority to their assertions. Moreover, both camps have accused the other of cherry-picking and purposefully ignoring key evidence, and members of both immediately express doubt about the objectivity of the findings of any research study, no matter who conducted it, that contradicts their expectations and perceptions. To the extent that I present information about the biological science of foie gras in the chapters that follow, it is to establish what is and is not known about waterfowl physiology and, more importantly, about how different groups have mobilized scientific discourses to suit their purposes; it is not about resolving the discrepancies in the science deployed by both sides.

Foie gras has struck a resonant chord for many—it has often (and polemically) been called America's most controversial food. Its politics reveal how ideas and concerns about morality intersect with markets, social movements, and state systems of law and regulation. The very topic of foie gras's existence, as well as its presence on menus, has galvanized some people—animal rights activists, chefs, industry members, consumers, and legislators—to action in ways that other issues have not. These politics involve deep, identity-laden concerns, and they illuminate the various ways in which institutions and organizations, as makers and mediators of morally grounded cultural meanings, are critical to contested tastes.

CONTESTED TASTES AND GASTROPOLITICS

Why do Americans consider grilled shrimp delicious and boiled insects repulsive? One answer is that we eat as much with our imaginations as we do with our mouths. Foods can denote very different things from table to table and across time and place. Subjective choice plays a role in what and how we eat, but these choices are conditioned by the social worlds in which we live. What we eat can reveal our national identities, our ethnicities, our social class, our subcultural loyalties, and even our political commitments. Cuisine offers both symbolic and substantive norms of group membership and belonging. Culinary practices and tastes can bring people together or push them apart, for example, through revulsion at others' food preferences.[38] Americans might call eating worms, grasshoppers, or eyeballs disgusting (even though entire television shows are now devoted to such culinary thrill-seeking), while members of other societies find casseroles or peanut butter—a quintessential American childhood snack—similarly unpalatable.

While we might chalk up examples like these to legitimate or idiosyncratic differences in culturally learned tastes, the phenomenon of disgust over food preferences also works as an instrument to construct social and political order. Disgust exposes the basic distinction between strange and familiar tastes, and it permits negative associations to be made between foods and their eaters.[39] In other words, we project moral judgments onto what, and who, we consider unworthy of respect or empathy—how could "those people" eat that? For instance, to rail against the supposed harms that McDonald's has wrought on the world is, today, a way for members of the professional middle class to show they are right-minded and virtuous consumers.[40] This phenomenon is nothing new. The history of American immigration and ethnic assimilation is replete with xenophobic denials of others' humanity, not to mention citizenship rights, signaled in part by disgust at food and taste preferences. Italian immigrants in the late nineteenth century, for example, were frequently stereotyped as unwilling to assimilate, infuriating social reformers across East Coast cities with their heavy culinary use of imported tomatoes and garlic (called "Italian perfume") and their refusal to espouse more mainstream American diets.[41] Similarly, over the last century, social alarms over other people's food choices have typically concerned the food—and thus moral standing—of the poor, as food studies scholars such as Charlotte Biltekoff and Melanie DuPuis have repeatedly shown.[42] Food preferences have also worked internationally to separate "us" and "them"—calling French people "frogs" or Asians "dog eaters," for example.

However, while we know from both personal experience and substantive research that people's tastes and opinions tend to be fairly stable over time, we also know that societal-level changes in tastes do happen. We, as both individuals and groups, do respond to the shifting norms and values of our communities. Foods are tools in these processes, materially, discursively, and symbolically. Something desirable can become disgusting, and vice versa. As *New Yorker* writer Adam Gopnik writes, "The good food of 25 years ago always looks unappetizing, and the good food of a hundred years ago always looks inedible."[43] Yet some foods and culinary practices become not only classified as old-fashioned or unappetizing, but also castigated as social problems that demand attention. As such, in a civil society such as ours, where do we draw the line against foods we consider wrong or immoral enough to fight over, to threaten other people over, or to seek legal means to prohibit others from producing or consuming? What influences and animates these processes?

These questions orbit around what I call gastropolitics—conflicts, both small and large, over food and culinary practices that are branded as social problems and that concurrently enmesh the domains of social movements, markets, and states. I see gastropolitics, a term originally coined several decades ago by social theorist Arjun Appadurai to describe food's semiotic and classificatory power within everyday social relations,[44] as a way to conceptualize food's cultural power in politicizing taste. Eating or eschewing certain foods can become overt ways of signifying moral anxieties about other people's actions and political concerns about the social order. For a food like foie gras to be simultaneously labeled a social problem and tendered as a symbol of national heritage lays bare the competing interests of movements, markets, and states at the heart of gastropolitics.

Importantly, my approach to gastropolitics purposefully refers to the term "gastronomy," rather than simply "food." Gastronomy has a double meaning, referring to the study and practice of culinary excellence as well as to culinary styles and protocols that are considered specific to places, cultural backgrounds, historical periods, or groups of people—what food studies scholars call "foodways."[45] In her foundational work on nineteenth-century French cuisine, sociologist Priscilla Ferguson calls gastronomy a cultural field, or a social arena composed of all those interested in food that is special or distinctive in some way, including producers, consumers, and food literati.[46] In this regard, gastronomic tastes serve as identity-locating social currencies.

Gastropolitics, as elucidated in this book, is a close sociological cousin to the large and excellent body of interdisciplinary academic research and popular writing on food politics published in the last two decades. A great deal of this other work has focused on the politics of nutrition advice, the power of food corporations, the consequences of agricultural policies for the natural environment and human health, the treatment of workers in the food system, and the creation of locally embedded food growing and provisioning systems that are alternatives to industrial agribusiness. Gastropolitics, however, also draws from sociological theories of culture and of "symbolic politics" to highlight how, why, and for whom certain foods become touchstones of moral and cultural, as well as political, contention.[47] Gastropolitics foregrounds why and how people try to claim authority and to convince others what is right or wrong to eat.

And because gastropolitics are about struggle over cultural meanings and group identities, they differ from these other types of food politics.

I use the term "politics" in a broad sense here, to mean the efforts of social actors, including and beyond politicians, to achieve particular and divergent goals. Conflict among these actors and over these goals (which can be contradictory) is implicit in politics. How people make, market, regulate, acquire, consider, and consume food involves struggles over food's substantive, material qualities as well as its symbolic dimensions. Anthropologist Mary Douglas was one of the first to make this connection by referring to eating as a "field of action. It is a medium in which other levels of categorization becomes manifest."[48] In other words, food nourishes our minds as well as our bodies as potent symbols of place, purpose, and identity. Gastropolitics, then, are everyday politics where people and groups actively engage to keep or change what is eaten, and they are also formal politics related to laws and governmental regulations that shape the food system. They lay bare *why* people are willing to fight over food and *how* they marshal cultural and material resources to do so. As such, gastropolitical battles are situated in time and place, a point that applies to the historically specific practicalities of markets. Indeed, in the last few decades, people worldwide have become increasingly cognizant of the political, as well as cultural, implications of their food choices and practices.

For these reasons, my analysis of foie gras's gastropolitics is also grounded in the sociology of culture, which obliges careful examination of language, framing, meanings, and the affective sentiments that food and culinary practices generate. Cultural sociologists have studied meaning-making in a variety of modes of cultural production, including media, art, rituals, stories, and beliefs. But the symbolic and substantive content of food has hardly been considered in this vein. This omission is surprising given how fundamental food and eating are to social life. Considering food through the lens of cultural sociology—especially how some foods become the foci of public sentiment—similarly sharpens our theories of how cultural categories are substantiated, and how cultural power is deployed, harnessed, suppressed, and contested.[49]

My analysis draws on the work of those who have studied contestation in other cultural markets and fields, such as markets for art, literature, or music. In each of these fields, battles over symbols, discourses, and cultural prescripts can have real effects on livelihoods and on markets. Symbolic politics work to reshape these fields, and to redefine culture, by moralizing their consumption. As sociologist Joseph Gusfield wrote regarding symbolic politics, "issues which seem foolish ... are often important for what they symbolize about the style or culture which is being recognized or derogated."[50] This is especially true when consumers (and their wallets) are solicited as powerful actors by an issue's defenders or detractors.[51]

However, food differs from these other cultural goods in several important ways. First, food has a special place in our lives; linked to our bodies and our health, the act of physical ingestion creates visceral responses—and anxieties—that most other cultural goods do not, despite how strongly some people might feel about country music or science fiction. Second, food is mundane—part of our routine, everyday lives—and is only one of a variety of concerns competing for people's attention. This everyday nature of food exposes a duality: we can be lulled into seeing it as unexceptional or innocuous, or we can ask whether its ordinariness belies important cultural and affective attachments.[52]

Most importantly, the food industry is a market of a vastly different scale than industries in these other cultural fields, with a greater number of people and organizations that are directly affected by changes in its political economy. Government policies, powerful transnational companies, and global financial economics all shape the production of food. Food is big business. In the United States, food and agriculture are the second largest industry (after defense). With the industrialization of agriculture and food production in the twentieth century came conglomeration, corporate appropriation, and increased political power.[53] Similarly, in Europe, an integrated market for agriculture and food products has been a core activity since the European Union's formation and currently absorbs about fifty percent of the EU's annual budget. Even though foie gras is but a minute fraction of the food industry, challenges or changes to policy can have implications for other industry segments.

Foie gras is an exemplary case of gastropolitics and contested tastes in the twenty-first century. Its significance as a social symbol has arisen not only from the varied meanings and values it indexes, but also from the affective sentiments it drives. Contestation around foie gras exposes acute political tensions around consumption, identity, and cultural authority in today's culinary world. These battles illustrate how the juxtaposition of moralistic concerns and the culture of markets makes our ongoing relationship with food—and with each other—invariably political. Some call foie gras historically and culturally irreplaceable for who they are, personally or professionally. Others find its very existence upsetting, offensive, and a reason for protest.

Gastropolitics as Moral Politics

There are two connotations to the term "moral" that bear on how people actually engage with gastropolitics as moral politics. "Moral" can denote universal considerations of right and wrong, and it can be taken to mean relativist or situational questions of appropriate actions or behaviors that vary among individuals or groups. Drawing on research traditions in the sociology of culture that theorize processes of making meaning around contested tastes, I construe these different ways of talking about what is moral as *ethics* and *boundaries.*

A key way the term is used, especially outside of academic circles, is as a synonym for "ethical." Ethical convictions inspire people to act in certain ways due to concern with judgments about right and wrong, just and unjust, good and evil. They establish ideas for what people *should* believe and do—and in the case of gastropolitics, what is or is not ethically good to eat or to condemn. In this view, moral persons and practices are just and fair and humane, and they avoid harm to others. Their opposite is "immoral" or "amoral"—corrupt, depraved, or wicked. The power of cultural choices or symbols, in this view, resides in their ability to signify virtuous or ethically principled tenets.

With regard to boundaries, morality refers to feelings of self-worth, often in relation to one's identity-laden social connections and solidarity with one or more groups. It is about group membership or belonging, and it is about the acceptability or appropriateness of certain ways of being. Culture, in this view, is a reminder of affective bonds. From a complementary perspective, culture is a body of representations and texts that provide symbolic referents for the things that people commonly do together, as groups or societies, in domains ranging from the arts to education to table manners. It is a way that social life is ordered, patterned, and organized into actions and events that become easily recognizable and understandable.[54] Moral tastes and apologetics are, in effect, mechanisms that make groups and break them.

Many experiences in our lives offer sources of moral meaning that help create and reaffirm the "symbolic boundary" lines demarcating our social identities. The concept of symbolic boundaries, popularized by sociologist Michèle Lamont, denotes the intangible lines people use to make categorical distinctions about the moral worthiness of persons, objects, and practices.[55] These boundaries are about sameness and about difference, and they can be drawn along ethnic, racial, gender, social class, regional, and other lines. Yet, as Lamont explains, people do not draw or stretch symbolic boundaries based solely on their personal experiences or beliefs about merit and value. Rather, they borrow heavily from others who have similar lifestyles and from the places, time periods, and societies in which they live.[56]

These boundaries shape collective understandings of "good" and "bad" taste, especially as these understandings articulate with consumer identities in the public sphere. Importantly, it is not necessarily what people have in common, but also what they *reject*, that serve as markers of taste boundaries and serve as bases for exclusion based on group identity. For example, a declaration such as "we eat pork; they don't" articulates tropes of religious or ethnic similarity and otherness through shared consumption patterns and prohibitions. Class-based versions of food-related taste judgments link to how rich and middle-class people assess poor people's food choices (often as societal problems and with great disdain).[57] Symbolic boundaries and politics that blend group identities with gustatory tastes can indubitably be more elastic or expansive in some places and for some situations than in others.[58] Yet, while culinary tastes around the globe have changed dramatically in the last few decades, disputes over whose taste is the right one (either as ethics or as boundaries) can still be extremely contentious.

In some notable ways, what I discern here as ethics and boundaries are complementary parts of a single phenomenon. Both orient the ways that people use culture to make social connections and to coordinate goals with others.[59] Primarily, they fuse when people take on a set of beliefs or practices not only as reflective of their personal or social identities, but also as a motivating source of honor, shame, or ostensibly righteous behavior. For example, avoiding shellfish for religious reasons, claiming a vegan identity, or feeding one's children only organic food all denote a combination of ethics and boundaries. And when the ethical status of a food or food-related practice becomes the focus of scathing public critiques and debate, the permeability of boundaries is indubitably moralized.

In all of this, consumption operates as a structuring force. Sometimes the choice to consume or abstain marks one's efforts or propensity for group belonging. Sometimes it constitutes a refusal to blend in with the crowd, or even an explicit act of ideological resistance. We can think easily of other consumer items that have proved morally controversial in both the recent and more distant past: alcohol, headscarves, cigarettes, cars, guns, diamonds, bottled water, and even plastic bags. Similarly, economic and cultural sociologists following in the footsteps of Viviana Zelizer have investigated markets for morally questionable goods and services that elicit questions of consumer and business ethics.[60] Examples include child labor, the creation of life insurance, sex work, and the medical market for human blood and body parts.[61]

This evocative body of research has shown that the success of attempts to legitimate such markets depends heavily on the interests, identities, and ideologies of the people and groups doing the legitimating.[62] This research helps us see how groups and organizations coordinate marketplace interactions and mobilize others who share their values, how economic interests are reassessed to meet new social and cultural demands, and how social and moral judgments become politically concrete. Additionally, conflicts over the legal statuses of the markets for these contentious products invoke the roles of social movements and government as influential moral actors. This is the framework that this book, too, highlights.

But food is different from cigarettes or life insurance, because we cannot imagine a world without food production. So moral arguments are not about food per se, but what kinds of foods are appropriate—we, of course, do not need to eat everything that could be eaten. Boundaries come into play in terms of cultural groups and the political uses of symbols, while ethics come into play in terms of protecting access to needs as well as preventing harm. Some foods become the bases by which activists see themselves as agents of change and others see themselves as upholders of the status quo.[63] Recent US history shows that frames of public health and consumer safety have been most successful in removing other controversial items from people's diets, such as trans fats from cooking oils and packaged foods and soda from school vending machines. On an international scale, ongoing disputes over seal hunting pit indigenous groups in Arctic regions against international animal rights groups and trade organizations. Shark fin soup, a de rigueur dish at Chinese special events, has seen legal bans in the United States and Canada and even criticism in China due to the practice of finning, in which sharks are caught, their fins sliced off, and the fish thrown back into the ocean, where they typically bleed to death.

These are but a few examples of recent gastropolitical conflicts. Our food choices—what we eat as individuals, as well as members of groups, of communities, and of society—are complex and multidimensional. And we also care about what other people eat. Judgments, actual and implied, about the "right" food choices affect when, where, and for whom different lines delineating moral identities are drawn. A gastropolitical perspective offers an analytical lens for seeing why and how our food choices matter for moral ties between people and markets, as well as between markets and states.

Markets, Movements, States

If symbolic and moral politics help orient us to the ways in which gastropolitics are about values and identities, we must also pay close attention to the institutional structures in which they are embedded. I argue that to fully grasp the concerns and consequences of gastropolitics, we can, and must, look at how foods and foodways sit at the intersection of markets, the state, and social movements.

At their core, markets are structures of exchange where producers and consumers meet. When we talk about sanctioning producers or consumers, we are talking about reshaping markets. The structure of the state provides a general rubric for understanding the authority and jurisdiction of elected and appointed officials to translate values, needs, and opinions into policy, from local laws to international treaties. For political sociologists, the state possesses symbolic power, or the cultural authority to set the rules of the game and ensure they are experienced as legitimate—although the extent to which state power intrudes into markets is a point of particular ideological contention.[64] Social movements are situated in the domain of civil society and provide a way to consider actors who are not directly involved in the actions of either the state or the market, but who work to influence one or both. Sociologist Sidney Tarrow offers a usefully broad definition of movements as "collective challenges based on common purposes, in sustained interaction with elites, opponents, and authorities."[65] The triangulation of these domains merits attention, especially for how social movements are essential to understanding consumer identities and changing tastes generally, and specifically in the realm of food.

The social organization of the food industry is highly pertinent here. Markets are economic spaces that limit and stratify foods' costs, availability, and cultural reception, and it is the state (in theory, at least) that codifies and enforces rules for food production, distribution, marketing, and sale. Of course, few if any of us are fully cognizant of the innumerable details and political interests that matter in getting different kinds of food to our plates. When we go out for pizza, for example, we don't typically think about all of the arcane regulatory codes that pertain to the wheat in the crust, the tomatoes in the sauce, the milk in the cheese, the meat and preservatives in the pepperoni, the water used to clean the pans, or the workers who produced those ingredients or wiped down the tables. Social movements are key here to understanding how people who are not directly involved in the state or in industry can influence either sector. Mobilization around social problems related to food and eating does not just happen; it takes planning, resources, and coordinated effort. And many of the groups that compel such actions today are established, large-scale organizations whose influences are, and should be, taken seriously. Today, for example, groups such as People for the Ethical Treatment of Animals (2014 revenue of $51 million) and The Humane Society of the United States (2014 revenue of $186 million)[66] retain teams of staff lawyers, hold enough stock in several food companies to introduce shareholder resolutions, and file lawsuits directly against individual food producers for violating state and federal laws.[67]

This brings us back to foie gras, the axis around which many adversarial ideas and interests—and this book—revolve. We might expect items that provoke such hostility to be culturally or economically important for many people, similar to the ways prohibition of alcohol or regulations on tobacco have spurred vigorous public debates and legal actions in the recent past. Yet foie gras—a food consumed by few Americans—has proved incendiary, disruptive, and a touchstone of activism over food ethics in the United States in a way that seems disproportionate to the scale of its market. This contrasts with France, where most people not only find foie gras production unproblematic, but underscore its centrality in their cultural and national identity. Even though foie gras is far from the most pervasive problem in the contemporary food system, the issues that surround it raise broad and thorny questions about the morals and ethics of eating. Of how we treat animals. Of tradition and troublesome heritage. Of the practices of the modern food industry. Of defining the common good. Of what others are permitted, or not permitted, to eat. These are issues that people hold close to their hearts, setting the table for conflict.

Today, foie gras is emblematically a French food. Chapter 2 tells how this became so, and discusses the consequences of this development. I argue that foie gras overflowed its original regional borders and came to denote French national culture at least in part *because* it is contentious elsewhere—a significant version of gastropolitics that I call gastronationalism. Yet how foie gras is marketed to the French public today, including by the French state, conveniently obscures the industry's capital-intensive expansion and transformations over the last few decades. In chapter 3, I argue that foie gras's status as a shared but imperiled treasure in the French collective imagination comes to the fore in this regard. In picturesque towns and regions that claim it as authentic tradition, local people and associations actively craft foie gras's moral worth in the face of intense international criticism. These sites create a physical and affective backdrop for provocative questions of how we "see" the production of both food and culture, as well as for making sociological connections among food, memory, and symbolic politics.

In chapters 4 and 5, I argue that in the United States foie gras has come to serve as a cultural barometer for complex issues of culinary moralism and gastropolitics. Chapter 4 analyzes what happened when Chicago decided to institute and then rescind a ban on the sale of foie gras in the city's restaurants. Reactions to the short-lived foie gras ban, especially humorous ones, underscored the profound connections between politics and eating. Chapter 5 shifts attention to the more general challenges and paradoxes of developing moral understandings around a contested food such as foie gras by asking, up front and center, "How do we know if a practice is cruel? For individuals who wish to be moral eaters, who is to be believed?" This chapter offers analyses of the moral discourses, empirical claims, perceptions, and political strategies that both sides of the foie gras debate have employed. The conclusion considers implications of this analysis for thinking about identities, cultural change, and how symbols energize people in new ways in today's world. It also predicts foie gras politics' ongoing relevance, not because people cannot live without foie gras cheesecake but because of the nerves it has hit for everyone with a stake in the worlds of food and consumer culture.

Foie gras's gastropolitics in both the United States and France show how tightly the material and social processes of food production and consumption are entwined. While an empirical understanding of the events surrounding it in both countries is relevant to disentangling these threads, I suggest that they also provide a rich context that exposes how people evaluate objects, ideas, and each other through a critical and sometimes disparaging moral lens. Contestation is an important cultural filter, especially for consumer tastes. In both France and the United States, foie gras has zealous defenders and opponents. The prospect that its production in the latter nation will cease one day soon appears likely. But to what end? What are these battles really about? And what can we learn from fights about liver?

This book is about how people have worked to construct a moral climate around the existence of a celebrated and troublesome culinary practice. It is about symbolic politics in action. Perhaps more fundamentally, it shows how small decisions can have dramatic and far-reaching effects. From a Chicago restaurant to the European Union, the gastropolitics of foie gras underpin boundaries of nation, culture, ethics, social class, and taste, even as it shapes them. When we fight about a food's existence, we necessarily find ourselves wrapped up in the fantastic ability of food to connect the personal and the political. The politics of foie gras permit us to understand how food can inspire and repel us—as individuals, as organizations, as communities, and as nations. I do realize that this book adds to the attention that foie gras has received in recent years. But I hope that it also proves valuable for readers interested in meaning-making and the politics of consumption, and in how moral politics are embedded in and reconfigured through markets, social movements, and law.

CHAPTER 2

Vive le Foie Gras!

*I*t was a brisk Saturday morning in November 2007, and I was at a factory on the outskirts of the city of Strasbourg in the North-eastern part of France. Jean Schwebel leaned forward in his office chair, gesticulating while explaining how his company, Feyel-Artzner, had adapted to recent market and regulatory trends affecting the foie gras industry. Slender and smartly dressed in crisp jeans and a sweater, with graying hair around his temples, Schwebel was relatively new to the foie gras business, but not the food industry. He had bought Feyel-Artzner—a company with €30 million in sales that year and recognized as the oldest foie gras "house" (or market brand) in France—in 1994 after spending twenty-five years as a senior manager with the multinational Danone Group, a food company known for its dairy products and bottled water brands. Since buying Feyel-Artzner, the company had created new foie gras product lines and developed new international marketing outlets. Sales had doubled. Due in part to his expertise in both French and international trends in food law and supply chain manufacturing, Schwebel had also recently been elected president of CIFOG (Comité Interprofessionnel des Palmipèdes à Foie Gras), the national foie gras industry association in France.[1]

When I asked Schwebel specifically about international condemnation of foie gras—namely, why he thought some countries in the European Union, Israel, and several US states had banned or were trying to ban its production and/or sale—he clasped his hands together and responded quickly, "I think the countries which have banned it did so because they have no real tradition of it." He then took a deep breath and further explained:

> I cannot imagine that foie gras could be banned in France because it's a very traditional product, consumed in this country for a long time. Our country and our law say that it has to be protected in our country. Consumers buy it because it's a ritual. You have to. It's exactly the same as in your country. At Thanksgiving, you have to have your turkey. There is no Thanksgiving without turkey. And we have no Christmas without foie gras.

This response was fairly typical among the French whom I questioned about contention over foie gras. Many in the world think of foie gras as a French food. Similarly, we know that food and cuisine have long mattered, more generally, for France's history and celebrated social identity. Like others, Schwebel bypassed the specifics of criticisms to focus his answer instead on foie gras's status as a French tradition and the role that it plays in French citizens' self-understanding. As I traveled around the country, people throughout the food chain—from small artisanal producers to managers at multinational corporations—were quick to call foie gras an "authentic" and "essential" part of French heritage and *terroir*. It was part of the country's moral economy. Charges of cruelty, when they were acknowledged, were often dismissed as poorly informed. Others—outsiders—simply did not appreciate foie gras's specialness.

The concept of terroir, especially, is a valuable one in the French food world and beyond. A term long used to categorize wines and now regularly applied to foodstuffs such as cheeses, terroir denotes the ways that the natural environment, including soil and climate, shapes a food's special qualities and unique taste. In other words, terroir offers a "taste of place," where the characteristics of specific places purportedly combine with human knowhow to produce inimitable flavors. A food or wine from one place would taste recognizably differently than that from another.[2] Foie gras's terroir regions are Alsace, in the Northeast, and a number of *départements* (administrative divisions, similar to states or provinces) in the Southwest.[3] Terroir also, importantly, includes a social, human element of local knowledge—of *savoir-faire*—that has developed over time. One of the farmers I interviewed echoed others, telling me, "It is the person and the family who gives the identity to the land and the terroir." Terroir, then, links special, unique, and sophisticated products with localized identities of a virtuous peasantry. Typically, terroir products are marketed in direct contrast to globalized and homogenous foods, wines, and liquors designed to taste the same everywhere.[4] Throughout the European Union and elsewhere in the world, the market for place-based terroir foods has grown—especially in France.

Foie gras is also recognized in France as an emblem of national value and pride. Websites and books sold in French bookstores, for both adults and children, describe it as an "authentic French product" and an "emblem of French gastronomy."[5] Such phrases appear in marketing and tourism campaigns, across the Internet, and in everyday parlance. Moreover, the law to which Schwebel referred was a relatively recent one that officially protects foie gras as French. Passed by large margins in the French National Assembly and Senate in October 2005 and implemented a few months later, it sanctions the production of foie gras (defined as the liver of a duck or goose specially fattened by gavage[6]) in the "officially-protected cultural and gastronomic patrimony of France."[7]

And yet, for something that is supposedly so exceptional, I was surprised to find it for sale just about everywhere I went in France. Every supermarket had shelves or aisles devoted to foie gras and other "fat duck" products (see Figure 2.1). The majority of restaurant menus listed it. There were stalls selling it at every outdoor food market I visited. In the Southwestern regions, you could even buy it in gas station rest-stops along the Autoroute. Even though it is held up as a special Christmastime food, I saw it being sold and eaten throughout the spring, summer, and autumn. Its ubiquity in urban and rural spaces alike seemed almost mundane.

I also learned that this national pride was not completely universal. Contention over foie gras production also exists inside France. Some smaller producers expressed tinges of bitterness about larger producers' market power and political influence, and how these firms have affected French consumers' perceptions of foie gras. And in the past two decades, French animal rights groups have become ever more vocal in their op-

2.1 Foie gras and "fat duck" product offerings at LeClerc in Auch, November 2007.

position to its production. As in other places, their appeals are grounded in arguments about cruelty and ethics. While small in membership numbers, they have received both moral support and in-kind resources from similarly minded (and better-funded) organizations around the world. Yet, when I spoke with Antoine Comiti, one of the leaders of France's main anti–foie gras group, Stop Gavage, it was clear that he understands the uphill battle his group faces, and that the fight to eliminate foie gras in France is unlikely to be won in his lifetime.[8] When I asked Comiti why this was so, he replied:

> There is a recent polarization on foie gras—it is the patrimony. It is the identity of France. It's like wine from here in Bordeaux. Development of foie gras production is within the last sixty years, more or less. It was there, but very weak, before. There was little consumption; it was not all that widespread. So the foie gras industry had a lot of work to do on the image of foie gras as something from the Southwest and later as being part of the image of France, like the Eiffel Tower.

Comiti's response is a telling one, for two reasons. First, it mentions the industry's promotion of foie gras's national cultural value, accentuating its similarity (from his perspective, an unjustified one) to other significant symbols of France. Indeed, at all levels of the contemporary French foie gras industry—from the handwritten, photocopied flier of a fourth-generation family-run *conserverie* in the Périgord to the professionally produced book that CIFOG sends to new members—declarations of foie gras's Frenchness and specialness abound. They rely on evocative narratives that imbue foie gras with themes of national history, holiday celebrations, and longstanding family and social traditions.

Second, Comiti's comment reinforces the contradictions inherent in foie gras's ubiquity on supermarket shelves. He calls attention to the capital-intensive and productivity-boosting developments that expanded and restructured the industry, which in turn made foie gras increasingly available and cheaper. While it has long been consumed by French people of most social backgrounds as a holiday and special occasion food—like Thanksgiving turkey in the United States—due to shifts in the production process, foie gras in France today is not nearly the same product that it used to be. And yet, as I found, only in the past half century has foie gras become fêted as a symbol of the nation—as Comiti proffered, like the Eiffel Tower. Depending on one's perspective, this status is a political accomplishment or an artifice.

This chapter explores how and why these transformations in French foie gras came to be, and demonstrates foie gras's flexibility as a nationalist object in the face of change and challenge. Foie gras's success should be understood as a social and cultural achievement, one made possible through the work of interdependent players and processes. While culture indubitably plays a pivotal role in the construction and reification of national symbols, the story of foie gras makes clear what can happen when markets and politics bolster explanations typically construed as cultural ones—in other words, when nations (and communities) see themselves reflected in their gastronomic choices.

Importantly, I am not interested in normative questions of foie gras's authentic Frenchness. Judgments of authenticity around foods or cuisines, like those of music or art or handicrafts, are social and situational acts. Appeals to consumer tastes for "authenticity" are often created ret-rospectively on the basis of current desires and interests,[9] and asserting authenticity is a tactic used to sell a wide range of things.[10] At the level of the nation, France is but one of many countries that has broadly ad-opted the discourse of authenticity in regard to food and cuisine in the late twentieth and early twenty-first centuries.[11]

Rather, my aims are to trace how the ties between foie gras and French national identity emerged and strengthened and to highlight how the former has become, simultaneously, a product and a producer of nationalistic sentiment with timely political overtones. This is a vari-ant of gastropolitics that I call gastronationalism.[12] In other words, in order to make sense of people's interpretations—and the potential ram-ifications—of foie gras's controversial and celebrated status, we first must discern how and why it *became* a French food.

The processes involved in defining any foodstuff as nationally valu-able are manifold. From the standpoint of gastronationalism, food is a fundamental aspect of collective national belonging; it can communi-cate symbolic boundaries between insiders and outsiders. It alleges gas-tronomic uniqueness vis-à-vis other nations and bolsters the work of particular food producers through state and civic support. A national cuisine, in turn, is far from synonymous with unchanged age-old tradi-tion, but it is nevertheless composed of real foods and dishes, with real meanings, that extend from the agricultural products and practices of specific geographic spaces. In the context of markets, especially today's global markets, gastronationalism throws the political dynamics of con-necting localized food cultures with nationalist identities into sharp relief.

An ethically divisive item, such as foie gras, makes parsing these re-lationships and their impacts all the more important. Several interlaced pathways converged to allow foie gras to rise to an elevated status in France by the beginning of the twenty-first century. First, its symbolic currency is grounded in historicized and fanciful origin stories. Second, foie gras entered into the tastes of French mass culture following a boom in innovative technologies spurred by state and private financiers' investments in the 1970s and '80s that expanded production into a large-scale, highly commercial undertaking.[13] This solidified the industry's standing as economically viable and politically valuable. The 1990s and 2000s saw two trends: the passing of protective policies by the French state and the growth of a foie gras–centered agritourism industry. These efforts put foie gras at a gastronational juncture of cultural, commercial, and state valuation. They modernized a food whose cultural value supposedly lies in ancient, historical traditions. Importantly, these efforts occurred within contested waves of pan-European integration and globalization. In the final part of this chapter, I suggest that foie gras has come to play an elastic role in broader political negotiations of what it means to be a French citizen today.

The Project of Patrimony

While Schwebel and Comiti used similar turns of phrase to describe foie gras's current status in France, and both recognized the industry's expansion from more modest beginnings, the tensions amid their contrasting beliefs highlight the stakes of protecting foie gras as patrimony, or what the French call *le patrimoine*. This is an idea entrenched deep within the French consciousness. Its root is in the word "father," and it is typically translated as cultural inheritance or heritage. Cultural patrimony is something that represents groups' self-defined collective identities. For example, old paintings can be thought of as cultural property, but Botticelli's *Birth of Venus*, which hangs in Florence's Uffizi Gallery, is Italian cultural patrimony. The concept links objects or places of the past with contemporary place-based identities.

Le patrimoine is an evolving project. Project is a germane term here, because it links patrimony with the social dynamics of culture, markets, and politics. And because patrimony is used to signify the uniqueness of certain natural landscapes and societal creations, it is implicit in our conception of what nations are. Manmade objects of cultural patrimony—such as artworks, buildings, books, bridges, and architectural remains—are catalogued by groups such as UNESCO as belonging to nations, which then have the responsibility to protect them for future generations. Taken together, these objects are supposed to validate cultural ideas about shared national and world heritage.[14] As an ongoing project, le patrimoine exists in interaction with its counterpart—namely, within the realm of fears about the homogenizing power of globalist enterprises, which have themselves transformed consumer and citizen expectations.[15]

Concerns about patrimony crisscross ideas about tradition, authenticity, and national autonomy. Tradition is often characterized as that which connects people to ideas of cultural continuity and a sense of historical belonging.[16] It has cognitive and emotional elements to it, and it is tied closely to claims about authenticity. Authenticity, broadly speaking, refers to a set of idealized expectations about how a thing, a place, or an event *ought* to be experienced to be credible, genuine, or even real.[17] Many objects and practices of the past do not, for various reasons, endure the test of time; there must be some sort of continued demand for a tradition to be sustained. Tradition, then, is also a process of selection. And traditions are malleable. They shift and transform, sometimes in surprising ways, as a result of being exposed to tests of their proponents' claims, to social judgments, and to fissures among the fields of culture, commerce, and politics.

When tied to ideas of nationhood, tradition and authenticity consolidate beliefs and stories that refer to shared history, independence, and autonomy. Yet, conceptions of national autonomy do not remain unchecked when it comes to the enactment and enforcement of laws and regulations. Since at least the creation of the League of Nations after World War I, for instance, we have become increasingly aware of the ability of some nation-states to pressure others to "toe the line."[18] Additionally, when tied to place, discourses of tradition and authenticity build on a deeply rooted sense of the homeland and of belonging.[19] This is central to political participation, as it suffuses state institutions with cultural significance,[20] but in France's case also reveals an irony: it ties symbolic boundaries around "Frenchness" as an encompassing national category to particular traditions that are limited in time, space, and participation.

At the same time, national frameworks have increasingly limited power in the modern world. Sociologists and others have pointed to ways in which a pervasive neoliberal ideology has afforded increasing power to transnational corporations and institutions of global political governance, overshadowing nation-states.[21] Some domestic policies are classified as marginal to international systems of governance. The notion of "place" for France is a complex one in this regard. France is made up of smaller places with their own needs and wants, and it is also an active member of numerous supranational governmental organizations, in Europe and beyond. These organizations have revised the roles, responsibilities, and functions of individual states as members of common political-economic enterprises.[22] Yet alongside profound changes in all aspects of French society since World War II has been a thread of strong, vested, and sometimes parochial interest in the virtue of unique places.

Since the nineteenth-century rise of nationalism, states have benefited from creating new traditions and symbols for building patriotic sentiment. Nationalism, in this vein, indicates the range of ways people self-define, or are defined by others, as a national group.[23] Such projects make effective claims to social solidarity and common descent, and to constituting an "imagined community" for people who will likely never meet each other.[24] Traditions were invented and strategically adopted to bolster the idea of the nation as a historically legitimated destiny.[25] Symbols such as flags, monuments, pageantry, parades, and anthems—and the practices that surround them, such as saluting or singing—work to link citizens emotively with each other and with their national states. Not only state-created symbols of independence and sovereignty imbue national cultural identities with political coherence—far from it. The banal language used in everyday media reporting or cheers for a country's sports teams at the Olympics or people's self-identification as "British" or "Brazilian" also work well in this regard.[26] Such everyday symbols help us better understand collective and political claims to a meaning-laden and relatively distinctive past.[27]

Traditions that are institutionally protected as patrimony today typically denote specially designated physical sites (both natural and man-made) or some form of performing, visual, or craft art—the collectively owned "cultural wealth of nations" that confers status and economic benefits on those able to make lawful claims to them. This has been especially apparent in Europe, where guidelines for countries to "protect national cultural treasures of artistic, historical, or archaeological value" were first instituted with the 1947 General Agreement on Tariffs and

Trade (GATT), the initial step after World War II to reduce trade barriers among European national markets. These "treasures" contribute to how people imagine nations as places to live or visit within the context of global capitalism.[28] Heritage is thus one way for nations to capitalize—symbolically and commercially—on cultural products and projects that distinguish them on the world stage. The story of heritage becomes a reason for visiting (and spending money in) particular places. The market for heritage, in turn, offers a paradox of its own, because identifying goods as inalienable or priceless gives them higher commodity value.[29]

When globalization started to sweep the world in the 1980s and '90s, the French were among the most fearful. Successive French governments enacted "cultural exception" policies, or nationalized protections within international trade agreements involving cultural goods such as film and music. This policy framework elicits the basic ideas that global markets for these cultural goods are unduly affected by stronger and better-resourced players, and that homegrown cultural industries need state production.[30] While such policies matter for those who may benefit financially, they also matter for "on the ground" pride in the pleasures of place.

Gastronationalist efforts to include foie gras as part of French heritage and patrimoine, alongside churches, famous paintings, films, and other gastronomic products such as champagne and Camembert cheese, are particularly significant. First, they are meaningful because foie gras production and consumption are not confined to the geographic territory of France.[31] But perhaps more importantly, the assertiveness of these efforts is significant because numerous communities—including many within the European Union—want foie gras production to stop altogether. For foie gras's opponents, "tradition" is not a compelling argument for continuing an arguably cruel and inhumane practice. What does it mean, then, to transform the fattening of ducks and geese into a celebrated symbol of national heritage when it is also so polarizing? What are the rationales and contradictions inherent in doing so? What is perceived to be in jeopardy, and what is really at stake?

It was not inevitable that French legislators in 2005 would designate foie gras a critical symbol of their national culture. That said, the law also offers no guarantee that the market for foie gras will be sustained. French society is confronting new challenges, including immigration, social stratification, and market liberalization. Lifestyle and professional desires are also changing: many longtime foie gras producers I interviewed lamented a dearth of younger farmers around them. These changes have opened new spaces for particular kinds of narratives about the nation to emerge. As we will see, these narratives—which weave foie gras into vivid and glorified tales of intense cultural belonging—indicate new tensions in an environment otherwise obliged to internationalism, and in how foie gras has come to matter for France.

THE FOIE GRAS ORIGIN MYTH

Foie gras's cultural beginnings are in many ways grounded in a mythical, even whimsical, past. And it did not even enter history as a French foodstuff. The tale begins, instead, in ancient Egypt and Rome, and follows the movement of people across Europe.[32] It was not until 1651, with the publication of *Le Cuisinier François* by François Pierre La Varenne (considered one of the founding fathers of French cuisine), that "foyes gras" began to appear in French recipes and then more regularly in local markets.

This irony does not matter for foie gras's modern Frenchness; rather, it is more like a preface for the stories that people tell about it. Independent of where I was in France, the size of the farm or organization I was visiting, or whom I was interviewing, I heard identical tales about foie gras's "discovery" and "extraordinary pathway" from the banks of the Nile River to the humble country barnyard to its role in the canon of French gastronomy and its current status as a symbol of the French nation.[33] These stories are recounted—with only slight variations—in books and on websites, in museums and tourist brochures. And they have left a lasting impression. People I interviewed often used the same words, phrases, and descriptive elaborations in telling them. I was in no way expecting this kind of uniformity. I even started jotting "FGFT," for "foie gras fairytale,"[34] in my field notes when someone launched into them.

As folklorists and anthropologists would insist, this is not a fairytale but an origin story, in that there are no magical creatures or imaginary places involved.[35] Origin stories are socially produced compositions of discoveries, claims of nationhood, and iconic figures. They are a special sort of narrative, one that indicates particular worldviews, and one that works to make the social world intelligible. The practice of telling them, not to mention taking them as objects of study, is revealing because of the ways such stories both articulate categories of identity and simplify some values of their respective communities while masking others.[36] Not everyone trusts or believes these foie gras stories. (The French animal rights group Stop Gavage is but one example.) Nevertheless, they both reflect and guide the way many French people think about this food as part and parcel of their shared history. I also found that these stories have been mediated largely through state, as well as market, institutions.

Over time, I came to see that the veracity of these stories was less important than the mythologizing work they did. They mobilized and marketed pride in national culture even—or perhaps especially—in the face of evidence that challenged the ethics of foie gras production. The "foie gras fairytale" does not just imbue livers with historical or fanciful roots that provide raw material for advertisers. It also serves three additional social exigencies of the present day. First, it holds contemporary culinary renown as a derivative of the "greatness" of civilizations past. Second, it contains multiple narrative plots of family, nation, class, and economic life. And third, it provides a way for foie gras's proponents to counteract moral critiques by conflating tradition with ideas about nature and by highlighting heritage as a counterclaim.

Discovery and Dispersion

According to the tale, the "discovery" of foie gras first occurred in ancient Egypt, where the ancients observed wild geese overeating to build up fat deposits before their migratory journeys across continents. This part of the story stresses evidence of a phenomenon from the natural world in order to challenge accusations that foie gras production imposes "unnaturalness" on the birds.[37] The English-language version of a video shown to tourists who visit the Musée du Foie Gras (Foie Gras

Museum) in the town of Thiviers declares that "Egyptians began to capture and eat wild geese just before the migration period, and they considered it a delicacy. They then learned how to harness the goose's natural tendency to overfeed and produced the first foie gras." The website of Rougié (France's largest foie gras producer) similarly highlights this "discovery of how the secret of foie gras came to be known."[38] Popular books on foie gras all begin with illustrations of what gavage presumably looked like in these ancient times.

Such accounts are not altogether fanciful or false. Bas-relief paintings found inside tombs from the fourth and fifth Egyptian dynasties (several of which are now housed in the Louvre Museum in Paris) depict slaves force-feeding geese with balls of grain through a hollow reed.[39] Ancient language and literature further depict ties to Roman and Greek agricultural practices,[40] inserting foie gras into early chapters of recorded history. The Greek and Latin term for liver was *ficatum*, which literally means "stuffed with figs" (*fici*). *Ficatum* is, in fact, the linguistic root for *foie*, *higado*, and *fegato*, the respective French, Spanish, and Italian words for liver. The earliest written reference to "geese-fatteners" is from the Greek poet Cratinus in the fifth century BC. Fattened geese were gifted to the king of Sparta around 400 BC, and the Emperor Nero served them at his banquets.[41] In Greece, Horace's depictions of the decadent aristocratic banquet mentioned fattened livers as a symbol of moral decay. Homer referenced them in *The Odyssey* in the scene where Penelope has a dream of twenty geese fattening in the yard.

According to some culinary historians, foie gras entered present-day France with the Roman occupation of Gaul, now Southwestern France.[42] Others claim instead that the Jewish people acquired knowledge of goose fattening practices during their bondage in Egypt and carried it with them as they migrated across Europe.[43] Because Jews had to adhere to the laws of *kashrut* (which prohibits cooking with pork fat or lard), these historians note, rendered goose fat provided a suitable solution to a religious problem.[44] Moreover, selling the fattened livers brought in extra money for families who were barred from owning land due to their religion. The Musée du Foie Gras's video tells viewers that "foie gras spread with the spread of the Gallo-Roman Empire, but for many centuries was kept alive by the Jewish community in central Europe, who raised geese more for their fat than for their livers."[45] This part of the origin story also underpins Strasbourg's early renown for goose foie gras, as the city was home to a large Jewish population in the Middle Ages.[46] To this day, goose foie gras takes a prominent place on Alsatian tables, though much of what is served is actually produced in Southwestern France or Hungary.

Foie Gras and the Advent of French Gastronomy

Foie gras's origin myth handily skips over centuries and recommences in Strasbourg in the late eighteenth century. Even though farm wives had long created dishes out of the livers of fattened geese and ducks in that region, and foie gras had been served at festive occasions, the next chapter of the tale begins when Jean-Pierre Clause, chef to the governor of Alsace, supposedly created and served his "pâté de foie gras de Strasbourg" at a state banquet. As the "foie gras fairytale" goes, the governor loved it and brought it to Versailles, introducing the dish to the royal table nine years before the French Revolution began. Foie gras then became an integral part of the new and culturally powerful field of French gastronomy.

This part of the origin story puts foie gras squarely within the historical context of the grand narrative of the French culinary enterprise and its nineteenth-century ties to nation-building. During this period, national unity was considered a critical political project, and state-led initiatives for projects such as standardizing language and education systems were designed to bring together disparate regions and peoples with diverse allegiances under a common patriotic identity.[47] With the aid of several esteemed chefs, state officials purposefully and systemically began to render regional ingredients, dishes, and flavors into a national "French cuisine." Like words or phrases that make up sentences, these "typical" dishes became connected to each other on the national "plate."[48] As Priscilla Parkhurst Ferguson writes in *Accounting for Taste*, "In contrast with the Ancien Régime, which coupled cuisine and class, nineteenth-century France tied cuisine to country. It urbanized and then nationalized the haute cuisine once sustained by the court and the aristocracy. It translated largely class-oriented culinary practices into a new national culinary code."[49] Importantly for the evolution of French gastronomy, this process was a recursive one. State support for growing, cooking, discussing, and eating particular foods and dishes also shaped local markets and consumer demand. This history is critical for appreciating the foie gras fairytale's cultural power and foie gras's place as one of these prized gastronomic items within the offerings of the French culinary field today.

Around this same time, as historian Rebecca Spang has shown, eating in France also gained new public prominence. The restaurant emerged as a distinct entity in Paris about two decades before the French Revolution and gained in popularity through the nineteenth century.[50] Paris saw the burgeoning of a novel cultural trend: a food scene. Bourgeois clientele and the first restaurant critics began to seek out new dining experiences. Bakers, meat roasters, and caterers opened specialty shops to sell cooked foods, including foie gras terrines, for home consumption. The gastronome ("judge of good eating") became an identifiable public persona.[51] Journalist and author Adam Gopnik remarks in his book *The Table Comes First* that it was in this particular period, linked to the end of a national famine, that "enjoying food for its own sake came to be regarded not as an instance of gluttony but a virtue of its own."[52] Yet it is important to remember that, at the time, "French" cuisine was mostly a jumble of dishes from different origins: the countryside, chefs from bourgeois families, places outside of France, and the foods of immigrants. And at that time, most French people ate a barely sufficient and unvaried diet thanks to a mixture of political and economic constraints: little or no meat, cabbage soup, potatoes, stale bread, mediocre wine, and water of questionable quality.[53]

Food writing was instrumental to the institutionalization of the French culinary canon.[54] Gastronomic writing emerged as a distinct and fashionable genre and informed public opinions, both elite and popular, about restaurants and culinary practices.[55] Menus, cookbooks, and even cartoons and books aimed at children helped bring together diverse culinary histories from France's territories. In regard to foie gras, a progression of celebrated writers depicted it as a consumable pleasure, a delicacy, and an indispensable ingredient of French haute cuisine (and later, nouvelle cuisine). Renowned chef Auguste Escoffier's landmark cookbook *Le Guide Culinaire*, published in 1903, contains thirty different foie gras recipes.

Print media continued to be important for the development of a national taste for foie gras as a component of a national French cuisine. By the beginning of the twentieth century, regional French culinary books were being published in Paris, and culinary guidebooks—such as the *Guide Michelin*—consolidated symbolic authority within the growing field of gastronomy. Train travel in the 1920s and '30s and automobiles after World War II were critical for the proliferation of romanticized sentiments and ideas about the rural landscape and small towns so often attached to French food "traditions" today. New rail routes and highways enabled food writers and more affluent urbanites to visit and sample different food products at their provincial sources. By midcentury, writers, geographers, and gastronomes avowed France's agricultural regions as guarantors of good eating. "Vaut le voyage," says the *Michelin Guide* to recommend regional French restaurants: "It's worth the trip." Vacations in the provinces became important in French consumer culture through this time period, as well.[56] Later in the century, other media—including radio, television, movies, and eventually the Internet—added to France's national culinary storytelling. In part due to its good weather and proximity to the ocean, Southwestern French provinces became destinations for gastronomic tourism and expanded their production of foie gras accordingly, alongside truffles, wines, local cheeses, and specialty liquors such as Armagnac. Regional governmental associations realized that tourists wanted to eat well when they traveled, and that hosting food-related events, such as festivals or specialty markets, encouraged local economies.

Cultural claims of terroir and culinary patrimony go hand-in-hand with the marketing of "authentic" places and people. Yet the work of foie gras production was mostly disconnected from the reality of daily life for many people. For it to be woven into the French landscape and social experience, it needed human anchors of recognizable and valued cultural familiarity. This challenge was answered with the image of the *paysanne* ("peasant" or "country") grandmother and with the popular establishment of foie gras as a celebratory dish linked to family and holiday festivities.

2.2 Image displayed in the Musée de Foie Gras in Thiviers of a
"traditional" gaveuse in Périgord, year unknown.

The Iconic Grandmother

The paysanne grandmother is an icon in the foie gras origin myth and
a tool of French national defense of foie gras production today.[57] Raising
and force-feeding geese, and caring for poultry more generally, was traditionally women's work. Old black-and-white photographs (and pho-
tographic reproductions) of elderly women sitting on stools, wearing
long skirts and sporting head scarves or buns in their grey hair—while
holding funnels in their hands and geese between their legs—are omnipresent in books, marketing materials, and on the walls of foie gras
shops (see Figure 2.2). Unprompted and often, the producers I spoke
with frequently mentioned the grandmothers, sometimes referring to
their own. Patricia, an *artisan-conserveur*, for example, spoke proudly of
foie gras as a female tradition in her multigenerational family business:

> My grandmother had a restaurant in Salignac, and behind her
> there was her mother, her grandmother, also in the gastronomy.
> Here, in Salignac, there has always been continuity. Look in this
> photo (pointing to an image in her marketing brochure), you see
> my grandmother, holding the goose by the neck. She did not ga-
> vage the birds herself, but she went to market and bought from
> other women to serve at her restaurant.

Among rural French families through the twentieth century, it would have been typically the job of an older female member of a household to raise small animals such as chickens, rabbits, or geese, to provide food for the family. Often, the livers harvested from fattened geese were sold at markets or to neighbors—one of the few income-producing activities available to women at the time. For example, one with whom I spent a week, was a female producer in the Dordogne who had learned to make foie gras from her grandmother and was now a grandmother herself. Danie told me proudly how, when she was a young woman, she used the money earned from foie gras to make her first major purchase—a set of dishes.

For some families, elements of this pastoral imagery remain a lived reality. At a multigenerational family farmhouse in the countryside just north of Toulouse, I met a seventy-seven-year-old *bonne-maman* who continued to raise about two dozen birds each fall for her family and holiday gifts, as she has done for decades. She delightedly led me around the farm she shares with her daughter and son-in-law and their teenage children, showing me her house (whose décor had not changed in decades), her vegetable garden, the cages of rabbits she raises in a barn, and the root cellar, which housed the family's larder of jarred foie gras, preserved meat, jams, and about one hundred bottles of wine from a neighbor's vineyard. She was not rearing ducks or geese at that moment, as it was June and that was—she explained—her autumn activity. She told me that she learned to gavage from her grandmother. Another family-owned artisanal foie gras business outside of Pau had the wife's eighty-one-year-old mother selling their products at a biweekly outdoor market. She said she enjoys driving the delivery van to and from the farmhouse twice a week, catching up on news with their longtime customers, and being the face of the farm.

It is fairly common for discourses of national history to be grounded—usually through rose-colored glasses—in figures or characters that emphasize virtue and resilience across generations.[58] Historical narratives that appeal to a premodern past or images of pure "folk" are actually selectively chosen, often by individuals or groups who are relatively aware of how they might be received by different audiences.[59] In part, these choices help make intelligible the nuances and confusions of ignoble history and give shape to the puzzle pieces of collective identity.[60] For foie gras, the imagery of the kindly grandmother helping to support her family serves a function in resisting accusations of cruelty. Yet, grandmothers producing a few livers in the family's barnyard today are few and far between. Those who persist generate but a small fraction of the foie gras produced in France today.

Familial Celebrations

The final, and crucial, component of the origin myth, one that under-girds its cultural worth, is foie gras's place on the table of family and holiday celebrations. As Jean Schwebel remarked, "we have no Christmas without foie gras." Similarly, a visitor to a food expo in Paris told me: "The foie gras traditions are the traditions of Christmas. I am thirty-five years old, and have had foie gras at every holiday."[61] Foie gras sales peak in December, and holiday promotions abound in stores and online. Smaller farms sometimes send a family member around the country to make deliveries to customers, and towns around the country host specially organized Christmas markets with foie gras vendors present.

In these links between culture and commerce, we see how a national food market becomes intertwined with otherwise "local" tastes or traditions. The story of foie gras is similar to that of champagne in the way that its consumption has come to mark special occasions and celebrations. Recent French marketing campaigns promote foie gras for other special moments throughout the year: Valentine's Day, birthdays, graduations. In early July 2006, for example, I noted large-scale, professional advertising campaigns from some of the nation's larger producers, such as Rougié and Delpeyrat, for including foie gras in upcoming Bastille Day fêtes.

In sum, the origin myth marries foie gras's production and consumption to the idea of French nationhood. It meshes selected bits of cultural history and nostalgic reflections on foie gras's connections to the "greatness" of past civilizations, the grand narrative of French cuisine, and family belonging. This works to propagate national taste as moral taste, marking who belongs to the nation (and who does not). It gives foie gras and its producers legitimacy. Yet, the myth's tenacity is increasingly vulnerable to challenges presented by opponents eager to point to the actualities of its multi-billion-euro industry. In the last few decades, the French foie gras industry has radically transformed in size and scope, making it an object of mass culture.

INDUSTRY SHIFTS

As a commodity, foie gras's national valuation gives those who control its production and distribution an extra layer of moral authority. Explaining its desirability today by referring to ancient glories and grand-mothers—as a number of my interviewees did—ignores the significant role that commercial and state forces have played in France's modern foie gras industry. Importantly, rather than destroying the origin myth, these shifts, which combine the resources of the state with those of commercial firms, have instead infused it with new vigor and new gastronational meanings.

In the latter half of the twentieth century, the French foie gras industry changed in fundamental ways. Beginning in the 1960s, the French state and commercial financiers underwrote capital resources for new technologies and infrastructure that led to the industry's expansion. Three major shifts occurred: consolidation of business ownership, changes in the technologies of production, and a switch in the type of bird used to make foie gras. These subventions lowered production costs and, in turn, the price point for products "du gras."[62]

Foie gras became an industry linked to strategic partnerships and financed equity. In part through bringing individual producers together into associations and collectives to supply different production houses, foie gras became a spatially segmented and vertically differentiated supply chain. Like most chicken production in the United States, tasks became divided among hatcheries (*écloseries*), raisers (*éleveurs*), feeders (*gaveurs*), slaughterhouses (*abbatoirs*), and processers (*maisons* or *fabricants*). Gendered associations of bird raising and fattening eroded; male gaveurs became more common in this new production model. Importantly, these industry transitions were contingent on technological changes: namely, a shift from fattening geese to fattening ducks, the adoption of pneumatic feeding machines, and the use of individual cages (known as *épinettes*) to hold ducks during gavage. With the advent of this model, the Southwestern regions of France—which had cheaper, less-populated land and a better climate for year-round farming—surpassed Alsace as the main locus of the country's foie gras production.[63] In 2004, according to CIFOG, the Southwest supplied almost ninety percent of the estimated 18,500 tons of foie gras produced in France that year, an estimate that has remained stable in years since.[64]

The 1980s witnessed further financing of growth-oriented research and active capital investment in the foie gras industry. In 1986, French investment firms Le Hénin and Compagnie Financière de Suez[65] trained a group of specialty food companies, including the foie gras company Labeyrie, to build larger-scale commercial distribution channels. Similar efforts were successful for other conglomerates. At the same time, this period saw a flood of lower-priced imports, primarily from Hungary, and increased domestic production that left many smaller-sized producers on the brink of bankruptcy. Several firms consolidated and quickly became market leaders. At the beginning of the 1990s, just four brands together realized forty-four percent by volume of the foie gras sold in France.[66] Hatcheries producing more than one million ducklings annually jumped from fifty-seven percent in 1995 to eighty percent of total production in 2001. Manufacturers making more than four hundred tons of foie gras per year went from forty-eight to seventy-six percent of total French production during this time period.[67] Today, the world's largest foie gras company, Rougié (which is owned by the multinational firm Euralis), raises and processes more than eleven million ducks in France per year (about thirty percent of the nation's total foie gras production).

One product in particular—the *bloc de foie gras*—contributed to this growth. *Bloc* is a smooth, emulsified liver paste that is cooked and either canned or sealed in plastic casing and sold ready to consume. Before its invention, foie gras producers worked with whole pieces of liver that could show imperfections in the production or preparation processes. Bloc eliminates these imperfections by blending lower-grade pieces of livers together into a single product with a consistent texture. It is less costly than other foie gras products, making it an attractive item for supermarkets and chain stores to put on their shelves, and it helped the industry expand its reach to middle-class and lower-end consumers. Bloc also helped address the industry's previous seasonality "problem" because, like other processed foods, it could be stored for longer periods of time. By 1992, more than fifty percent of the foie gras sold in France was bloc.[68]

Due to these supply chain transformations, foie gras production rates within France tripled between the early 1970s and the early 2000s. Moreover, new markets were created for duck meat, feathers, and fat— the byproducts of liver production. CIFOG's summer 1996 newsletter reported:

> French foie gras production has had a veritable revolution. Links in the chain have benefited from the advances of fundamental techniques and permitted response to consumer demand, notably the entrance of foie gras into large-scale distribution venues, and for the development of secondary meat markets and the valorization of magret [duck breast].[69]

Marketing campaigns and consumption have followed suit. One foie gras farmer I visited said similarly: "Foie gras was really expensive until the 1980s. It was only for Christmas and New Year's then. Now you can get it anywhere, and the demand has gone up and up." Several other industry members referred to this as "the democratization of foie gras." With this "democratization," however, came a shift in the very animal being used.

From Geese to Ducks

Foie gras is made from either goose (*l'oie*) or duck (*le canard*). Historically, geese were much more commonly used. As of 2010, however, ninety-five to ninety-eight percent of France's foie gras producers use ducks, up from fewer than twenty percent just half a century ago. Farmers with whom I spoke considered geese more challenging and more costly to raise in large numbers. Geese do not breed year round, as ducks do.[70] I was also told that geese need more space while in gavage because their immune systems and esophagi are more "delicate and sensitive," and that they "do not adapt well to mechanized gavage." Geese require three daily feedings during gavage, compared to two for ducks, requiring more human labor and more feed. Farms that raise geese are typically smaller in size, usually employ artisanal feeding methods, and have higher costs for producers and price points for consumers.

The director of international exports at Rougié, Guy de Saint-Laurent, explained that an additional reason for the switch was that "all the money from goose production is concentrated in the liver. To sell goose meat is very difficult. Consumers don't like it as much. To sell duck meat is much easier." He anticipates French goose foie gras production decreasing even further. Yet goose is still vaunted as being more refined (and is slightly, but not prohibitively, more expensive). Much of the goose foie gras sold in France now originates in Hungary.[71]

Not only have ducks surpassed geese in number but, in the 1960s and 1970s, researchers developed a special hybrid duck just for foie gras—the mulard (sometimes spelled moulard and translated as "mule duck"), a sterile crossbreed of the male Muscovy and female Peking duck. Farmers told me they consider mulards "hardier," "more disease resistant," and "less temperamental" than other breeds of ducks. They produce a "more reliably consistent" liver and also have "tougher esophagi," making gavage "easier for bird and feeder alike."[72] Only male mulards are used in foie gras production; the females' livers are considered "too veiny."[73] Today, some producers raise and gavage Muscovy (*Barbarie*) ducks, but the vast majority (as high as eighty to eighty-five percent) of foie gras ducks in France and elsewhere are mulards.

The mulard's sterility has had significant implications for the social organization of control in the industry. Egg fertilization happens through artificial insemination, because these two types of ducks are otherwise sexually incompatible. The associated costs of artificial insemination make this viable only on a larger, consolidated scale. Moreover, this means that production of eggs and ducklings can be centrally controlled. Farmers who raise mulard ducks, either artisanally or industrially, must buy hatchlings from purveyors rather than breed them themselves.

At the other end of the chain, chefs' practices and consumer tastes have evolved concurrently. A few decry the change, bemoaning the loss of goose foie gras's texture and flavor, but others recognize culinary opportunities in mulard livers. Goose foie gras is generally cooked over low heat in a *terrine* or *torchon* and served cold. As an *artisan-conserveur* explained: "With goose there is more fat. So it makes it less advantageous than a duck, because it melts a lot more. It's less firm. Beautiful, but gives off more fat."

By contrast, mulard duck liver can be prepared cold or hot. Emil Jung, a Michelin-starred chef in Strasbourg, described the mulard as "versatile" and as "the duck whose liver doesn't shrink." Consumer tastes for hot foie gras dishes made from non-shrinking mulard duck livers grew at restaurants in France and elsewhere. Chefs created new dishes to feature it, ranging from slices of seared foie gras with fruit garnish to toppings for seafood or steak and foie gras baked into pastry dough. Several told me that it was an "easier" product to serve than terrines, which can take several days to prepare. Some have even extended the mulard's "versatility" to sweets, such as foie gras lollipops, doughnuts, crème brûlée, and ice cream.[74]

Many French producers, chefs, and amateur gourmets noted taste differences between the two. When I asked which he prefers, renowned nouvelle cuisine chef Michel Guérard responded:

> I like them both, for different reasons. For me, it's a very different taste. The goose, it is the finesse. The duck, it's more rustic, more musky, and it has more sensibility. If I was going to compare them to wine, I would say that the liver of duck is Burgundy and the liver of goose is like Bordeaux.

A shopper at a Parisian food expo combined cost and symbolic distinction in how he values goose liver and how he rationalizes others' preference for duck, saying:

> I think goose foie gras is finer. The taste is less strong, more delicate. That of the duck is stronger, spicy, and this pleases people who aren't educated a lot to taste. They see a product that is still festive and less expensive than goose.

These changes in animal type and breed are important to foie gras's Frenchness for several reasons. First, they helped a previously expensive and prestigious food become cheaper in price, "democratizing" it. Second, they show that the cultural meanings and understanding of "what foie gras is" are flexible.[75] Yet this flexibility has also created new modes of aesthetic distinction through taste-based assertions about flavor, texture, and connoisseurship.

The Logistics of Industrial Foie Gras

While the previous section demystifies *what* foie gras is made of, this section explores transformations in *how* it is made and who is involved. The 1970s saw the invention and rapid adoption of a mechanized feeding process that uses hydraulic or pneumatic pumps instead of the previously used combination of a funnel, an auger, and gravity (see Figure 2.3). These machines calibrate the amount of food each bird will get in a feeding depending on its stage in gavage (which increases gradually from a few tablespoons to about three-quarters of a cup of a slurry of ground corn[76]). Twice a day, the gaveur rolls the machine (about the size of a washing machine on a wheeled platform) down a barn's aisles of ducks. At several farms, I watched as a gaveur grasped a duck by the back of its head, opened its beak, inserted the tube into its esophagus, and pressed a button for the machine to dispense a premeasured amount of slurry into the bird's crop.

Alongside the shift to these machines, the industry began using individual confinement cages to hold the ducks during the twelve-to-fifteen-day gavage period. During gavage, the ducks are kept side-by-side in individually sized metal cages sized raised waist-high off the ground in long barns with low lighting and ventilated air. They are unable to turn around or fully spread their wings. A trough of water runs continuously underneath their heads, and the temperature in the barn is chilly compared to the summer day outside. Several different gaveurs told me that the colder air and low lighting keep the birds calm. Raising the ducks off the ground serves a dual purpose: it lets their feces fall underneath the cages and allows the feeder to have the

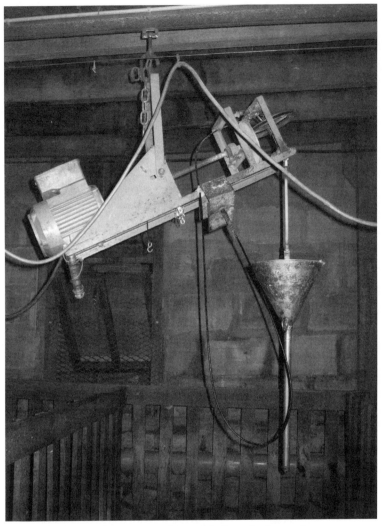

2.3 Artisanal gavage machine with funnel, pipe, and auger.

ducks within arm's reach as the machine is wheeled down each aisle (see Figure 2.4).

Using this combination of feeding machine and individual cages reduces the time for each duck's feeding to just a few seconds, rather than the thirty to sixty seconds of artisanal producers, where the gaveur must

2.4 Industrial gavage machine, which grinds and dispenses feed.

measure the food for each feeding, catch each bird in a larger group enclosure, and move it into a feeding position.[77] In this system, called industrial by opponents and practitioners alike, one person typically feeds eight hundred to one thousand ducks twice daily, compared to one person feeding twenty or so birds a few generations ago or in smaller, "artisanal" production facilities. Farms elsewhere in France (many of which are contracted by firms headquartered in the Southwest) sometimes use several gaveurs to feed up to two thousand birds at a time.[78]

These practices quickly became part of manufacturers' standards for their suppliers. By 2007, they accounted for around ninety percent of French duck foie gras production. One farmer in the Gers region justified this near-ubiquity with a conventional supply and demand argument. "Overall," he said, "it's not a choice. Before, everyone fed like my neighbor (who is an artisanal gaveuse) does. To make a living, you have to optimize, and the solution is the individual cages. Demand has exploded, and so production has exploded." When I asked him to clarify why he himself chose to produce ducks in this way, rather than use the older, traditional methods, he responded, "We decided to gavage so many ducks in this way so my wife, who does the feedings, could have a salary here instead of having to look somewhere else for work." The decision to join the industrial supply chain—while requiring capital investment in machinery and setup—was framed as an issue of family livelihood.

These industrial logics have permitted a few manufacturers—some of which operate as firms and some as producer-owned cooperatives—to control production throughout the supply chain, beginning with breeder contracts and networks of *éleveurs* who receive and raise day-old ducklings. Rougié, the largest of the brands, contracts out raising its birds to eight hundred farmers around the country. Others are contracted for gavage and follow manufacturers' standardized rules for feed and housing conditions. Still others do the killing and butchering. Processing and packaging then occur at centralized locations, typically at one of several large, factory-like firm headquarters that distribute the final products through wholesalers and retail stores. None of the gaveurs I visited who worked within this supply chain could pinpoint what happens to their ducks after they leave their farms—not where they were processed, what brand would be on the packaging, or at what store I might find them.

Observers dispute whether this shift has negatively affected the quality of the product and the lives of foie gras producers. Mitchell Davis, a coauthor of *Foie Gras: A Passion*, told me that during his on-the-ground

book research in France, he saw that mechanization had "not only affected quality, but has affected the economics to the point that it becomes a political issue because of the ways the birds are kept. A lot of
the smaller farmers we met with there were feeling as though they were
being pressured out of the business, because they couldn't compete with
the huge producers." Antoine Comiti similarly noted that some French
consumers draw stark moral lines between "industrial" versus "artisanal"
foie gras. On the other hand, some chefs and industry members think
that these changes have been beneficial, and that overall production
quality today is higher. Sitting at his dining room table, André Daguin,
a celebrated chef and restaurateur perhaps most strongly associated with
promoting foie gras in the Gascony region, recounted the difference
between foie gras "then" and "now":

> When I was ten years old, my mother used to buy geese and ducks
> whole. In the kitchen, we opened them. Out of ten, we had two or
> three nice livers, two or three medium, and two or three *pffffft!*
> Now eighty percent or more are good. That's because the ani-
> mals are healthier. An animal that is sick or ill cannot make good
> foie gras.

From his perspective, mechanized feeding methods have been a positive
turn of events, not a drawback. The birds are "healthier" because there is
more knowledge about, as well as care taken with and consistent over-
sight of, the gavage process.

Perhaps unsurprisingly, mechanized gavage operations are not the
ones promoted to tourists. While such operations are located throughout the countryside, they are hidden in plain sight. My visits with these
producers had to be arranged through intermediaries, and I was often
regarded with suspicion as an outsider and sometimes as an American.
On my very first visit to one of these farms, I was accompanied by the
neighbor with whom I was staying. Walking up to the unmarked barn,
we were greeted by a woman sporting short blonde hair, reddened
cheeks, and work overalls. My host explained why we were there, introducing me as "an American who is interested in foie gras." Her immedi-
ate response was "je ne veux pas d'une problème" (I don't want a prob-

lem). My host reassured her, saying, "No, no. She likes to eat foie gras," and then said to me, "You see, there's yet another person who is suspicious of an American who is interested in foie gras. It's not typical." What did prove typical throughout my fieldwork at these types of operations was this response to my presence.

On a separate occasion the following year, Guy de Saint-Laurent of Rougié offered to take Mark Caro, my journalist colleague, and me to what he called "a typical foie gras farm" as part of our visit to his firm, whose headquarters are in the town of Sarlat. Even though we had already visited a number of farms, we agreed, interested to see where he would bring us. The next day, we drove fifteen minutes out of town to a picturesque farm on a hillside. Guy was behind the wheel, explaining how his industry needs to be better at "showing" and not just "telling" people that gavage is not as bad for the birds as they might believe, and that he needs to work harder to "reverse the negative publicity." The farm where he took us raises about 1,200 geese at a time, most of which were out in the fields, wandering under trees, when we arrived. 180 were in the gavage barn, grouped in threes in pens raised up on metal grates.

The farm's proprietor—an older man wearing dusty overalls and scuffed boots—came out to greet us. He showed us around the fields, gesturing at the open spaces and the geese pecking at the ground. We then ventured into the barn, where he set up a three-legged stool next to the raised pens to demonstrate gavage. He used a thirty-year-old machine that seemed on its last legs. It shook and rattled as he fed one of the geese, kneading the bird's neck as damp corn kernels went into its crop. He invited me to come over and to put my hand on the goose's neck and crop as he was doing this, to feel where the corn was landing.

Mark commented that the process seemed slow for feeding so many birds. In response, the proprietor pointed to another, newer and pneumatic machine in the corner that he said he uses for everyday gavage. What we had just seen was a demo for visitors. It also turned out, after a few more pointed questions, that Rougié uses this as one of its "show farms," and that this farmer was not actually a Rougié supplier. Guy defended this discrepancy, saying that Rougié's suppliers were located too far away for a quick visit (but also did not offer information or contacts for us to visit them). Hidden in plain sight.

Industrial feeding operations with individual cages have proven politically acrimonious. In 1999, the Council of Europe, the organization that promotes pan-European integration of legal standards, endorsed a proposal to phase out their use in France. (The proposal stated no acquisition of new cages after 2005 and no further use after 2010.[79]) Jean Schwebel, however, insisted it was "well known" that this was a "recommendation" and not an "obligation," and that the industry agreed to it "willingly." CIFOG and the French Ministry negotiated a five-year delay, arguing that the timetable was too short for farmers whose livelihoods depended on this type of production. This extension—which currently stands to remove these individual cages from use by December 2015—will indubitably affect how the industry operates, if it happens. Meanwhile, in 2006 and 2007, I noted that the farms I visited were not actively phasing out the cages, and I heard hints from farmers and activists alike that new ones were still being installed. And as of December 2015, individual cages still remained in use.

Consumption and Price

France is a land of foie gras plenty. Though it is produced and consumed in other countries,[80] as of 2005, eighty percent of world foie gras production and ninety percent of world consumption occurred in France.[81] In 2006, it was a €1.9 billion (about $2.5 billion) annual industry and has proven economically important for rural regions and national export markets, the latter of which net about €40 million per year (about two percent of total revenue).[82]

A December 2008 survey of French consumers by polling company TNS Sofres found that eighty percent of respondents had eaten foie gras at least once that year, if not multiple times. Foie gras can be relatively cheap, no more or less costly than many other specialty food items. A small can of industrially produced mousse or bloc de foie gras at a grocery or chain store costs €3–5 (around $5–9 US) for sixty to eighty grams (two to three ounces). Artisanal foie gras and *d'entier* have a price premium, ranging between €18 ($22–26) for a 120-gram jar (4.2 ounces) and €64 ($74–78) for 450 grams (15.9 ounces). A large piece of deveined and vacuum-sealed artisanal duck liver with a PGI label available at the 2006 Salon Saveurs food expo, complete with the image of an older man wearing a beret on the label, was priced at €22 (around $35 US). On restaurant menus, a foie gras appetizer was often only few Euros more than the next most expensive choice. The range of prices and available products—from mousses and bloc to *mi-cuit* (chilled, semi-cooked livers) and whole cooked or fresh livers, not to mention to various ways foie gras has been incorporated into other products— makes it affordable for a majority of French consumers. In addition, demand for the rest of the duck—*magret* breasts, *rillettes*, and *confit* legs—has also grown.

These prices and products are representative of the industry's relatively new conditions. They denote an expanded tradition as well as a common story about commodification and market growth. For foie gras, this led to opaque understanding about the industry by some of the very people it employed. Many people I interviewed or spoke with throughout the industry's supply chain lacked a complete picture of what was happening outside of their own positions within it or those positions most proximate to themselves. For example, gaveurs could not identify what happened to their birds after they left their barns, and retail shopkeepers often only vaguely recognized the shifts that have taken place in the industry. But economic investments in the supply chain alone cannot create and sustain the nationally emblematic status of a food. Political legitimacy is also essential.

POLITICAL LEGITIMATION

According to the origin myth, foie gras is a French tradition that evolved "naturally" over time as more and more consumers fell in love with it and the market grew to meet demand. However, such a narrative overlooks the ways that policy decisions have been indispensable for cementing foie gras in the French gastronational imagination. The concept of gastronationalism—how national sentiment and food production build upon and strengthen each other—necessarily invokes involvement by the state.

As the foie gras industry grew throughout the second half of the twentieth century, attempts at quality regulation lagged sorely behind. It was not until 1993, the same year that saw the official creation of the European Union via the Treaty of Maastricht, that French agriculture law first specified criteria for grading and categorizing different types and preparations of foie gras. Prior to that time, the market was mostly unregulated and products were easily—and often—misrepresented to consumers.[83] The 1993 criteria were published in the *Official Journal of the French Republic*.[84] CIFOG president Jean Schwebel explained that while they took time to affect labeling practices, they allowed consumers "to better understand, and appreciate the contents of the products they were purchasing" and allowed producers to develop shared ideas about their collective interests. CIFOG itself was not founded until the early 1990s, remarkably late for a national trade association representing a product of ostensible historic value.[85]

Animal agricultural practices throughout Europe are overseen by the EU's Commission on Animal Health and Welfare under the Directorate General for Health and Consumers.[86] EU standards for hygiene and humane animal treatment must be met in husbandry and slaughtering facilities across all member countries.[87] In 1998, the EU Scientific Committee on Animal Health and Animal Welfare published a report on foie gras production that has proven to be an important document in the debates over its moral status. The ninety-three-page report's conclusion, that "force feeding, as currently practiced, is detrimental to the welfare of the birds," is often cited by animal rights organizations as irrefutable evidence that foie gras production is inherently cruel and should be prohibited. If read more closely, however, the report condemns not foie gras itself, but rather the use of individual cages and the industrialization of the feeding process. It recognizes the need to limit "avoidable suffering" and includes several recommendations to improve production conditions. It also sanctions limiting production to where it was a "current practice" and recommends "continued scientific study" of welfare standards, pain and stress indicators, and alternative methods that do not include gavage.

The year after this report was released, CIFOG and the French government received from the European Union's new "designation of origin" (DO) food labeling program a Protected Geographical Indication (PGI) label for "canard à foie gras du Sud-Ouest."[88] This PGI allows producers of any size in the Southwest to apply to use a special symbol on their packaging indicating its terroir. It registers foie gras within a respected pan-European program created in part to safeguard gastronomic "diversity" across the continent. Producers from other regions of France, and other parts of Europe, can still call their offerings "foie gras"; they simply cannot label them "canard à foie gras du Sud-Ouest." This came around the time that French public opinion polls and social observers showed heightened concerns that globalization and Europeanization were threats to national identity.[89]

This label, however, contains three puzzles for foie gras's status as a tradition, each of which contrasts image and reality. First, the application for "canard à foie gras du Sud-Ouest" was contested not by animal rights groups or other national bodies, but by small-scale, artisanal foie gras producers in Southwestern France. According to research conducted by French anthropologist Isabelle Téchoueyres, these producers criticized the application for its nonspecificity regarding the size of production operations and lack of quality measures for the resulting products. Many feared that they would be put in economic jeopardy.[90] Second, the Southwestern regions are only one location within France that claims foie gras production as historic tradition; there is no equivalent label for foie gras produced in Alsace. Finally, this application and its reception are significant for the material basis of what foie gras has become—canard means duck. As mentioned previously, ducks only surpassed geese as the primary bird used in the late twentieth century. But the official protection is for ducks.

In the first decade of the twenty-first century, international criticism of foie gras production intensified. The French group Stop Gavage began to receive increased media attention and to draw resources from international animal rights organizations. In 2002, Cardinal Joseph Ratzinger, the future Pope Benedict XVI, declared in an interview regarding the industrial fattening of geese: "This degrading of living creatures to a commodity seems to me in fact to contradict the relationship of mutuality that comes across in the Bible."[91] Protesters in Britain targeted, boycotted, and vandalized department stores and restaurants that sold foie gras. Several well-known celebrities became outspoken opponents. In 2008, Prince Charles issued a letter asking his chefs not to buy it for the British royal residences. The Dutch royal family issued a similar statement. The Supreme Court of Israel—a country that had goose foie gras producers—banned production in 2003 after pressure from Israeli animal rights activists.[92] And legislators in several places across the United States considered and passed city and state prohibitions on production and sale.

Laws banning foie gras production also exist throughout Europe, which its opponents around the world highlight as evidence of the practice's immorality. Today, foie gras production in Europe is limited to France, Spain, Belgium, Hungary, and Bulgaria. Germany, Italy, Luxembourg, Poland, Finland, Norway, and several Austrian provinces have laws prohibiting the force-feeding of ducks and geese for foie gras. An Austrian animal rights group, Four Paws, organized a media campaign and successful boycott in Austria and Germany against foie gras and poultry products from Hungary (a country with a relatively weak farmer lobby) in 2008.[93] Laws in Holland, Switzerland, Sweden, and the United Kingdom do not explicitly ban the practice, but interpret general animal welfare laws as applying to gavage. Yet, the majority of these countries were not foie gras producers in the first place. Passing these laws assuaged the desires of activists without causing adverse economic effects.

At the same time—and this is important for the French industry's doggedness—retail sale and consumption of foie gras *cannot* be banned in those countries.[94] Due to the EU's regulatory principle of mutual recognition, a food product that is lawfully marketable in any one EU member state must (subject to a few limited exceptions, most around public safety related to health) be lawfully marketable in *all* of them. And foie gras continues to be legally produced in several countries, primarily in France. This makes foie gras production *within* France problematic for opposition elsewhere in Europe. Activist groups have appealed, so far unsuccessfully, to the EU to ban foie gras production. While the EU *has* expressed concerns about the specific practices of its production (beginning with the 1998 report), no direct moves have been made to outlaw it completely. In response to a 2001 inquiry posed by a member of the European Parliament, the Commission stressed that "it should be mentioned that a ban on force-feeding is neither foreseen by the Directive nor by the recommendations" made by the committee.[95] But, presumably, this may not always be the case.

It was in this transnational context that the French National Assembly and Senate voted on an amendment in 2005 to protect foie gras as part of France's official cultural and gastronomic patrimony. The amendment noted that foie gras "perfectly fulfills criteria" characterizing "the link to terroir that characterizes the originality of the French food model." The Assembly provided an accompanying explanation to the amendment, which passed 376–150, that "Foie gras is an emblematic element of our gastronomy and our culture." Testimony by senators over the draft law suggested that the declaration was preemptive and anticipated "any initiative from Brussels" (the European Union's headquarters) on the matter. In response to one senator's concern that the "advertisement of foie gras in law" seemed somewhat unnecessary and foie gras need not be endorsed by the French state, another responded that "it is because gavage is contested that it is necessary to inscribe it in law; otherwise, the good spirits of Brussels will come and ban from us all that is our terroir."

Without acknowledging the empirical reality that French foie gras production has transformed into a highly mechanized, multi-billion-euro industry, these leaders were responding to what many felt was the diminishing and vulnerable role of French national culture within European integration politics and broader global affairs. Their words illustrate hopes that they can shield foie gras preemptively—as a cultural symbol and as a commodity—from censure. Its inclusion within French patrimony law was thus designed to send a galvanizing message to French and international audiences alike that cultural, patriotic, and market actions are one and the same.

Gastronational Adversity

Contentiousness over foie gras is anchored within timely social frameworks about French national identity. This food became a potent gastronational symbol in a world where borders and boundaries between countries seem progressively obsolete in many different markets. Foie gras's current status suggests tensions in how cultural belonging is reified and in how certain beliefs come to be not only cherished, but intensely so.[96] We can also see that no single institution or group alone had the power to characterize what foie gras is today. This makes this food especially "good to think with," to borrow a turn of phrase from anthropologist Claude Lévi-Strauss,[97] because of its fraught and contested nature. Whether treasured or despised, foie gras is a multivocal symbol: it is imbued with narratives, imagery, tastes, and meanings that are widely available for public use and that people find useful.[98] And its industry is just as much a product of a particular historical trajectory as it is an instigator of it.

Yet, such beliefs also require sponsorship; tradition must be continually reappraised. And nationalized protections require more than mere presence within institutions. They also matter in everyday experience, parlance, and tastes. If we look at marketing campaigns around specific foods as evidence of gastronationalism, we see attempts to filter nostalgia and protect certain tastes through a modern lens: new "traditional" foods based in part on modern technologies of production and distribution and marketed directly in relation to what they are *not*.[99] As we will see in the next chapter, this sponsorship for foie gras has become visible in various ways from farmyards to tourism campaigns to governmental offices. Willingness to interpret foie gras as an indelible and endangered resource depends on its cultural brokers. Though its meanings are increasingly slippery, the work of these brokers shows the strength and the flexibility of nationalist objects associated with authenticity, tradition, and autonomy—and with markets. When connected to the idea of the nation, such moral sentiments have power.

Commemoration of and nostalgia for the past can be mercurial processes.[100] In expanding such contestation to include certain foods or cultural products, the concept of protecting heritage serves as a rallying cry for fostering the unique values of certain places, people, or industries as they find themselves in new global relationships.[101] Institutionalized support for foods signifying a worthy past also sends audiences a message that law and policy are valuable, even necessary, tools of defense. We see state actors and private interests working together to facilitate this. They elude critics' accusations and instead rely on symbolic politics derived from a sense of infringement on the nation's moral sovereignty.

Accounts of the past influence and reflect the way we think about the future. French historian Pierre Nora wrote that for the belief systems of the French nation, "memories become valuable just as they vanish" ("On ne parle tante de mémoire que parce que qu'il n'y en a plus").[102] I posit that foie gras became iconic *when* it did, at least in part, because it coincided with other shifting meaning systems in French society. The industry's buildup as a public-private enterprise, the lowered price point, the PGI application, and the 2005 declaration occurred at historically contingent moments. For the French Parliament to officially include a polarizing food like foie gras in its portfolio of national assets equates challenges to its moral status with perceived attacks on French culture. Foie gras's origin myth—its historicized ties to discovery, family, place, and cultural canon—in public narratives is key here. This is because the origin myth emphasizes *intra*-national coherence and similarities at the expense of organizational and supranational disjointedness.

French commitments to the idea of political unity in Europe are longstanding, with some French political figures being, to a large extent, responsible for the overall European project past and present. Yet, a vein of national self-interest also runs deeply through political rhetoric of the last half-century, and has surfaced yet again with rising approval ratings for the country's far-right political party, Le Front National.[103] Numerous public opinion surveys show that while many French people approve of the European community, they also have doubts about the ways its structures and institutions have evolved. Even with fallout from the recent global economic crisis, an integrated Europe is considered by many to offer a competitive market, a powerful and moderating voice in international relations, and a shared system of liberal values. But the idea of creating a European consumer or a singular European identity still has a long way to go.[104] Additionally, while food and cuisine are central to buttressing France's historic identity as a culinary trailblazer, the nation can no longer declare itself the indisputable international leader of gastronomy. Competition in this cultural field has become ever more intense.

As a challenge to the modern-day processes of European markets and institutions, then, foie gras matters. Gastronationalism helped to transform it from a regional, small-scale, and seasonally produced foodstuff into a multi-billion-euro industry linked to the geopolitics of national identity. The age and details of the tradition of gavage have come to matter less for "authenticity" than what is today proclaimed as an asset of national cultural wealth. With this positioning, perceived and real threats to foie gras production and consumption have become equated with challenges to French heritage and sovereignty. Moreover, foie gras has become a repository for projected fears about the dissipation of French identity and culture, at least in part *because* it is ethically contentious and vilified elsewhere. To some observers, France's actions read like condescension and unwillingness to deal with opponents' concerns in a diplomatic way. But at the same time, for France to engage those concerns head-on means undoing an industry it has worked hard to develop and legitimate as a national cultural good. Preserving foie gras is a small but significant way for the French to defend the idea of France.

CHAPTER 3

Gastronationalism on the Ground

I was thrilled when a Michelin-starred chef in the city of Bordeaux responded positively to my email requesting an interview about foie gras—one of the only chefs to do so during my first fieldwork trip to France. Jean-Pierre Xiradakis has been the chef and owner of La Tupina (which means "kettle" in Basque) since 1968. The restaurant specializes in "the cuisine of [his] mother and grandmother—simple, honest country cooking with good products from the region." He was also an expert on French food: he had authored a book on Bordeaux's culinary heritage, several cookbooks, and a guidebook to regional vineyards (as well as a murder mystery novel). And in 1985 (when French foie gras production was industrializing, as discussed in the previous chapter), Chef Xiradakis organized a regional chefs' association to "defend Southwestern culinary traditions" and revive the use of endangered "quality" foods. Foie gras was one of the first items brought under this umbrella. His work and prolific writings, not to mention his invitation, led me to believe that he would be welcoming.

I arrived at La Tupina at 11:30 on a Monday morning, before the lunch service began. In a call earlier that morning, Xiradakis sounded friendly but serious. I was led through the restaurant's dining room and upstairs to his empty office. The room was small and cramped, but an open window permitted fresh air and noise from the traffic of the city's historical *quartier* below. A large wooden desk was strewn with books. Stacks of papers took up most of the floor. A large framed image of

Che Guevara, signed by photographer Albert Korda with a personal note to the chef, hung on the wall. In the next room, several fashionably dressed young women worked on computers next to tall, overstuffed bookcases.

The chef arrived and sat down behind his desk after shaking my hand. A middle-aged man with wire-rimmed glasses and graying hair on his temples, he was wearing a buttoned dress shirt rather than a chef's jacket. Our conversation was stilted, to say the least. His answers to my questions were short and gruff, and he seemed exasperated by what I was asking. He explained the principles of fattening as mimicking the birds' migratory habits, the geography of foie gras production as split between the Southwest and Alsace, and that he had gotten his foie gras from a nearby cooperative for the last twenty years. Customer demand for foie gras at La Tupina had increased over the years and extended beyond the winter holidays.

When I brought up the controversies around foie gras in the United States, Xiradakis went from exasperated to indignant. "In the United States," he declared, "the principle of gavage is considered a crime, whereas for us it is an old tradition of twenty centuries." He then noted what he perceived as the overemphasis on animal rights activism regarding foie gras relative to other social problems. "You could do an analysis in the United States," he said, "of the lack of limits to people's behavior—the violence, the racism, the homelessness, and they go looking for things to ban, something that is part of our traditions. It seems absurd. They demonstrate caring about ducks when they don't seem to demonstrate caring about people." I pressed back, saying that in fact foie gras has opponents within France too. Without missing a beat, he replied, "Yes, but America doesn't have a monopoly on imbeciles. There are assholes in every country."

After a few more minutes of such piqued answers, Xiradakis asked if I would have lunch with him. I agreed. We went downstairs, where he spoke with the maître d' about a table. I was shepherded to a beautifully set table in the corner of the main room, while the chef disappeared into a back room for a few minutes. The painting above the table was of a lobe of foie gras wearing a smiley face, sitting on a piece of lettuce, signed D. Rosa 1988. A server came over with a pitcher of water, a plate of charcuterie, a cigar along with a cigar cutter, and two glasses of white wine. No menus.

Over the course of the next hour, I was tested. After sitting down, Xiradakis asked the nervous-looking server to bring out several dishes, which arrived shortly thereafter—a large piece of seared but runny foie gras, a plate of fried tripe, and patties that looked like hamburgers but were really made of congealed chicken blood. The chef handed me each platter, expectantly. After watching me put a portion of each dish on my plate and then in my mouth, he smiled. Then, he began talking, really talking, in an utterly effusive way. He asked me how my interest in food began, about my family, why I was interested in foie gras, and what I hoped to do with my degree. I brought out my voice recorder again, and he recounted his visit to New York City for a gathering of foie gras producers and chefs organized by Ariane Daguin of D'Artagnan, a gourmet food purveyor and daughter of André Daguin, an esteemed chef in Auch, a city south of Bordeaux. He spoke of his admiration for the Union Square Greenmarket in New York City and for the quality of American beef. Eating these dishes in front of him counteracted any suspicions that I, as an American interested in foie gras, seemed to generate.

By eating these foods, I was engaging in "boundary work," playing with the conditions that delineate insiders from outsiders—those who can be trusted versus those who cannot.[1] The boundary here was a gastronational one, in that it tethered sentiments of national attachment and pride with the material and symbolic realities of cooking and eating food. I argue in this chapter that gastronationalism appeals not just to macro-level political and business interests but also to a micro-level of collective identity that is shaped through cultural scripts and is contingent on actual and embodied consumption. In this particular instance, I was deemed "safe," at least temporarily, through my visible act of eating these special dishes. As such, these foods are social objects that have a life of their own—they reflect the interests, spaces, and sentiments of the people who make and use them.[2] The story of foie gras in France is a story about the social construction of national taste, and it is also a story about people's lived, emotional experience and their vested interests in the symbolic politics of food.

Through the nineteenth century, the French state invested in gastronomy as a nationalist endeavor, bringing regional items together and transforming them into a grand cuisine that became one of France's greatest sources of domestic and international pride. An educated palate became a vehicle for characterizing national identity.[3] In contemporary France, I posit, foie gras has similarly come to convey identity. The catch here is that, as explained in the previous chapter, although foie gras has also been "democratized" through mass production and consumption, the specialness to which its adoption by both opinion leaders and the larger public attests depends on its visibility and its materiality. In other words, it needs also to be a material container of cultural meanings for various social uses "on the ground." Further, these sentiments are situated in opposition to international social movements that would prefer it not exist at all. Reiterating one of this book's main premises, foie gras is not solely a product of gastropolitical contention; it has also proven to be an independent producer of it in its own right.

In this chapter, I use an ethnographic lens to explore how gastronationalist sentiments crisscross the social worlds, landscapes, and local economies of the French regions that celebrate foie gras production. By immersing myself with people involved in its production, I sought to make sense of their stories, motivations, and challenges. I underscore the affective relationships that both producers and consumers have toward this food, and I also analyze tensions over foie gras's moral disapprobation as a modern and contested industry.

My inquiry is guided by several overarching questions: How do micro-level practices of production and consumption articulate with the more macro-level politics of identity, especially in places where foie gras "traditions" are classified as heritage? What if the heritage being celebrated is a dissonant one? How do the people involved in the production of foie gras experience the dissonance of nostalgic romanticism and the industry's empirical realities?

To investigate these questions, I conducted fieldwork throughout France in 2006 and 2007.[4] When I first began this research, I did not expect to find foie gras to be as abundant and omnipresent as I did. Its shops were part of urban streetscapes; it was available on the majority of restaurant menus and advertised in magazines and on television and billboards. I spent between a few hours and five days at twelve foie gras farms and six production facilities in the Southwest. These operations ranged in size from two-or-three-person family-run businesses to farm operations that were parts of vertically integrated production chains to a factory that employed several hundred on-site workers. I also spent time in tourist offices, retail shops, outdoor markets, amateur-created foie gras museums (complete with repurposed department store mannequins dressed in old-timey clothing), professionally run food expos, and people's homes. I talked with people involved in foie gras's social world: tourism employees, tourists and consumers, restaurateurs, chefs, researchers, anti–foie gras activists, and local government officials.[5] I also collected French news and magazine articles, industry reports and association newsletters, producer sales catalogues and advertisements, tourism brochures, popular books aimed at children and adults, restaurant menus, and French anti–foie gras social movement materials. Since then, I have remained in contact with informants and abreast of events reported in the French and European media that have sparked similar introspection about the politics of foie gras's value in the face of international contention.

In the previous chapter, we saw how state policies and new capital investments bolstered the industry and embedded foie gras in national patrimony law. But what, exactly, is this law protecting? Its passage throws into sharp relief the interplay between localized food cultures and the twenty-first-century institutions that set the terms of markets and mediate issues of national sovereignty. This chapter shows how contention over foie gras is played out across national, and nationalistic, boundaries. Importantly, what any group categorizes as "authentic" or "heritage" is a moving target. Across Europe, some foods are labeled as cultural traditions by certain communities. As described earlier, many are protected as a type of national intellectual property under a European Union program for "designation of origin" (DO) that licenses the historicized link between their production and particular places and communities.[6] "Terroir" has become a buzzword with global reach. These foods' culture, commerce, and politics are intricately linked to transformations in, and questions of, collective identity.

Foods that are labeled and marketed as national heritage give people—often geographically, socially, and politically divided—the gustatory means to participate in the idea of a nation. Across the world, many foods marshaled for such a cause originate in peasant food cultures. Some have been key cultural symbols in the work of inventing nations. In Mexico, for example, maize—originally associated with pre-Hispanic society and peasants, rather than colonial elites—became central to the development of a national Mexican cuisine.[7] Today, efforts are underway in Mexico to recognize items such as nopales and chiles as official geographical indication (GI) products via the World Trade Organization's TRIPS Agreement. (Tequila was the first GI registered product outside of Europe.[8]) Ghanaian elites under British rule turned from consuming European to African foods as an expression of nationalist sentiment.[9]

Some such foods are heralded, and are classified as "endangered," by a prominent international effort named the Slow Food Movement, which promotes itself and its member businesses as an alternative to industrialized "fast food" and the global disappearance of old-style culinary traditions. For instance, in the 1990s, *lardo di Colonnata*, a cured pork fat specialty of a tiny marble-producing Italian mountain village, was inscribed as one of the first items in the Slow Food Organization's "endangered foods" campaign—the lunch of an impoverished quarry laborer reinvented as an exotic item for gourmet consumption (and with the town of Colonnata playing the new role of host to an influx of international culinary tourists).[10] Importantly, it is also the way some foods are produced that has mattered for identity. In Mexico, an argument could be made that tortillas made by hand are more authentic than industrial ones. Lardo di Colonnata has been held up as simultaneously threatened and treasured because townspeople consider the practice of curing the fat in locally sourced marble basins in dank cellars the only way to obtain its true flavor, yet this process does not mesh with modern European hygiene and sanitation policies for food production.

These cases (and others) clearly show that "heritage" is relational, meaning that people both have a stake in it and also need to "pitch in" for it to be achieved on a grander scale. Successfully crafting foie gras as a crucial part of French heritage and patrimony today involves the labor, interests, flexibility, and buy-in of many different people and groups. It means crafting history.[11] As a relational process, heritage is both social and situational, expressed through objects and markets that aim to represent particular ways of life. It is concerned with legitimizing social identities for the present. As detailed in the previous chapter, this helped national affinity for foie gras to supersede class divides.[12] Foie gras production and producers matter for popular national self-imagining, not just that of the country's elite.

In most of the industry's flowery rhetoric, which strives to connect foie gras's symbolism with certain aspects of a culturally appropriate history, the gritty realities that reflect about ninety percent of the foie gras produced in France today are actively obscured. Its origin myths extol the resilience of the paysanne grandmother and the enticing terroir of the countryside. They also draw on, and contribute to, longstanding claims about the iconic value and perceived superiority of French cuisine in world history.[13] The story being told and sold fits with narratives that create binaries contrasting mass production to tradition, fast to slow food, and globalized trade to local production. Holding these narratives up to empirical scrutiny, however, shows the considerable implications they hold for people who have a stake in foie gras's future.

As a topic of conversation in the places that claim it, foie gras elicits perceptions of threatened identity, sometimes triggering displays of jingoistic pride. For example, one potential informant—an academic whose research combines anthropology, marketing, and food studies—told our intermediary that she would only meet with me if I "enjoyed eating foie gras." When I asked her why she had solicited this information, she responded, "Because you came with the category of American. And, some Americans are against the production of foie gras. So, I didn't want to invite one of them, because I didn't want to meet someone who doesn't like foie gras. It's a question of national solidarity. I don't think I am especially nationalist, but in this context, I defend it." Her response surprised me, because we might think that an academic, of all people, would possess more critical distance than most. But for her, as well as for others, foie gras elicited nation-based defensiveness.

This makes the story of foie gras a clear case of gastronationalism. Disputes over foie gras's production and consumption—as they manifest in France and elsewhere—raise questions about the shape of "national culinary heritage" in modern times. Part of the foie gras industry's reality today is that it faces new ethical challenges, namely animal welfare and rights concerns that include direct accusations of torture and cruelty. These ideas in turn are intertwined with French mindsets on the benefits and drawbacks of globalization in the twenty-first century. This is significant because, of all the European countries, France's leaders have been especially successful in deploying ideas about protecting "culture" in the face of what are seen as encroaching political institutions and powerful transnational corporations.[14] Is French society ripe, as fearmongers bemoan, for Americanization? McDonaldization? Homogenization? At the same time, however, these concerns often fail to consider the new diversity France confronts as an immigrant destination and a leading member of the European Union.

DOWN ON THE FARM: THE (RE)INVENTION OF THE FOIE GRAS ARTISAN

Darnat is a small, artisanal foie gras farm located in the hills outside of La Roche-Chalais, a village of about three thousand people in the Dordogne region of Southwestern France. It is on an unmarked country road, with only a small sign at the end of the driveway. It was midmorning on July 14, 2006—Bastille Day. I had just spent the previous evening and the early part of the morning shadowing Darnat's owners, Dominique and Michèl Jaumard, as they gavaged several pens of ducks (see Figure 3.1). Now, with assistance from their adult son Julien, they were about to process four ducks in their small, tile-covered abattoir. These particular ducks had been deemed "ready" during their handling the night before, and each had feathers clipped from their heads with a small pair of scissors to indicate that fact. Overfeeding past the time when the liver is ready produces bad foie gras, Michèl had told me. Before they began, Dominique handed me a blue plastic apron and asked if I would be okay watching, with a warning not to faint: "Ne tombe pas sur les pommes!" (Don't fall on your apples!) (I didn't.) The three moved energetically around the room, speaking little except to tell me the details of what they were doing—rendering an electric shock to stun the ducks, bleeding them out, dunking them in boiling water to make the

3.1 Gavage at Darnat.

feathers easier to remove, defeathering with a circulating vacuum and a blowtorch for the pinfeathers, and hanging them to chill (see Figure 3.2). The boiling water steamed up the room, and the air smelled biliously sour. They handled the ducks expertly and spoke matter-of-factly, neither glorifying what they were doing nor excusing themselves for it. It was their everyday work.

After that, I stood in the "cold room," sandwiched between the abattoir and a small kitchen, where I was indeed shivering as Michèl and Dominique butchered the four ducks. Wearing plastic gloves, Michèl sharpened a knife and made slow, careful cuts to remove the first duck's "jacket," or *paletot*—the skin and fat, to which the breasts and legs are attached as a single piece. He then sliced the breast meat, or *magrets*, out of the paletot, put pieces of fat into a small pile, and laid the legs flat in a ceramic dish that Julien put in the refrigerator. Julien explained to me that every part of each duck would be used in some way. Some of the meat and livers would be vacuum-sealed or canned in an autoclave to sell in their small on-site shop or at the weekly outdoor market Dominique attended. The feathers removed earlier would be dried and sold (for seven cents per duck) to a distributor who sells them to pillow and quilt makers. The carcass was wrapped in plastic and put in the walk-in

3.2 Cutting the carotid artery in the abattoir.

refrigerator. Julien explained, "It will be good for soups, barbeque, rillettes. Everything is used. The intestines and all those things, even the veins, go to a friend of ours who raises dogs. Delicious for the dogs. They will eat well."[15]

Some of the meat and innards—like the legs now in the refrigerator—were put aside for Michèl to cook for lunch patrons at their twenty-seat *ferme auberge* restaurant.[16] At least seventy-five percent of what a ferme auberge serves must come from the farm. (The family also has a vegetable garden, some egg-laying hens, and a small coffee roaster.) The menu was fixed-price, with three entrée-plat-dessert choices, most of which involved duck. Michèl was the cook and Dominique the server, and they typically planned their days around reservations. Julien helped out when he was home from the hotel management school he attended, as did his sister Anaïs, a high-school student. That particular day, they had one lunch reservation for seven people. Then I accompanied the family to a friend's home for an afternoon Bastille Day fête. After that, the ducks in the barn had another gavage around sunset.

I asked Michèl how they learned to do all of this. "Petit a petit" (little by little), he responded. Dominique—a former schoolteacher who grew up in a Parisian suburb—said she learned by watching Michèl. Unlike most other farmers with whom I spent time, foie gras did not run in this family. They had purchased and renovated this farm in the early 1990s, after a few years of leasing nearby land and teaching themselves the craft. "At the beginning, we lost a lot of meat on the carcass. We did not know exactly how to get the most out of it, like we do now," she told me, as she trimmed some white fat. She pointed out the heart and the lungs. "Et voilà, le foie gras," Dominique said, cracking the carcass open to remove the liver, which she placed on the metal countertop in front of us.

Darnat was one of several farms in Southwestern France where I learned firsthand about the work, lives, and perspectives of artisanal foie gras producers (who account for about ten percent of the nation's production). Most, but not all, were intergenerational, family-owned businesses. Many had been fattening geese or ducks for twenty years or more, and told me in detail how they had learned to raise and gavage the birds from their parents and grandparents. Some raised geese, some ducks, and some both. They sold their products at outdoor markets, to restaurants, at retail shops on the farms or in nearby small towns, at terroir food expos held in cities around the country and, increasingly, online. Commonly, many (but not all) artisanal foie gras farms raise, gavage, slaughter, and process the birds themselves. Some were certified PGI (Indication Géographique Protégée) in the EU's national labeling program. Some belonged to producer cooperatives. A few had a family member make deliveries to long-time customers around the country. More than one told me that they occasionally send small shipments to friends in other countries, including to Americans, labeled as "conserves." I also spent time with two artisan-conserveurs, whose businesses bought, processed, and sold products made from ducks and geese raised and fed by gaveurs in their communities.

The term "artisan" has archetypally been used to describe a skilled craftsperson who works with his or her hands in the production of consumer items such as pottery, jewelry, and furniture. It is typically characterized in relation to what it is not—modern, technological, large, fast.[17] When used in connection with food and cuisine, it conjures an image of seasoned individuals handcrafting small batches of foods using time-honored techniques. Throughout France, names of villages and provinces designate artisanal foods as unique local specialties (whether or not they are actually produced on a small scale).[18] Artisans thus become standard-bearers of a sort of traditionalist, localized pride.[19] I argue they have also become producers of contemporary gastronational identities, built from reliance on the idea of "the nation" without necessarily forsaking localized interests." By the beginning of the twenty-first century, branding foods as attached to place names, identities, land, and terroir—grounded in the nation's soil and people—had turned into a politically defensible cause.[20]

To produce foie gras, artisanal gaveurs operate on a small scale in terms of the number of birds they raise and feed. They use mostly old-fashioned techniques and tools, including slower, hand-feeding methods that rely on gravity and a rotating auger inside a funnel attached to a metal tube. They feed the birds with scoops of whole-kernel corn that has been soaked in water to soften it.[21] A couple of artisanal farms I visited did use machines that were variants of the hybrid-pneumatic machines used in industrial gavage. (One gaveur rationalized using it as "a more exact calibration, so better for the geese.") The gavage period for artisanal birds is longer than the twelve days of industrial production, and feeders increase the amount of food at smaller intervals. In artisanal gavage, the birds are held in group pens or cages, not the individual cages described in the previous chapter. I watched several different gaveurs physically get into ground-level pens and sit on stools to hold the birds between their legs while massaging their necks during feedings, or sit down next to raised cages and pull the birds toward them one by one.

Several artisanal gaveurs spoke of their work as craft, describing the nuances of their techniques and the learned skills of touch, sound, taste, and smell. For example, I watched a gaveur named Gilles gavage geese one evening on his multigenerational family farm. He moved skillfully through the pens, telling the geese "doucement, doucement" (softly, gently) in a low voice as he stepped over the dividers between groups of geese, moved the feeding funnel into position as he sat down on his stool. He showed and explained how he massages each bird's abdomen to know exactly how large the liver has become before feeding it. Similar to what I saw at Darnat, he took a small scissor from the breast pocket of his weathered, blue work jumpsuit and snipped the forehead feathers of geese that were destined for the abattoir the next morning.

Using such hands-on techniques permitted small-scale producers to distinguish their practices from those of their industrial counterparts. These producers consider their products to be "of quality," their animals better cared for, and their farms to have unique taste profiles. This legitimates the higher cost of artisanal foie gras for consumers. One producer drew this contrast: "Every product we have is different. Every duck is a little different, so the taste from liver to liver might be different." This allowed them to affirm their own integrity by producing foie gras "the traditional way" and "the right way." They also reveal the complex reality of negotiations between traditional skills and modern commercial needs. For example, at a food expo in Paris that included nineteen foie gras producers of various sizes, one artisanal producer displayed a large poster with photographs of its farm's rolling hills and the slogan "Escapades d'authenticité" (Getaways of authenticity). Another distributed brochures to expo-goers with photos of her family's ancient farmhouse and an *attestation de provenance*, which explained that she chose to "bring the most transparency possible to guarantee the authentic quality" of her products, which she noted were also certified by Qualisud (a sixty-year-old French organization that inspects and certifies agricultural activities as being "of quality").

Most of the artisanal producers I interviewed or followed offered detailed interpretations of how various factors—including their parcel of land, the microclimate, their rearing practices, the types of feed they used, and the lives and bodies of the birds themselves—influence the quality and taste of their products. Several also spoke of intangibles such as community memory and family history. Most downplayed their own commercial motivations for being in the foie gras business. And yet, the former themes matter for a successful business. For example, one artisan-conserveur told me of her family's innate "savoir faire" for the business, showing me old black-and-white photographs of her ancestors' restaurant, *conserverie*, and trips to market, saying that "since always, our family prepares *produits de terroir*."

There is little doubt that nostalgia and romanticism permeate thinking about what artisanal foie gras production is and is not.[22] Farming has many joys, but consistent cash flow is not always one of them. Yet, artisanal foie gras producers are not arguing for a return to the days of yore. Far from it. The realities of those days were far bleaker, with much greater hardships than the bucolic scenes painted in children's storybooks and films portraying the virtuousness and innocence of the French countryside.[23] Instead, as I witnessed, these producers are reformulating artisanship for the twenty-first century. They are updating their expectations, seeking out new market opportunities, and eschewing provincial political attitudes. Living modern lives with modern conveniences is also important. Many have renovated and updated their homes. They email, surf the Internet, use cell phones, and watch satellite television. Their production facilities must meet health and hygiene standards set by the European Union, and many have begun using social media to advertise their product lines. Yet, in and through their work, they are persistent in linking cultural claims of foie gras's terroir with the marketing of "authentic" people and places.

The cultural work surrounding this product as place-based is neatly reflected in a statement made by Fabio Parasecoli in his 2008 presidential address to the Association for the Study of Food and Society. "Local products," he said, "reveal their historicity and their developing nature, always pulled between tradition and innovation, cultural value and economic potential." To this wise observation we might add the importance of shifting local contexts. In the 1980s and onward, small foie gras producers feared state-financed industrialization and a flood of cheaper livers imported from Eastern Europe. Indeed, this happened and many lost or sold their businesses. Grassroots efforts to sustain quality and market share—such as Chef Xiradakis's association of regional chefs, begun in 1985—helped alleviate some, but far from all, of this trend. In one *commune* in the Dordogne, for example, I was told that a few decades prior there had been forty-five working foie gras farms but as of 2007 only three, including the one "full process" facility I was visiting.

However, those farms that remained by the early 2000s saw new interest in their methods and their products. This was part and parcel of a broader response to modernization and globalization, especially by those deeply concerned with the fate of local and national food cultures.[24] In France at the turn of the twenty-first century, globalization was widely perceived as a threat originating outside national borders—an image of French land, sovereignty, and identity under attack. Writers, artists, and cultural critics, along with supportive politicians, were strident in challenging the perceived encroachment of American companies. "Cultural exception" policies protecting markets for French film, television, and music were inscribed into national law in the 1990s, limiting foreign media on screens and radio dials. These policies were often positioned by pundits and legislators alike as the country's right, and even duty, to preserve and promote its cultural heritage and prevent irrevocable loss.[25]

Food and cuisine have similarly been sensitive subjects. As but one example, observers of France's pushback against the forces of globalization often mention the Confédération Paysanne, one of France's largest farmers' unions and led by a man named José Bové.[26] Bové became famous in 1999 for driving a tractor into a McDonald's restaurant. He did so to protest the World Trade Organization's decision to penalize Europe for prohibiting US-produced hormone-treated beef and to support US sanctions on European (primarily French) food products, including Dijon mustard, Roquefort cheese, and foie gras. This action—and the deluge of public support that Bové received then and since—juxtaposed issues of agriculture and culture with the physical destruction of an icon of globalization.[27]

Other promotional strategies for safeguarding French foods as heritage have reverberated at national levels. In 1989, the French Ministry of Culture created the Conseil National des Arts Culinaires (National Council of Culinary Arts) with a mission statement of protecting French gastronomy and new initiatives such as teaching the development of a national palate through "taste education" programs for children at public schools. French citizens have also seen the growth of a veritable "heritage industry"[28] organized by regional and local governments in conjunction with national initiatives to promote physical sites, rituals, folk museums, the arts, and foods celebrating French history and culture.[29] The number of appellations granted through national labeling programs such as Label Rouge (awarded by the French National Institute of Origin and Quality as a guarantor of premium, superior-quality food produced using traditional and environmentally sound methods[30]) and the EU's designation of origin program for "artisanal" foodstuffs— including cheeses, meats, vegetables, fruits, and olive oil (not to mention wine)—is one of the highest in Europe and still rising.[31] French cities finance and host gastronomic expos highlighting these foods. The *Salon Saveurs* in Paris, for example, is a biannual three-day event that hosts twenty-five thousand visitors and two hundred and fifty to three hundred smaller and medium-sized producers of terroir food products from around France, as well as a few from Italy and Spain.

And demand for these foods is growing. A 1998 Eurobarometer survey found that thirty percent of Europeans said that identifiable origin, either by country or region, was an important food purchasing criterion and that seventy-six percent claimed to consume food produced "traditionally" on a semiregular basis. In 2014, Europeans said "quality" was the most important purchasing factor, with fifty-three percent being prepared to pay more to see origin information on labels.[32] According to reports from CIFOG, artisanal foie gras sales and, in particular, of *foie gras entier* (whole foie gras sold in cans or jars or fresh), have jumped since the 1990s. This trend mirrors dynamics of other specialty craft food production within France and elsewhere.[33]

Values and claims associated with an idealized rural past—such as artisanship, quality, authenticity, sustainability, community, local economies, craft, nature, and skill—are increasingly promoted by these food producers and their supporters as antidotes for the anomie and placelessness produced by globalization and industrial agribusiness. The notion that heritage is innately valuable is reflected in consumers' beliefs. A 2004 study by Christy Shields-Argèles that compared French and American self-understanding in relation to food habits found that among her French respondents these values represented not only "good eating," but a logic for sustaining national gastronomy.[34] Similarly, one visitor to the expo mentioned above, a Parisian man in his early sixties, told me, "There are some products like foie gras that follow the place.

Two businesses that are twenty or thirty kilometers apart can taste different. Not like McDonald's, which has the same taste everywhere in the world. It's for this that it [artisanal foie gras] is a fantastic product."[35] Another interviewee told me, "Here, in France, you don't eat just to feed yourself. It's culture. It is totally different."[36]

Connoisseurs and producers claim to be able to distinguish easily between artisanal and industrial foie gras. I had been invited to Darnat after a telling interaction several weeks prior with the owners' son, who was a master's student at a hotel management school. The school's director had invited me to their "foie gras day," when representatives from Rougié, the world's largest foie gras company, were visiting to introduce their firm to the school's students. I went with the goals of observing how Rougié pitched itself to hospitality students and obtaining an "in" to collect some data from the company itself.

During the company's presentation at the sit-down dinner that evening, the student sitting to my right introduced himself as Julien and said, "That is such a funny coincidence that you are here next to me; my parents own a foie gras farm!" At that moment, student servers brought in the first course—an appetizer of three different foie gras preparations. A plate was set in front of each of us, and a Rougié representative explained the order in which they should be eaten: a pâté, foie gras entier, and one flavored with champagne. Julien asked me (in English) if I understood how they were described. Without waiting for my answer, he pointed to my plate and said, "The first one is crap, the second one is whole foie gras but still doesn't look good, and the third has champagne." I asked him what he meant by "crap." "Well," he began:

> It's only thirty percent foie gras and then has a lot of other stuff. And it's too salty. The finish is a bit sour and bitter—that's the word, right? Bitter? *Amer*? The second is also crap. Look at it. It's all foie gras, but you can see from the different colors that it has different livers put together, not from the same duck. It's good, I guess, but from my point of view, it's not that good. The third is good, but the quality of the liver isn't very good. But, it's better soaked in champagne because the liver taste is not very strong. If you're going to use a good quality liver for this type of foie gras, it's

a waste. So it's okay. But this is a truly industrial product. There is a big, big difference for me. They grow the liver in twelve days. My parents do three to four weeks and feed only with corn. I don't know what these ducks are fed.

He then invited me to visit their farm and "see real foie gras being made."

Language around "realness" came up repeatedly in my fieldwork. It specifies a moral valence of authenticity, one that has enabled artisanal foie gras to be "rediscovered" as special and worthy of national-level attention. In addition to emphasizing quality, what matters for "real" foie gras is the sense of social rootedness in particular landscapes and connectedness to the people involved in its making. State-based promotional campaigns, travel guidebooks, and culinary websites similarly valorize these people as "real" and "authentic" stewards of French heritage.[37] Yet unlike other specialty products with dedicated enthusiasts, such as chocolates or cheeses, foie gras production is also vilified as a cruel and torturous practice. It is a *bête noir* of the international animal welfare lobby. Artisanal or industrial, it does not matter. They want it gone. And this is a problem that the industry, and the nation, must confront if it wants foie gras production and consumption to persist.

Visit with the Ducks: A Neo-Rural Landscape of Tourism

Seeing gavage in person, foie gras's foes adamantly proclaim, will disgust and repulse even the most hardened of meat eaters. Yet, what has been established in Southwest France in the last few decades is a tourism industry dedicated to doing just that. As an interloper in this world, I found that tensions in the social practices that order food preferences in a morally hierarchical way—such as what others might regard as unpalatable, disgusting, or unethical—tempered the ways that gastronationalism around foie gras manifested in everyday practices. One of the main ways foie gras is crafted as nationally valuable—and at risk—is through the framework of terroir tourism, which works to connect sympathetic outsiders with the physical places and cultural spaces of artisanal production. From a bird's-eye view (pun intended), the relational nature of heritage work becomes clear in this framework. It valorizes particular sets of social ties and claims of belonging, while also masking the dizzying realities of what most production is really like.

In general, tourism creates social expectations about place. Culinary tourism in particular enhances the status of food and agricultural practices in several ways: it makes them better known and appreciated, it links them with pleasure and desire, it implicates participants in shared cultural tastes and symbolic meaning systems, and it connects them with (i.e., brings resources to) their places of production.[38] Contemporary culinary tourism initiatives create a specific vision of rural, agrarian France and serve this vision onto people's plates. It is consumption, and eating, that activates the experience of an "authentic" France. It reveals how gastronomy is used consciously to tout a sense of timeless continuity with history, even when it elides contemporary realities. And tourism is indubitably a source of change for the very sites and practices that made them appealing in the first place.

Rural tourism has a long history in France.[39] Importantly, in contrast to American environmental discourses that promote nature as a pristine wilderness, French visions of and desire for nature are predicated on notions of *social* rural life, which establish the paysan farmer as a cultural expert and spokesperson for the sustainability of the landscape.[40] Beginning in the 1980s and 1990s, France's rural areas experienced a new wave of interest among French city-dwellers and other Europeans who wished to learn about French country life and the provenance of traditional dishes.[41] In a recent essay on the importance of place in the modern French "foodview" of the *goût de terroir*, anthropologist Amy Trubek quotes from an interview with a small regional publisher of books related to the Dordogne, who told her that emphasis on "terroir has increased in the past thirty years, and it is primarily a form of nostalgia; people are searching for their roots as an antidote to their increasingly fast-paced, urban lives."[42]

Foie gras producers of all stripes have been able to capitalize—symbolically and economically—on the cultural power of this desire for agrarian landscapes and old-timey experiences and on stories about shared savoir-faire.[43] Yet, provenance is a tricky issue. Scholars have long critiqued tourism for oversimplifying complex cultural histories and for manipulating physical places so as to seem more authentic to visitors.[44] While traveling to small towns in search of authenticity might bring people to new places and offer them novel experiences, it will not bring them back in time. Heritage is marketed to tourists as something old and longstanding but is actually a relatively new form of cultural production that works to inject a "second life" into otherwise-fading places.[45] These "authentic" people must square a number of roles in this new world: food grower, entrepreneur, citizen, community member, ecological steward, cultural host. They must negotiate between personal desires and market logics, demonstrating that heritage is indeed a churning cultural process. It is not only *what* is interpreted through these practices, but also how, by whom, and for whom.

What I observed in the Southwest of France related to culinary tourism was a mélange of old and new. Besides foie gras, these départements—which encompass Aquitaine and the Midi-Pyrénées, as well as Périgord, Landes, Gascony, the Gers, and the Dordogne—are promoted as being replete with gastronomic treats such as Armagnac and black truffles. They are also home to prehistoric caves, ancient churches, stunning panoramas and gardens, vineyards galore, outdoor activities such as hiking and cycling, and generally beautiful weather. Vacationing there is relatively inexpensive compared to city-based holidays, and people can purchase quality products for lower prices than they could find in shops at home.

The départements and communes of Southwest France have strong incentives to support tourism. Local chambers of commerce and of agriculture classify tourism as an important facet of economic development, especially in areas that are historically agricultural and not as monetarily prosperous as others.[46] Many of these towns participate in Bienvenue à la Ferme (Welcome to the Farm), a branded national network of chambers of agriculture and more than six thousand farmer-members, or "ambassadors of sustainable and responsible agriculture," as they are called by the program, throughout France.

Driving in cars, riding public buses, and hopping trains between rundown stations around the Southwest gave me numerous opportunities to observe the regions' culinary offerings and to consider what remained invisible in this social landscape. Professionally designed billboards for

3.3 Farm sign for Ferme du Courdou and its small foie gras
museum, from the road.

large companies such as Rougié and Valette lined the main highways,
advertising "foie gras from Périgord." Signs for small-scale foie gras
farms and their attached shops dotted the narrower, winding roads
throughout the countryside. Some were hammered into the ground on
wooden posts, hand-drawn to evoke rustic charm. Others showed car-
toon images of smiling ducks wearing bowties or playing musical instruments. Sometimes the sides of buildings were painted with the
name of a producer down the road.

I took this photograph of one artisanal farm's sign to document the
saxophone-playing duck, its invitation to visit the farm's "small foie gras
museum," and the icon for the Bienvenue à la Ferme campaign (see
Figure 3.3). It was only later, after looking at the photo a number of
times, that I noticed how the sign was mounted directly on top of an
older, muted, hand-lettered and duck-shaped wooden sign. This juxtaposition of the old with the new frames the farm as both historically
grounded and relevant in modern times. It also shows ways in which
tourism has recalibrated the artisanal foie gras farm, using the past to
negotiate new ways of being in the present.

Importantly, the foie gras farms that are conspicuous, self-promoting,
and welcoming are artisanal farms, which together account for only

about ten percent of the foie gras produced in France. My visits to industrial producers all had to be arranged through gatekeepers. Artisanal farms offer a sanitized version of foie gras production. While they still have a lot of birds—and all that their lives and deaths entail—they do not have the quantity that industrial operations do, nor do they use the individual cages that foie gras's opponents vociferously condemn. Yet, even these farmers are trying to figure out how to position themselves for the future, not for the past. The value and pleasure of their work emerges in the interactions they have with each other and with their customers, as well as from positive depictions of their families, their villages or towns, and their country. Most did not begrudge industrial producers their market share. Some were their neighbors and friends. Instead, they described themselves as serving a different market and their offerings as based more on quality. Financially, foie gras production has helped some to stay on their land and others to renovate their ancestral homes and provide for their families.

At these small, often picturesque farms, one can meet the farmer, purchase duck or goose products fresh or in cans or jars, and sometimes eat at ferme auberge restaurants or stay overnight in inexpensive *chambre d'hôtes* guest rooms or camp on the property. Tourism information offices in the historic centers of many towns in these regions distribute fliers from nearby artisanal foie gras farms. These fliers entreat visitors to stop by, admire the idyllic property, have a "tasting" of the farm's products, and perhaps buy a few things. The visitor does not just purchase meat in this exchange. He or she also purchases a connection and a story that has symbolic value.[47]

If visitors time it right, they are often welcome to watch gavage, slaughter, and/or butchery. This witnessing is offered, and welcomed, by many producers.[48] Many follow routine scripts explaining foie gras's origin myths and do a quick demonstration of gavage. One producer expressed sentiments similar to those I heard from others in this regard: "It's a really good education for people, to come and see the whole process. For the older people especially, it justifies the higher price [of artisanal foie gras] to see the amount of care taken with each bird." Care is an important concept here. As anthropologists Deborah Heath and Anne Meneley argue, an "ethics of care" considers the well-being of both humans and animals in the artisanal foie gras equation as "co-producers" that come to know each other, and where "careful" treatment is also a marker of respect for tradition.[49] Similarly, the owner of La Ferme du Courdou, depicted in figure 3.3, explained that "not many still do it my way." She said she doesn't want to change her practices because "I want to remain traditional. It's also better for the ducks."

Watching foie gras production did not horrify the French tourists I observed on these farm visits. Instead, it seemed to do the opposite. As but one example, I arranged a visit to a small farm in the Périgord with three older, middle-class French couples who were in the area vacationing—one from Paris, one from Alsace, and one from Reims—all fellow residents of the guesthouse where I was staying. I was excited to observe their reactions. Only two of the six, the oldest of the couples, had witnessed foie gras production previously. The next day, I recorded the entirety of our visit to the nearby Ferme de la Gezelie, which raised, gavaged, slaughtered, processed, and sold products from both ducks and geese on site. Together, we watched workers gavage ducks and geese in one room and then butcher several chilled duck carcasses in another (Figures 3.4 and 3.5). The farm's defeathering machine, used earlier that morning, sat full nearby waiting to be cleaned. The six asked the farm's owner and the three workers present a number of detailed questions, and they kept responding "how interesting" while politely stepping over duck feces and splatters of blood.

The owner, a heavyset and grizzled man wearing a stained work smock, then suggested a tasting in a quaint one-room stone building on the other side of the gravel courtyard (see Figure 3.6). I wondered how the couples would respond, having just witnessed "dirty" scenes of production. He led the group into the room, which was ringed by tables stacked with cans of foie gras. None seemed apprehensive about tasting the *foie gras d'oie en entier* (whole goose foie gras) and *mousse de foie gras de canard* (duck foie gras mousse) from the cans that he opened. One member of each couple then picked up a basket. As I wrote in my field notes: "Even though they had just witnessed first-hand the process of gavage, evisceration, and butchery, things that might turn a lot of people off, they approached the tables like children in a toy store and filled their baskets. I doubt that any of them spent less than 100 euro."

3.4 Geese in gavage at Ferme de la Gezelie near
Sarlat in June 2006.

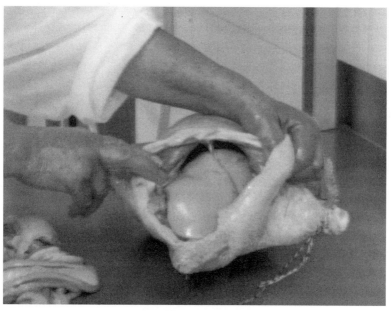

3.5 Voilà le foie gras!

3.6 Degustation (tasting) room at Ferme de la Gezelie.

By welcoming visitors, one might argue, these farms open themselves up to being considered living museum exhibits. In doing so, according to sociologist Elizabeth Barham, they put terroir at risk of "Disneyfication": making these farms into quasi–theme parks, generating a static sense of culture, and benefiting visitors more than locals. In this critique, producers function not just as purveyors of heritage, but as props.[50] Indeed, just as curators at art or history museums select and organize which objects to display and suggest interpretations through accompanying texts, these producers' lives and livelihoods are objectified. They follow particular scripts and perform for visitors. Moreover, the accessibility of these farms, as well as artisanal producers' public prominence at outdoor markets and gastronomic expos and in the French media, also masks the vastly uneven divisions of resources, labor, and market share between them and those that supply most of the nation, who are definitely not as visible.

But in spite of these issues, this encouragement of agritourism as heritage, alongside other initiatives such as geographic origin-labeling programs and quality-based certifications, has the potential to contribute to meaningful rural development.[51] And it can work to garner sympathetic audiences for this problematic product. Particularly as the market for foie gras expands beyond local regions, recognition and reputation become ever more meaningful. By permitting—and even encouraging—observers to watch their day-to-day work, artisanal foie gras producers foster particular moral arguments in a marketplace where "authenticity" is highly valued, yet hard to pin down.[52] They deploy "care" in combining their self-promotion with responses to indirect critiques. These cultural sentiments, in turn, give producers' identities new relevance in the modern landscape of Southwest France.

A few entire towns use foie gras as a tourist attraction in this regard. Sarlat-la-Canéda, a well-preserved medieval town in the Périgord, is a popular summertime tourism destination, a UNESCO World Heritage Site designation nominee, and a veritable foie gras Disneyland. Thousands of visitors use Sarlat every year as a base to visit cultural and natural heritage sites in the region. Its tourism office is significantly larger than those of nearby towns and offers a number of area tours with local guides. The town's center is a pedestrian zone, and cobblestone streets spoke out from the medieval cathedral. Visitors can meander through a maze of immaculately restored stone buildings and sit and drink wine at outdoor café tables in the plazas. The storefronts housed in many of these buildings are packed with duck and goose products, as well as duck-themed children's toys, cookbooks, ceramic figurines, linens and kitchenware, keychains, souvenir postcards, and other knick-knacks. (Many other storefronts, as I will discuss in a bit, are real estate offices.) Every restaurant in the town center, including a pizzeria, advertises foie gras dishes. The only thing missing is people dressed in bird costumes.

Yet, Sarlat is a case of contrasts. There are around fifty artisanal foie gras conserveurs and two hundred artisanal foie gras farms in the vicinity. The town is also the home base of Rougié, the world's largest foie gras producer, who moved their headquarters there in 1875. Rougié's factory and offices, which do not permit tourists, are currently located in an

3.7 Statue and photo prop donated by Rougié in
Sarlat's central plaza.

industrial park a few miles from the town's historic center. As I noted
during my time in Sarlat, it is common practice for travelers to have
their photographs taken with a bronze statue of three geese donated by
Rougié in the town's central plaza (see Figure 3.7). We can thus understand visitors to these places as engaging in cultural performances of
their own, as they celebrate "tradition" in the presence and shadow of
modern industry.

Marchés au Gras

Local officials in the nearby region of Gers have similarly recognized
demand for artisanal foie gras and created special markets for showcas-
ing it. These *marchés au gras*, or "fat markets," are held one per day of the
week in each of seven towns in the late fall and winter months. No two
are scheduled on the same day. These are not regular farmers' markets,
because the only things sold there are raw duck and goose carcasses and
fresh whole livers—no vegetables, no breads, no cheeses. Everything is

sold by weight, and all vendors charge a price set by market operators. They are draws for restaurant chefs, tourists, and locals alike.

The mayor of Samatan (population 2,000), also a member of the Conseil Général of the Gers region, told me that Samatan's Monday marché au gras hosts thirty to fifty small-scale producers from Garonne, the Gers, and the Hautes-Pyrénées, and that they sell about twenty tons of meat and two to three tons of liver each week. He called it "a market of quality, of tradition," and said that it is

> a good thing economically for Samatan, and for Gers also. It is good for small producers in the region. Fat and the production of fat are very important for people here. We have three hundred producers in the Gers alone. These products bring more tourists to the region to experience our high quality of life, to see quality and tradition being made.

Clearly, this comment was to some extent made to me as an outsider, but it also prompts an important point—for artisanal foie gras to be commercially viable, it has to be, in large part, about happy workers as well as happy ducks.

At one November marché au gras in the town of Gimont (population 2,900), I watched about two hundred people gather midmorning outside the doors of a large, unheated municipal building. The atmosphere was festive despite cold temperatures. Hung outside and over the doorway to the back room were large placards of a smiling woman holding a live duck and a basket that read "Sunday morning, make it a 'fat morning' in Gimont!" (see Figure 3.8).[53] People chatted, munching on rolls from a nearby bakery, and a few tried to keep warm by jumping up and down. Most had brought heavy-duty shopping bags. Two women sold paper cups of hot coffee. Just inside the open double doors was a rope separating buyers from the vendors, who were setting up their wares on folding tables and greeting each other with handshakes and *bisous* (the traditional French cheek kisses). On the room's left side, three men wearing spotless white butcher jackets and paper hats stood in a raised area, waiting with sharp cleavers to chop off heads, wings, and feet. A

3.8 Gimont marché au gras sign hung outside the market space.

few people jokingly called out to the man in charge to blow the ten o'clock start whistle a few minutes early and "let us in already!"

I was there with Mark Caro, the *Chicago Tribune* reporter, who was writing his own book about foie gras. Mark and I introduced ourselves to the market manager, who allowed us to come in and talk with vendors before the selling began. We walked among the tables, where men and women were neatly arranging their white plastic bins of livers and their birds, hanging the latter's heads off the table edges. White paper napkins were wrapped around the necks, with each bird's weight in kilos scrawled in marker: 7.6, 7.5, 6.7. There were about a thousand birds for sale that day (most, if not all of which sold). Carcasses cost €2.20 a kilo and livers €35 a kilo.

We chatted with one older woman who proudly lifted the lid off a plastic bin to show us "yesterday's livers." She told us she had been producing foie gras for over thirty years, and that she wakes up at 3:30 in the morning to feed her ducks before driving almost two hours to this market. She sells at three markets a week and is glad for a steady supply of customers. Other sellers came from around the region, a few as far away as the Pyrenees. Another vendor, an older man wearing a beret, told me that this market offers "a good business for everyone here."

3.9 Gimont marché au gras vendors prepare themselves
for the opening whistle.

Five minutes before ten o'clock, the vendors returned to their places
(see Figure 3.9). The manager came and found Mark and me and told us
that we had to stand to the side. He joked about us getting trampled. He
then walked to the front of the building and, on the dot of ten, blew his
whistle and opened the rope. The crowd barreled toward the tables,
shopping bags in hand. Animated buying lasted just over an hour. Customers took their birds to the choppers and then to the back room to be
weighed, where they also paid the cashier. Children chased each other
around the room, weaving through the tables, and tried to weigh themselves on one of the big scales next to the choppers' stalls. The vendors
would receive their payments—minus a fee for table space—after the
market ended.

I spoke briefly with several shoppers about their purchases. Most
people I observed bought several livers and/or a few carcasses after
quickly surveying the different tables. One man, who bought seven livers "to make provisions," was part of a small group of friends from Avi-
gnon (about four hours away) who came together to this Sunday market
twice a year. It was, for them, a fun occasion. A middle-aged woman
showed me the five geese she had selected "for everyday use." She lived
nine kilometers away and first came to the market three years prior "out

of curiosity"; she returns three times a year "because of the quality." By 11:30, there was little left on the tables, and vendors were already packing up their things.

These marchés au gras are a striking venue for the ways foie gras "traditions" manifest as relationship-building devices at the turn of the twenty-first century. Like the peasant markets of yesteryear on which they are modeled, they involve active face-to-face conversations and encounters between customers and foie gras's "happy" producers. They provide a charming break from everyday life for the visitor, where one is given over entirely to the specific activity of discussing and shopping for foie gras ducks and geese. However, these markets are in reality a modern phenomenon, staged by village associations looking to tempt visitors—and their wallets—to their environs. According to my interviews with two different local government officials, including the mayor of Samatan quoted previously, the main goals of supporting these initiatives are to acquaint French people with the men and women engaged with foie gras production, to increase consumption, and to "prove" to them foie gras's national cultural value. They are promoted by the French for the French.

Weekend Foie Gras

Another recently developed opportunity for heritage-interested tourists is called "weekend foie gras." Organized and promoted by the Southwestern regions' government-sponsored tourist associations, one can spend a night or two on a working artisanal foie gras farm. ("Weekend" is not taken literally.) The main activity during one's stay is a lesson from the farm's proprietor on butchering and cooking a foie gras duck or goose to take home. Farmers sign up as potential hosts with a local tourist association, and guests are "assigned" to a farm based on availability. At the end of their stay, each guest receives a certificate proclaiming them a "foie gras expert." The idea for this experience is relatively new, beginning only in the mid-1990s, yet it has grown quickly in popularity.

The "weekend foie gras" I attended in November 2007 was at a farm in the Gers that had been hosting them for two years and renting rooms as a chambre d'hôtes for four. Myriam, the proprietress, lived there with her teenage son and seventy-five-year-old father, a former boxer with a cauliflower ear. Myriam, however, did not fit the image of the foie gras granny. She was a slim woman in her early forties with a nose stud and dyed auburn hair pulled into a curly ponytail. Parts of their peach-colored farmhouse dated to the early 1800s, when their family first ac-quired the land. She had contracts with two tourist associations, Gîtes de France and Loisir Accueil Gers, to host "weekends" between October and April. During the summer months, she worked on renovating the farmhouse and rented out rooms to European tourists who come for the area's music and Armagnac festivals. Family and guests alike ate on benches around a long wooden table and drank wine made from local grapes and served in large ceramic jugs.

Myriam was a gaveuse, a feeder, and did not raise the birds herself. This was different—she said—from the way it used to be, when all farms in the area did everything themselves. Now, as she explained, it's be-come more specialized, even for artisanal producers such as herself. She gavages forty-eight ducks six times per year in a raised communal cage system that her father devised and built in 1976 in a building next to the main house. The system uses a moveable wire clamp to hold the bird being fed temporarily in place. Each of the eight pens, which held be-tween three and seven ducks, was raised up to hip-level, with metal grates as floors. As her mother and her grandparents did before her, Myriam gavages Barbary rather than mulard ducks. (She said she is one of the last ones in the area to do so.) She feeds them for sixteen days, then takes them to a friend's slaughterhouse nearby, as she does not have the right permits, and then bring them back to butcher and prepare for sale. She primarily sells her products in the farm's shop, to her guests, and to a restaurant in the next town. Her boyfriend also "does" foie gras and sells some of his products in her shop. She was not PGI-certified because it "requires too much homework," and because she does not sell her products widely and saw little use for an additional expense. Her father takes care of much of the rest of the farm, including a few thou-sand chickens elsewhere on their property, and drives his grandson to and from motocross practices and events (because, he explained with a wink, many of the other boys are taken by their grandmothers).

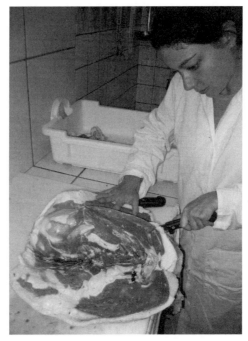

3.10 Butchering a duck at a "weekend foie gras" at a farmhouse in
the Gers, November 2007.

There were four of us present: myself, Mark Caro, a French colleague
and anthropologist named Isabelle Téchoueyres, and a fifty-something
heavyset man named Dany, an avid amateur cook from Montpelier, recently retired from his job at Goodyear Tires. Dany, who spoke little
English, had signed up "to know more about foie gras" which he "loves
to cook and eat." He had never seen gavage before. Mark and I, we were
told, were the first Americans to ever visit the farm (which perhaps explained some of the funny looks we received from Myriam's father).
Dany, on the other hand, was exactly the intended target for this experience. This also became obvious in our kitchen abilities. Immediately
upon arriving at Escala, we donned work smocks and were instructed by
Myriam how to break down a duck and put the pieces of meat and liver
in jars to be cooked in the autoclave overnight. Myriam demonstrated
her quick and precise knife skills and suffered patiently through Mark's
and my attempts to mimic her (see Figure 3.10). Dany, on the other

hand, approached his ducks like a well-oiled professional. "You've done this before?" asked Mark. "No," replied Dany in English, "my first time."

Besides cooking, eating, and watching her gavage her ducks, our group visited two other nearby farms at Myriam's arrangement—another artisanal farm (Courdou, whose sign appears in Figure 3.3) and a neighbor's industrial gavage operation (which did not have a sign at all). At each, we asked about production methods and discussed opposition to gavage. Piled into the car afterwards, Mark asked Dany, who had been fairly quiet through the visits, what he thought about all of it. This French, food-loving amateur chef had never seen gavage before and had just witnessed it in three different places over the course of two days. Dany shrugged. "I see the animals before gavage, and I see them after," he said slowly, in stilted English. "And I do not see the difference. They look very much the same. The animal after the feeding seems just like the animal before. So, for me, it is not a problem. One doesn't have the right to ban this. This is in the tradition." And with that, alternative considerations were ruled out. For Dany and others, willingness to identify foie gras as a valuable and imperiled resource depends on preexisting, identity-based affinities. And it clearly shows the cultural work tied to cultivating a national taste for foie gras.

Symbolic Boundaries in Time, Place, and Space

When a food becomes valued as a national symbol, threats to its production and consumption can be perceived as insults to national identity or even as threats to the nation itself. It becomes a symbolic boundary marker. The institutional promotion and protection of foie gras help us see the intensification of "invented" traditions at times when old and cherished practices (and thus old identities) are perceived to be in some sort of jeopardy. As such, they reflect a distinct moral politics of food, one that is set within broader concerns about changes in French culture and identity in the twenty-first century. In other words, foie gras is a resource that both affects and responds to political agendas.

Throughout my fieldwork in this region, I noted tensions around claims to space and place, both vague—such as offhand but pointed remarks—and strong. This was just a few years after the implementation of the euro as common currency, yet before the global financial crisis had set in. Many of the people I interviewed or spent extended time with were aware, to varying degrees, of three simultaneous trends—the purchases of property and farmhouses in the countryside by the British and other Northern Europeans, the growing power of the animal rights lobby in Europe and the United States, and the influx of Algerian and North African immigrants to French cities. These trends were conspicuous and often mentioned when I asked about the communities I was in.

The first was centered in the countryside. In the town centers of Périgueux, the capital of the Dordogne region, and Sarlat-la-Canéda, the foie gras Disneyland, I took special note of the many storefronts that were real estate offices. Most of the descriptions in their windows of houses for sale were in English as well as French. Listings were concentrated in the countryside, rather than the towns, and cited the amount of property and types of amenities, such as fruit trees and swimming pools, accompanying the houses. For British buyers, these purchases are relative bargains because the pound remains stronger than the euro. Presumably, those who choose to relocate to this region would be sympathetic to French ideas about culinary tradition. But some industry members with whom I spoke were a little worried, because foie gras production is illegal in the UK and British animal welfare groups have been especially active in fighting against it, lobbying the EU to consider an outright ban.

Driving around the countryside with French hosts, I asked about this trend and received varied answers. A few worried out loud about the loss of "French" ownership of the land. One eighty-year-old woman, who had lived in the area all her life, complained about what she felt was a diminishing sense of community: "They're buying it all, old houses, and restoring them. Then, they come to live here during the winter, when it is cold in England. It's cold here too, but not as cold. It's too bad, because they keep to themselves and don't join our clubs. They stay at home." Her fifty-year-old daughter, however, retorted, "It's just as well that they bought those houses, because they were empty and run-down."

On a separate occasion, I was taken to lunch by the mayor of the town of Thiviers (which claims one of the region's three foie gras museums) and his wife. The restaurant they chose was in the neighboring town of St. Jean, population two hundred. Upon sitting down at our table on the patio, I realized that most of the diners around us were speaking English. Mme. and Mr. Jaccou listened to their conversations, trying to ascertain whether they were British or Dutch. Mme. Jaccou pointed out the paper placemats to me, which advertised a local real estate firm's property offerings, written in English. "About thirty percent of residents in this area now are English!" she told me chattily. "It is a good thing in some ways, because it brings money to the area and some of these beautiful old houses get restored."

Mme. Jaccou then paused, looked more closely at the placemat, and asked her husband, "Michel, umm, isn't this your grandparents' home?" He examined the photo, and confirmed that indeed it was their farmhouse, albeit transformed. "They did not have a swimming pool there," he said. "They were poor farmers." "Isn't that funny!" remarked Mme. Jaccou, who then quickly changed the subject. Thus, viewed either positively or negatively by long-time residents, the British foray into property ownership in this region was notable. It has provided jobs in construction, but simultaneously increased the costs of land ownership and amenities for the French who remain in their ancestral homes.

It is not only physical spaces that reflect social and demographic changes. French foie gras producers large and small are aware of social movements that liken their work to animal cruelty and suffering. Fourteen European countries (many of which were not producers in the first place) have foie gras production bans on their books, and animal rights activists have successfully petitioned the European Union to pass new restrictions on the cages in which the ducks are kept.[54] Antoine Comiti, the head of anti–foie gras group Stop Gavage, told me he believes the French state made foie gras part of official patrimony "because they are scared of campaigns like ours in the context of the evolution of opinion, as more and more people are speaking out for the well-being of animals during their raising."

When I asked people about bans and critiques, their levels of knowledge of foie gras's politicization varied, mainly (but not always) along the spectrum of their organization's size (small farm versus large producer). In fact, many repeated incorrect information, such as "foie gras is banned throughout America, is it not?" and "The mayor of Chicago banned foie gras!" Some took seriously the prospect that the anti–foie gras movement might prevail in Europe and they themselves might come down on the wrong side of history. One lifelong artisanal producer expressed this concern, saying "It's already begun," and adding, "Brigitte Bardot!" referring to the famous actress-turned–animal rights activist whose eponymous foundation has mobilized against foie gras in France and Britain. "In France, yes. It's unfortunate, but it's possible."

Producers of all sizes frequently responded to accusations of cruelty by insisting on foie gras's naturalness and their commitments to their animals' well-being, in addition to the importance of their role in maintaining tradition. When I asked the owner of La Ferme du Courdou if we could watch the gavage, she responded emphatically to a different question (cuing that she was prepared for a challenge): "It's not a malady. It's a natural process." One industrial gaveur visibly tensed when I asked if I could take some photographs of his ducks. I could, he warned, as long as I promised "not to use them for bad things." He was "very wary" because several years prior, people had come to the farm saying they were curious about gavage and took photos. He later found the pictures on an animal rights website and said that his father had received threats in the mail. Several artisanal producers I interviewed seemed flabbergasted at assertions that they were torturers or villains, and more than one explained that a "good feeder" has to earn the birds' trust.

Many attempted to make sense of anti–foie gras arguments by fitting them into a broader world political-economic context. The United States frequently served as a gastronationalist boogeyman, tied to deteriorating global views of US policies—particularly among European allies—during George W. Bush's presidency.[55] For example, a tourist office employee in Toulouse was immediately responsive when I described my research. He had not heard of the Chicago foie gras ban and asked whether it was due to a boycott of France or fear of avian flu. An artisanal producer similarly said that she believes foie gras is under attack in the United States "because it's a food very much identified with France. So, if they want to punish the French, they are going to suppress, moreover with a good conscience, because they construct the logic of animal welfare behind it."

Important in this regard is the fact that foie gras entered the American political stage in California right around the time French troops withdrew from fighting in Iraq and the US House of Representatives' cafeteria began selling "freedom fries." While animal rights activists in the United States rarely if ever made this connection explicitly, my French respondents believed it to be a driving force in anti–foie gras activism there (that foie gras equaled France for Americans in the same way that it did for the French). One long-time employee of an artisanal foie gras producer in the Hautes-Pyrénées region said flat-out: "I think that it's because of the war in Iraq. There's a sanction in the US of the French products." A customer at the Salon Saveurs in Paris who worked in international wine sales and described himself as on the political right, spoke similarly: "When people care about tradition, they care about food. We saw on the television Americans opening bottles of French wine and pouring them on the street. It's combined—the war, French wine, foie gras!"[56] These comments evoke the words of renowned anthropologist Sidney Mintz that the "conception of an invader or interloper helps to collectivize the society symbolically—it creates a national cuisine, so to speak, by generalizing a specific identity to a foreign enemy."[57]

The United States and the EU are not the only targets for some of foie gras's strident defenders. Foie gras has served as a referent for ultranationalist groups seeking to draw starker lines around what they consider legitimate citizenship in France. France has long been a nation that prides itself on *liberté, égalité, fraternité*, but at the time was struggling to figure out how to integrate its estimated four to five million Muslim residents, the largest population on the continent, into national life. (In myriad ways, it still is.) Conflicts over unemployment, language policies, and women wearing headscarves or burqas, for example, raged in the public sphere and included riots in November 2005 in the *banlieues* (suburbs) of Paris and other urban areas.[58] This has implications for cultural markets, and for the symbolic politics of taste. One warm June afternoon in the city of Toulouse, one of the larger cities in the Southwest, I followed up on a hunch and walked through the entirety of the historic city center surveying restaurants. The large majority of restaurants that were not cafés or bars were of two types: those offering "traditional" French cuisine such as *cassoulet*, a heavy meat and bean stew typically eaten in the winter, and those selling kabobs, spit-roasted meat identified with Middle Eastern and North African populations. This was, to me, a stark contrast about what types of cuisine were prospering in this place (and who was living or visiting there to eat it).

Labeyrie—one of France's largest foie gras producers, with a current market share of about twenty percent—became a target of ultranationalists in late 2006. Founded in 1946 in the département of Landes, Labeyrie was the first foie gras brand to be advertised on French television in the late 1980s. Its foie gras is PGI-certified, and its advertisements read "pure terroir" and "foie gras the ancient or old-fashioned way," attempting to position its products to consumers as authentically and traditionally French. Since 2004, the company has also been a subsidiary of ALFESCA, a French-Icelandic agri-food firm that produces, distributes, and supplies specialty and luxury food items, mainly smoked fish products, to retailers around Europe.

In late 2006, Labeyrie was at the center of an Internet firestorm, when French nationalists from Bloc Identitaire, Forum Nationaliste Français, and several other right-wing political groups condemned the company for labeling and marketing some of its foie gras products as halal, meaning suitable for consumption by Muslims.[59] Their base complaint was that by paying a required certification fee to a French mosque to be able to use the halal label, Labeyrie was funding Islamic worship. More to the point, it was marketing foie gras to people in France whom these groups see as decidedly not French. Islamophobic websites and online message boards called for a boycott and protests against retailers of Labeyrie products. One website's "call to action" declared that buying halal was "to take the risk of supporting Islamic terrorism" and that a French company marketing products as halal was "absolutely inexcusable."[60] The regional press and national radio stations picked up the story just before the winter holidays (typically the busiest time for foie gras's producers and retailers). In December 2006, these groups organized a "gourmet action" protest at a Labeyrie shop in Paris, distributing leaflets and videotaping themselves protesting "the Islamization of our gastronomy."[61]

Within a few weeks, after several other widely publicized protests and boycott threats, Labeyrie abandoned using a halal label, but only temporarily. They reverted the following year and were again subject to ultranationalist denunciations. Labeyrie was then criticized by members of France's Muslim community for being vulnerable to the pressures of right-wing media, because the company's website, promotional materials, and e-shop (launched in 2007) no longer showed images of halal foie gras labels, even though the products remained available in retail stores. A popular blog following trends in the Muslim consumer market accused Labeyrie of trying to play both sides to protect its "huge market that is the Muslim community" but in a way that would not inflict harm on their image as a French company producing a French product.[62] Similarly, an ultranationalist website charged Labeyrie with wanting "Koranic money" but not wanting anyone to know.[63] Since then, Labeyrie has continued to serve from time to time as a target for anti-Islamic voices and conspiracy theorists on French social media.[64]

The halal case is important here for its multiple layers of gastropolitical meaning. It shows that consuming foie gras has become such an important way of performing Frenchness that there is actual resistance to perceived outsiders doing it. Along with brandishing wine and pork charcuterie as rallying symbols of identity, for these extreme voices, it is about defining who is, and is not, French. "Voilà comment on vend notre identité!!" (This is how we sell our identity!!") exclaimed one poster on a political website in 2013 about the false claim that Labeyrie had ceased using Armagnac (a kind of brandy produced in Southwest France) as a foie gras flavoring specifically to appease Muslims, who cannot consume alcohol.[65] Yet, not everyone is on board with such a xenophobic mindset. Halal foie gras is available all the time at national supermarkets and chain stores such as Carrefour.[66] Six other large French foie gras companies also obtain halal certification for some products for sale in France and for export. (Dubai, Kuwait, Qatar, and the United Arab Emirates are growing markets.) News articles have reported on the rise of halal foie gras consumption among Muslims in France, especially upwardly mobile Muslims, in the last few years.

Quotes from leaders in the Muslim community attribute this rise to a desire for symbolic integration, and consuming foie gras—the national food—being seen as a way to do that.[67]

CONCLUSION

Even amidst looming questions about EU-level political disarray and an uncertain future arising from the global economic crisis and imposed austerity policies, protecting foie gras remains a priority of many. Successes in institutionalizing it in the French gastronational imagination—in the face of international condemnation—relied on a great deal of intensive and coordinated cultural work. Much of this work, as I found, has centered on building emotional sentiments around this particular food—stories emanating from the notion of the "imagined community" (as defined by Benedict Anderson) and the cultural opportunities and constraints of markets. This chapter, in particular, has sought to explain how foie gras's continued—yet shifting—valuation in France depends not only on its cultural utility for the present but also on the moral identities of the people who claim it as their own. Gastronationalism can be defensive, and it can also be enrolled in political projects that work to assert national allegiances and affirm social exclusions.

Disputes over foie gras across Europe continue to make headlines, recurrently showing the food's endangered status. In December 2007, an activist group in Switzerland calling itself "The Masked Ducks" claimed responsibility for throwing paint in a gourmet food store to denounce foie gras. In 2008, the Animal Liberation Front vandalized a two-starred Michelin restaurant in England for having foie gras on the menu. Chefs and retail stores in Britain and elsewhere are repeatedly petitioned, even threatened, by animal rights groups.

In July of 2011 in Cologne, Germany, officials at Anuga, a biannual food trade fair considered one of Europe's most important food shows, decided to disallow foie gras producers—artisanal and commodity alike—from displaying and selling their wares that coming October, causing what one international news outlet described as a "high-level diplomatic spat" with "angry missives" flying between Berlin and Paris.[68] Producing foie gras is legally prohibited in Germany (and has been since 1993), but distribution, marketing, and consumption are not, and cannot be, due to the mutual recognition clause of EU trade law. The "ban" on foie gras at Anuga came following pressure on event organizers from international animal rights organizations. The head of the foie gras campaign at Austrian-based group Four Paws called the decision "a major success for all animal protectionists" and said in a press release (that was reported everywhere from the group's website to *Poultry Production News*), "Now we can call off our planned protest around the exhibition." Indeed, two years earlier, animal welfare groups had caused "security issues" at the food fair; an Anuga spokesperson said that the idea of excluding foie gras had been discussed since then, and that they "didn't expect diplomatic reactions."[69]

But diplomatic reactions were what they got. French Agriculture Minister Bruno Le Maire wrote an open letter to his German counterpart calling the decision "unacceptable," asking her to overturn it, and intimating that he would boycott the fair's opening ceremony. "Products that respect current EU legislation should all have access," he wrote, "If this exclusion is confirmed, I cannot see how I will be able to take part in the opening."[70] The German minister responded that it was up to the fair's organizers to decide on the issue. Anuga's spokesperson said, "We decided not to allow something that is banned in many countries . . . This product is the object of virulent criticism; animal rights organizations and others reproach it as linked to animal suffering, and consumers are more and more interested in what they eat."[71]

The announcement became a public sound bite. Political missives from government officials flew back and forth. Actress turned animal rights activist Brigitte Bardot wrote a public letter to the German minister, asking for her and the show's organizers to resist French pressure. A member of France's Senate hyperbolically labeled it a "totally discriminatory measure" and wrote that "It's like banning German sausages in France." France's external trade minister called the Anuga decision "anything but anecdotal" (implying its political undercurrents) and implored Germany's ambassador to France, Reinhard Schäfers, to get the fair's organizers "to respect European law."[72] Antoine Comiti of Stop Gavage (and more recently president of L214, a broader animal rights group) wrote Schäfers as well, saying that the group was "very happy" to learn of the "respectful" decision and "dismayed by the reaction of French authorities, in particular the minister of agriculture, who does not hesitate to lie to support the behemoths of French agro-industry."[73]

In the end, the two sides came to what some called a compromise, but was really more of a stalemate. Just before the trade show was to open, Anuga's organizers conceded to allow foie gras producers to attend. However, they maintained that the term "foie gras" would not appear in the show's official directory. The public debate had mostly run its course; people who wanted their voices heard on the issue had made their points. Compared to the thousands of websites, blogs, and news outlets that picked up the initial story in July, very few reported on the outcome just three months later. It was the conflict itself that proved newsworthy.

The concerns raised in these public rebukes seem to be more about national pride and dignity than market share (though of course the latter matters at such a prominent event) or individuals' ethical beliefs about the production of animals as food. Such disputes over the moral worth of particular products serve to mark, challenge, or harden divisive cultural tastes. They provide images and ideas that contribute to collective introspection about which and whose values are legitimate in today's world. As such, gastronationalist attitudes permit national justifications for legally protecting culinary traditions as salient markers of identity, even when others consider those traditions loathsome. While it is true that contemporary marketing efforts offer a misleading view of what the foie gras industry truly looks like in France in the twenty-first century, this chapter shows that the sustained power of French taste for foie gras comes not just from "invented" traditions but also from the visible and visceral performances of producers and consumers themselves.

Clearly, France is far from a closed society. And yet even the academics, international business students, and others I talked with whose mindsets otherwise leaned heavily toward the cosmopolitan promises of a united Europe told me repeatedly about their incredulity and even horror about foie gras's being banned in some places and potentially, someday, in France too. For people working in the industry, these challenges have sent a polarizing shudder up a collective spine. Even as the

French adapt to and benefit from modern-day global forces, they are not necessarily prepared to accept all of their consequences. Nor is France the only place ill-prepared to accept the repercussions of a ban on foie gras. As we see in the next chapter, bans elsewhere can also have unintended gastropolitical consequences, albeit for much different reasons.

CHAPTER 4

Foiehibition

*D*oug Sohn grew up in the 1970s in a northwest suburb of Chicago, Illinois. He attended college in New York City, where he was exposed to a range of cuisines far wider than his family or his suburban upbringing had offered. After returning to Chicago and working for several years in odd jobs he wryly describes as "unsatisfactory," Doug took the plunge to change careers and earned a degree from a local culinary school. He then bounced among different cooking jobs in the city, from line cook to corporate dining to catering, and traveled in Europe before spending five years as a cookbook editor at a small suburban press. In the late 1990s, a few years into this job, one of Doug's coworkers described a terrible hot dog he had eaten the previous weekend. They hatched a plan. Once a week, along with two other colleagues, they visited different hot dog restaurants in the area over their lunch breaks "not so much for the best food, just for the different experiences." Afterwards, they would write up "funny little reviews" for each other. Over two years, they sampled hot dogs from more than forty different establishments. About halfway through, as Doug recalled, an idea began to percolate. In January 2001, with a small business loan and a name suggested by his dad, Hot Doug's Sausage Superstore and Encased Meat Emporium opened in the Roscoe Village neighborhood on Chicago's North Side.

The beginning was tough. Doug took on debt and didn't pay himself a salary for months. The business was primarily sustained by his location near a large high school. The menu consisted of a mix of hot dogs and

4.1 Doug Sohn mans the counter at Hot Doug's (courtesy of Hot Doug's Inc.).

specialty sausages with different sauces and toppings, several named after celebrities (such as The Elvis, a "smoked and savory" sausage, and The Jennifer Garner, a "mighty hot" fire dog). He rotated the specials on a weekly basis and cooked the French fries in duck fat on Fridays and Saturdays.[1] The *Chicago Reader* wrote a "nice little piece," and things "really took off" after the *Chicago Sun-Times*'s dining section gave Hot Doug's a glowing review. Doug gained a following. Then, in 2004, a fire in a neighboring building caused irreparable smoke and water damage to Hot Doug's. Doug reopened eight months later in a new location a mile away. On reopening day, people showed up en masse. Word spread. Even in a location a bit off the beaten path, without other commercial businesses close by, Hot Doug's became a pop-cultural hotspot and a lunchtime destination for office workers, hipsters, families, and out-of-towners alike. Wearing black plastic framed glasses and a welcoming grin, Doug sat at the counter and took orders. He was always the only one to do so, guaranteeing every customer a bit of face time. Saturdays could see a two-hour wait, with lines of people stretching around the block. When I sat down to talk with him at his townhouse in 2007,

4.2 Hot Doug's line on a typical Saturday (courtesy of Hot Doug's Inc.).

Doug told me he found his cultlike fan base "incredibly flattering and awe-inspiring."[2]

Contributing to Doug Sohn's reputation in Chicago and beyond is the fact that, in 2007, he became the only person in the city to be cited and fined $250 for selling foie gras. The Chicago City Council had outlawed the sale of foie gras at restaurants a year prior, making it the first major American city to do so. The ban was repealed in 2008. During its short lifespan, nineteen restaurants (including Hot Doug's) received cease-and-desist letters from the city for selling foie gras. But Doug was the only recipient of an actual ticket.

Before it became a lightning rod in the Chicago food scene, Doug regularly served foie gras–themed concoctions:

> I would do different stuff, like a truffle sauce, goat cheese, and foie gras, playing around with it. Then we started doing a smoked pheasant sausage where I would do sautéed cubes of foie gras on top, with a little mustard. So, we were serving a lot of it.

In between the ban's passage in April 2006 and enactment that August, Hot Doug's featured foie gras with greater frequency, and received

4.3 Hot Doug's foie gras hot dog (courtesy of Hot Doug's Inc.).

two warning letters from the city during that time for doing so. As Doug explained, "The real intent was just to be a smartass and sort of provoke, poke fun at the ridiculousness of it." The day before the ban took effect, he put foie gras in three different specials. After that, he put a foie gras hot dog on his specials menu, calling it "The Joe Moore" after the alderman who had spearheaded the city's ban.[3] He recounted:

> That gained a little bit of publicity. But nothing happened. We sold a lot of it. We didn't get any protests, just a handful of calls. We were on AOL.com or one of those sites. And there's where I got most of the emails. My favorite one started "Dear Asswipe" and called my mother a whore. Yeah, like that's going to make me change my mind.

Doug believed that the warning letters and the fine for violating the ban were due to someone's monitoring his website and calling the city repeatedly to complain. This was a common strategy for anti–foie gras activists. On that particular Friday, Doug posted that weekend's specials at seven a.m. Before the restaurant opened for lunch a few hours later, the city inspector arrived, confiscated thirty pounds of foie gras sausages, and served him with the ticket.

Within a couple of hours, the cat was out of the bag. By happenstance, a *Chicago Tribune* reporter was having lunch at Hot Doug's that day and overheard what had happened. News vans started showing up outside. According to Doug:

> I told the guy who answers the phone to say yes, we got the ticket. But we've got a line out the door, so no. No interviews. I've got a business here. I need to make a living. I made my point. I was doing it to be a smartass. It's not the core of my business. I didn't think it was that big an issue to warrant this kind of nonsense.

For many other people, however, the citation was newsworthy, remarkable for its multiple symbolic meanings. At one level, Hot Doug's was the first—and only—restaurant to actually be ticketed by the city for the offense of selling foie gras. At another level, the Joe Moore Special was a way for people to thumb their noses at the city's ban. Hot Doug's having a foie gras hot dog was itself a gag for people who knew about the topping's more typical association with gourmet cuisine. These foodies understood Doug's tongue-in-cheek playfulness in using foie gras to garnish one of the most plebian of American foods.[4] This blurring between high and low tastes contributed to the citation's newsworthiness. The sole business to be fined during Chicago's "foiehibition" was a laid-back, hipster hot dog joint and not a high-end restaurant, even though Doug was far from the only restaurateur in the city flouting the ban. Doug himself told me he thought this twist was the reason he was "specifically chosen" by animal activists as a target. Even though Hot Doug's menu items were pricier than other hot dogs in the city, a $7 foie gras hot dog is still a reasonably priced lunch for many people. People who did not have other opportunities to eat foie gras could try it if they wanted to. Doug felt that this fact helped the ban's supporters demonstrate that "it can affect anybody."

Hot Doug's ticket—which gained a plastic frame and a home on the restaurant's countertop next to the cash register—received an impressive amount of attention from foodies, animal rights groups, and media

outlets across Chicago and throughout the country. The story was reported in the *International Herald Tribune* and on the CNN news crawl.
Doug did not contest the fine, even though people wanted him to. As
he told me, "I was like, at this point, I'm washing my hands of it. If it was
$10,000, yes, then I'll argue it. But $250? I told my attorney to walk in,
pay the fine, say thank you, and leave." Doug also told me he wasn't putting foie gras back on the menu until the ban was overturned. When I
spoke with him a few years later, after the repeal, the foie gras dog was
back on the menu (with a different name) and business was great. Doug
told me he took "a weird sort of pride" in his contribution to Chicago
history.[5]

Hot Doug's ticket marked the apex of foie gras's gastropolitics in
Chicago. In the time between the first City Council's Health Committee draft of the ban in 2005 and its rescindment in 2008, its promoters
lauded it as tackling an important ethical problem in today's world—
that of alleviating the cruel treatment of animals that are raised to become food. The ordinance was pitched to legislators and the general
public as the humane thing to do, and as a step toward making the city
a kinder and more compassionate place to live, work, and eat. But efforts
to establish foie gras as a significant public issue in and for the city of
Chicago also inspired detractors. Clashes over the ban's legal and ethical
status occurred within the staid walls of the Council chambers, on the
sidewalks outside of numerous restaurants, and online. Right after the
ban passed in 2006, the Illinois Restaurant Association filed a lawsuit
against the city, and then-mayor Richard M. Daley publicly referred to
it as "the silliest law" the City Council had ever passed. As exemplified
by Hot Doug's foie gras hot dog, it became a local quirk and subverting
it a game of sorts for a number of Chicagoans.

The ordinance's baseline purposes were to establish a legal norm in
the city against foie gras—a dish that most Chicagoans did not eat or
even know about—and to give city officials the authority to enforce a
ban on its sale at restaurants. But governmental acts can also offer new
reasons to mobilize, as well as beget unintended consequences. After
local media began reporting on the ordinance as a real possibility, activists' efforts to generate public awareness of foie gras (relying on information gathered during California's decision to ban its production and

sale the previous year) actually worked to undermine their goals. With its newfound infamy, foie gras came to engender new and significant meanings based on people's different value orientations in the cultural and culinary landscapes of Chicago.

Initially, the dominant framework used by and about the city concerned the ethics of foie gras's production methods. This narrative focused on compassion for ducks and the overtly moralized idea that the United States, as a twenty-first-century society, needed to do better—much better—by the animals we eat. The appalling conditions of livestock at CAFOs (concentrated animal feeding operations) were becoming a hot topic in the politics of food at this time, in Chicago and elsewhere around the country. This was due, in large part, to the combination of a growing local food movement, popular authors such as Eric Schlosser (*Fast Food Nation*) and Michael Pollan (*The Omnivore's Dilemma*), and the work of animal activist groups such as The Humane Society of the United States. In various ways, these reformers and critics have worked to inform and reshape people's values about the food system. Importantly, this has involved championing consumer empowerment through the act of making ethically sound, virtuous consumption choices—making food a personalized way to "do" politics.[6] Through this lens, foie gras is the epitome of inhumane and egregious agricultural practices suffered by animals in our food system. Chicago was tagged as a brave pioneer in the field of farm animal protection. The proper moral response was not simply to make foie gras an undesirable consumer choice: it was to make it illegal. Simply promoting abstention was not enough.

But the debate over foie gras's ethical status quickly morphed into one about jurisdiction, introducing questions about whether the city had the right to ban the sale of a food and the relative significance of the foie gras "problem" as necessitating government involvement. The Illinois Restaurant Association's lawsuit against the city, filed the day the ban took effect, argued that the city law interfered with interstate commerce, because the foie gras sold at Chicago restaurants was produced legally in another state. Other stakeholders soon got on board. Many leading voices in Chicago, culinary-related and otherwise, did not like the idea of the City Council's proscribing a ban on *any* food item based on one group's moral principles, and not on public health or safety. Foie gras became a buzzword—in Chicago and elsewhere—used in denunciations about the city's self-granted latitude to police food (and by extension, people argued, the personal freedom of consumers).

The question of significance also became a prevalent one in guiding people's responses to the ban. Not everyone—even people for whom CAFO and "factory farm" were indubitably pejorative terms—believed that animal rights activists and concerned legislators were pointing their fingers at the correct target. Foie gras was small potatoes, so to speak, compared to the breadth and depth of problems and issues in the industrial food system that feeds the large majority of people. Of course, we know that issues that "go viral" do not necessarily arise out of wholly objective conditions; nor do the most deserving causes necessarily see the limelight.[7] But, in this case, people in Chicago and elsewhere watched an amazing amount of time, money, and emotional energy being devoted to fighting against something that the vast majority of Americans had never even encountered.

Moreover, as more arguments and evidence defending foie gras production and challenging activists' exhortations came to the fore, questions of truthfulness began to complicate things further. Is foie gras production truly as cruel as activists purport it to be? Or should we listen to people with agricultural and culinary expertise who say it is not? Many of the latter—such as chefs and food journalists—also desire morally based food system reforms, yet they consider foie gras an ingredient whose special, "artisanal" character and rich culinary history make it a morally acceptable choice. The concept of artisanship stresses hands-on craftsmanship—where care, skill, and knowledge are brought to the physical making of material objects. Americans defending foie gras have stressed that its artisanal production methods starkly differentiate it from large-scale, mass-industrialized meat production (which is true in the United States, at least). For example, prior to the implementation of the California state foie gras ban in 2012, one chef there told a reporter, "Like most foie-gras proponents, I don't serve beef from factory farms or that has antibiotics and hormones. Why through one appetizer would I blow my whole ethos?"[8]

As I found over the course of several years of fieldwork in Chicago, foie gras—while a non-issue for many people—hit genuine nerves for a few influential individuals. I found several interlaced and tension-laden themes in the rise of social interest in foie gras's legal and moral propriety: the purview of city government over consumers, the autonomy of chefs as culinary experts, the nature of ethical and social responsibility, market-based notions of the primacy of individual choice in the marketplace, and the relative significance of foie gras as a social problem in both Chicago and the American food system. What made foie gras a volatile and combative symbol for Chicago had as much to do with how people made sense of these themes as it did with the identities of the groups pushing for them. While its passage was initially framed as being about the humane treatment of ducks, its repeal in May 2008 was instead undergirded by arguments about the city's reputation and priorities.

Moreover, actors in both camps all relied heavily on explicit cultural codes embedded in the discourse of American civil society, pitching this issue as one that should be regarded as a moral imperative: trust versus suspicion, compassion versus choice, freedom versus constraint. This chapter argues that foie gras was rendered strange, salient, and compelling because of a discernible absence of care—as opposed to the French national "ethic of care."[9] detailed in chapters 2 and 3—for something that is clearly not part of the United States's cultural traditions or even a chapter of the story of the culinary "melting pot" of ethnic food traditions finding their way into mainstream American tastes. Events surrounding the ultimately unsuccessful ordinance banning foie gras—a little-known, luxury food item—in Chicago's restaurants also offers us a prime example of how chance and contingency can affect the cultural evolution of a city's politics of food.

A Brief History of Chicago's Foiehibition

Introduction & Passage

In the early twentieth century, Chicago was the setting for Upton Sinclair's muckraking exposé of the meat-packing industry, *The Jungle,* and was nicknamed the "hog butcher of the world" in Carl Sandburg's poem "Chicago." The city's stockyards and slaughterhouses touched about eighty percent of the meat consumed by Americans at that time. Today, Chicago's Mercantile Exchange, the largest futures exchange in the world, annually confers sales contracts on millions of cattle and hogs. With such a deeply livestock-tinged past and present, it seems somewhat unlikely that this city would become the site of the first ban enacted in the United States on selling foie gras, a food typically associated with gourmet cuisine and upscale restaurants. Yet, Chicago served this pioneering role, offering a portrait of what can happen when gastropolitics galvanize a city's imagination.

Chicago was the first, and is so far the only, American city to ban the sale of foie gras in restaurants.[10] The ingredient first became contentious in March 2005, when the *Chicago Tribune* published a front-page article by a journalist named Mark Caro with the title "Liver or Let Live."[11] The article focused on acclaimed (and infamously hot-tempered) Chicago chef Charlie Trotter's decision to stop serving foie gras at his eponymous restaurant. Trotter was a pillar of Chicago's burgeoning restaurant scene and nationally recognized as a gastronomic visionary.[12] He was among the first in the city to champion organically and locally produced ingredients, and it was he who introduced the concept of the "chef's table"—where guests can eat in or next to the restaurant kitchen while watching the cooks at work—to fine dining restaurants nationwide.[13] Trotter's résumé included cookbooks, a PBS television series, Michelin stars, and multiple chef and restaurant awards from prestigious culinary organizations such as the James Beard Foundation. Many other highly regarded chefs in the city did stints in his kitchen. Trotter told Mark Caro that he had visited a few foie gras farms and was turned off by what he saw.[14] He also said that he felt the decision whether or not to serve it should be up to the chef, and that he was "not trying to preach" to others.

In the course of his reporting (which was itself later nominated for a James Beard award for food writing), Mark called several other high-status chefs in the city for comments. Most felt that what Trotter did or did not do at his restaurant was his own business. They would continue to serve foie gras. A couple of them said they found Trotter's decision a bit surprising, because his restaurant became renowned in part for the large variety of specialty and artisanal meats on its menus and because

Charlie Trotter's Meat and Game Cookbook, published in 2002, included fourteen foie gras recipes, as well as photos of Trotter at a foie gras farm smiling and holding fuzzy yellow ducklings.

But Rick Tramonto, the chef-owner of another award-winning fine dining restaurant, TRU, diverged from these more detached responses. Tramonto had previously worked for Trotter, so the two men knew each other well (and were not the best of friends). He called the decision "a little hypocritical" because "animals are raised to be slaughtered" and Trotter still served many other types of meat. Mark relayed this comment back to Trotter, who fired a "shot heard round the culinary world." Trotter questioned Tramonto's intelligence, calling him "not the smartest guy on the block" and his statement "an idiot comment." Then, he threw out an insult, suggesting, "Maybe we ought to have Rick's liver for a little treat. It's certainly fat enough."[15]

Mark had stumbled into an ongoing reputational battle and inadvertently put a spark to these acclaimed Chicago chefs' fuse. The article, and foie gras, quickly became hot topics across the city. Before that, foie gras had not really registered in most people's minds beyond a few chefs trained in French techniques and a small group of people who enjoyed eating at upscale restaurants. And yet, many found the issue compelling because both perspectives made sense. We shouldn't treat animals cruelly for the whims of gourmet palates. But at the same time, if a person believes the food industry causes animals to suffer, foie gras is but the tip of a huge, hulking iceberg. The war of words and its subject matter were the "talk of the party" at a *Food & Wine Magazine* event in New York City that week. Several chefs I knew told me friends from around the country were calling them to ask "what's up with Chicago?" The culinary world lit up further when it became known that foie gras had actually been served at a special event held at Trotter's restaurant a few weeks prior. (Trotter said that he was being ideologically consistent by not trying to impose his own feelings on the event's guest chefs.)[16]

Then, even though Mark's articles quoted Trotter as saying that he did *not* think legislators should get involved, a Chicago alderman named Joe Moore took up the issue.[17] Two weeks later, Moore—known for championing populist causes that rarely saw the light of day—introduced an ordinance to the City Council's Health Committee to prohibit the sale of foie gras at Chicago restaurants.[18] Moore told Mark that it was his article that made him aware of the issue and led him to propose the ordinance. In his public statement, Moore declared that voluntary efforts to avoid foie gras "do not go far enough" and that he wanted "to make this dish both unpopular and unavailable."

This caught Chicago-area animal rights activists off guard. Foie gras had not been a focus of their campaigns until that point. Moore had not contacted local groups to obtain information about foie gras production, nor had they reached out to him before that Health Committee meeting. One local leader told me later, "We didn't pick this battle. It picked us." Another activist, who had previously been involved in a campaign to improve living conditions for the elephants at the Lincoln Park Zoo before jumping into the foie gras fight, told me that they "needed a crash course" on foie gras production.

But the game was on. Two groups, Mercy for Animals and the Animal Defense League, reached out to the San Diego–based Animal Protection and Rescue League (APRL), the group that had made headlines in California two years before. National groups, namely The Humane Society of the United States (HSUS), People for the Ethical Treatment of Animals (PETA), and New York State–based Farm Sanctuary, took note of the opportunity that the ordinance presented to put farm animal welfare on a major city's political agenda. The HSUS bought ad space in the *Chicago Tribune* and *Chicago Sun-Times,* calling foie gras "gourmet cruelty." Farm Sanctuary hired a Chicago-based lobbying firm, contracted local activists to gather resources, developed a website (http://www.nofoiegras.org) and began contacting chefs to sign public pledges not to serve foie gras. They also ran a full-page ad in the *New York Times* to raise awareness and to encourage readers to "Say No to Foie Gras!" and donate money to the anti–foie gras campaign. PETA (which claimed over one million members at that time) sent out email blasts and began raising funds from followers around the country.

The City Council's Health Committee held two hearings in July and October regarding the proposed ordinance. As a matter of city policy, separate hearings are typically held for supporters and for opponents for issues such as this one. Both sides may attend, but only one is given the floor. At the first hearing in July, only ban supporters testified. Several were animal rights leaders, including the heads of APRL and Farm Sanctuary, who traveled from their home states at Moore's behest. A few sympathetic Chicago chefs also testified. Even though his name was invoked in the ordinance's text, Charlie Trotter was notably absent. He later said he was "appalled" that his name was included and that he wanted nothing to do with the anti–foie gras movement.[19]

Then, in October, to the ban opponents' surprise, the Committee again invited supporters to speak at the hearing's beginning and end. These included veterinarian Holly Cheever, who had also testified at the July hearing and at those in California, and celebrity activist Loretta Swit (best known for playing Major Margaret "Hot Lips" Houlihan on the TV show *M*A*S*H*). Swit's testimony, in which she compared the treatment of ducks on foie gras farms to that of prisoners held and tortured at Abu Ghraib prison, especially captivated the aldermen and -women present. Moore also screened a PETA-produced video narrated by Sir Roger Moore on the horrors of foie gras production. Several letters opposing a ban were introduced as evidence but not read aloud.

Directly after the testimonies, without allowing time for the committee to discuss the issue or to examine the submitted evidence, Joe Moore asked the chairman, longtime alderman Ed Smith, to "move that this committee recommend to the full council passage of this ordinance." Smith agreed. The motion and vote took less than thirty seconds, passing seven to zero to send the bill up to the full Council, after which applause erupted on one side of the room.

Neither supporters nor opponents knew when the bill would appear on the City Council's monthly docket. News reports, opinion pieces, and Internet commentary regarding the city's involvement with foie gras remained intense during this time. Animal rights organizations rallied supporters (whether residents of Chicago or not) to call or email aldermanic offices in support of a potential ordinance, which they did en masse. Every alderman received a copy of the PETA video. Moore pushed unsuccessfully for the bill to appear on the December agenda, and a number of activists showed up for a rally outside the City Council's chambers that month. Chicago's restaurateurs realized the ban might actually be enacted, and several began promoting foie gras dishes in response. For example, one restaurant advertised their "Au Revoir

Foie and Cigarettes" special in *TimeOut Chicago*, linking it to the city's newly passed (but not yet implemented) ban on smoking in restaurants and bars. Diners could "double up on controversial indulgences" and pair a foie gras appetizer with a fancy European cigarette to smoke on the restaurant's heated patio.

Then, at the City Council's April 2006 meeting, the foie gras ordinance was included as a late addendum to an omnibus bill. Joe Moore had not told reporters ahead of time that he intended to push for a vote at that meeting, the way he had in December. The Health Committee chairman, Alderman Smith, announced it as a measure that had been approved unanimously by his committee. The ordinance's text fit on two pages and read: "All food dispensing establishments as defined in section 4-8-10 of the Municipal Code shall prohibit the sale of foie gras" and that this ban was necessary "to ensure the ethical treatment of animals who are the source of food offered in our restaurants."

Omnibus bills are routine and hefty pieces of municipal legislation. They include multiple ordinances and bills that have passed the city's various committees and are voted on through an aldermanic roll call. Voting against an omnibus means voting against a whole month's worth of Council work. This omnibus was approved 49–0 at the end of a three-hour-long meeting.[20] No formal discussion about foie gras occurred. Some aldermen later admitted they did not realize the foie gras ban was in there. Regardless, selling foie gras at restaurants was about to be forbidden within city limits, as an amendment to Chapter 7-39 of the Municipal Code of the City of Chicago. The Department of Public Health—which reports to the mayor and which is tasked more generally with food safety—would enforce the ban, set to begin a few months later. Policing was to be done by citizens who would call the nonemergency police line to report noncompliant restaurants. For the first offense, the restaurant would receive a warning letter. For a second, it would be fined between $250 and $500.

Compliance & Defiance

Of course, most restaurants in Chicago didn't serve foie gras in the first place. The Chicago food scene has been better known for hot dogs, Italian beef sandwiches, and deep-dish pizza than for fine dining. Joe Moore's own district of Rogers Park had no restaurants that sold foie gras at that time (a fact that became a talking point for his critics). But Chicago was also a city gaining new levels of culinary acclaim. Its chefs and restaurateurs were carving an important niche as tastemakers in the American culinary universe, luring talented new cooks, investors, and tourist dollars. Restaurants have been a notable twenty-first-century component of revitalizing American cities' reputations as "culture capitals."[21] City planners and media heralded Chicago's flourishing downtown and neighborhoods, of which restaurants were an important part. Upscale establishments such as Charlie Trotter's, TRU, and Alinea (an avant-garde restaurant that features a culinary style known as modernist cuisine and has since received three Michelin stars) were receiving glowing international publicity. Chefs such as Rick Bayless and Paul Kahan became media darlings for their restaurants' many accolades, as well as for their support of the city's growing local food movement. Chicago was becoming a foodie town.

Between April and August, when the ban took effect, the Chicago restaurant scene experienced what the dining critic for the *Chicago Tribune* called "the foie gras backlash."[22] As cultural sociologist Nicola Beisel has argued, artistic communities (which have many commonalities with culinary communities) are often roused by legal actions that have the aura of censorship or that seem paternalistic.[23] Indeed, instead of quelling the demand for foie gras, the ban spawned new market behaviors. People who had never heard of the food were now intrigued and eager to try it. A number of restaurants promoted reasonably priced "farewell to foie gras" specials, whetting appetites for this soon-to-be-forbidden delicacy. Amateur cooking schools offered classes on how to prepare it. News articles and letters to the editor kept appearing, and debates over foie gras's ethics and the rationality of passing such a ban sprang up on online message boards and in the comments sections of online articles.

At those restaurants in the city that served foie gras before it became a hot and contested topic, some chefs looked at the evidence put forward by animal rights groups and took it off their menus voluntarily. Some did so to follow the law, and some to avoid protests or harassment by activists. Others were directed to do so by their corporate owners. A number kept it in their kitchens. Some of those kept it on their menus. And several of those thrived on the notoriety they gained for doing so.

During this time, a few chefs in the city and surrounding area formed a small, short-lived group called the Chicago Chefs for Choice as a chapter of the Illinois Restaurant Association, which began hosting foie gras dinners (see Figure 4.4). The group had two specified goals: first, to demonstrate their disapproval of the city's role of "morality police," and second, to raise money to fund a legal challenge to the ban. More broadly, their aim was to deny city officials and animal rights activists alike cultural authority over food and cuisine. To do so, their leaders and followers purposely employed the language of choice.

While small in membership and ill-defined in its organizational structure, the group succeeded in keeping the issue on the city's front burner. Its most active members and its cofounders—Didier Durand and Michael Tsonton—were independent chef-owners of their restaurants. Durand, a quirky chef of Southwestern French origin with a flair for the dramatic, interpreted the ban as a personal insult. His restaurant was twice vandalized during this period, including the night after the second Health Committee hearing. Tsonton, a charismatic, bull-headed art school graduate–turned-chef, had recently opened his own fine dining restaurant near Navy Pier after years of working in others' kitchens. Several nonmember chefs told me they supported the group in principle, but said either that they did not have the time to put into it or were told explicitly by their bosses not to join.[24]

On the day that the ban took effect, some restaurants that had never sold foie gras added it to their menus just for that one day, in what the *New York Times* called "an unlikely demonstration of civil disobedience."[25] Chicago landmark Harry Caray's offered a "farewell to foie gras" special, Connie's Pizza had deep-dish foie gras pizza, and BJ's Market and Bakery on the South Side served soul food–style foie gras. The main point was not to offer this expensive food in more "democratic" settings, but to respond symbolically to the City Council's move to prohibit an ingredient.

The city did not respond to the day's counter tactics.[26] When asked at a morning press conference if he would eat some foie gras that day,

A Very Special Thanks To…
Chicago Chefs & Friends:
Chef Allen Sternweiler – Allen's – The New American Café, Chicago, IL
Chef Dean Zanella – 312 Chicago, Chicago, IL
Chef Shawn McClain – Spring/Custom House/Green Zebra, Chicago, IL
Chef Paul Kahan – Blackbird/Avec, Chicago, IL
Chef William Koval – Culinaire International, Dallas, TX
Chef Hubert Seifert – Spagio, Columbus, OH
Chef Jean-Francois Suteau – Adolphus Hotel, Dallas, TX
Chef Chris Perkey – Sierra Room, Grand Rapids, MI
Chef Chris Desens – Racquet Club Ladue, Ladue, MO
Giles Schnierle – Great American Cheese Collection, Chicago, IL
Didier Durand – Cyrano's Bistrot/Cafe Simone, Chicago, IL
Chef Michael Tsonton – Copperblue, Chicago IL
Chef Ambarish Lulay –The Dining Room at Kendall College, Chicago, IL

Contributors:
Heritage Wine Cellars, Ltd.
Southern Wine & Spirits
Vintage Wines
Maverick Wine Co.
Chicago Wine Merchants
Pinnacle Wines
Pasture to Plate, Inc
Hotel Allegro

Contributors:
Illinois Restaurant Association
Gabby's Bakery – Franklin Park, IL
Chef John Hogan, Keefer's – Chicago, IL
European Imports, LTD – Chicago, IL
Distinctive Wines & Spirits
Louis Glunz Wines
Hudson Valley Foie Gras, LLC– NY
3X Printing – Niles, IL

A Festival of Foie Gras

Allen's –The New American Café & Friends
will be hosting
"A Festival of Foie Gras"
Tuesday, July 11th from 7:00pm – 10:00pm.
at

Allen

The event will take place at **Allen's –The New American Café**
located at 217 W. Huron, Chicago, IL.

For $150/person, guests will have the opportunity to enjoy a variety of foie gras
preparations, beverages included. Net proceeds from this event will be donated
to the Chicago Chefs For Choice, a chapter of the Illinois Restaurant Association,
Freedom of Choice Fund.

Table reservations are available for 6, 8 or 10 guests. Make your reservations today
by calling Allen's – The New American Café at 312-587-9600.
(Credit cards and checks accepted in advance, or at the door. No refunds.)
Donations Accepted.

4.4 Chefs for Choice event flyer.

then-Mayor Richard Daley said no. However, he was rumored to have eaten it at lunchtime at a downtown restaurant that was serving it openly for that one day. Also that day, the Illinois Restaurant Association filed a lawsuit in Cook County Court asserting that the Chicago City Council had overstepped its "home rule" powers under the Illinois Constitution.[27] The lawsuit was later amended to add a federal Interstate Commerce clause claim, because foie gras was produced legally in other states. The district court found in favor of the City, holding that the ordinance did not violate the Constitution's Interstate Commerce clause because it did not discriminate in favor of local or in-state businesses, nor did it affect foie gras production or pricing, only sales. The IRA appealed, but the appeal became moot and was dismissed in 2008, two weeks before it was to be decided, by the City Council's decision to repeal the ban.

After that initial display, most Chicago restaurants stopped serving—or at least visibly offering—foie gras to diners. Suburban chefs, who were able to sell it without incident, told me that they saw orders of foie gras dishes increase two- or threefold during this time. Yet, a few chefs and restaurants within the city limits continued to serve it, some more blatantly than others. The prospect of a relatively small financial penalty did little to deter them. The newly constituted "crime" of eating foie gras quickly entered the popular consciousness of a segment of Chicagoans. The ordinance was written such that it required citizens to serve as the city's eyes and ears.[28] Restaurant patrons would have to see and recognize foie gras, disapprove of it enough to report it, know whom to call, and then follow through. But only a few people viewed foie gras as a serious social problem, and others chose to react in creative (and, for some, tongue-in-cheek) ways. This offers us the means for thinking about how law's symbolic power can spur reaction, and how contested tastes can create certain types of consumers as well as ways to profit from controversy. It lets us see how some people respond when a consumable object becomes newly censured based on one group's moral beliefs.[29]

The text of the ordinance became a subject of flexible—and spirited—interpretation among a loose network of cooks, media, foodies, and Internet discussion boards. Businesspeople found ways to justify offering foie gras on quasi-legal grounds by tinkering with the language of the law, which stated that "all food dispensing establishments ... shall prohibit the sale of foie gras." First, what is a "food dispensing establishment"? A literal reading meant that Fox & Obel, a gourmet grocery store located in downtown Chicago, could not sell foie gras because it had a salad bar and a few tables where customers could sit and eat their lunches. But Binny's Wine Depot could and did. Commercial distributors of gourmet food products were not constrained by the ordinance in the way that restaurants were, and they were not required to report to city officials. A few underground and pop-up supper clubs—not technically "food dispensing establishments"—hosted foie gras–themed dinners in art galleries and industrial lofts. Sometimes the chefs sponsoring these dinners had rarely or never cooked with foie gras before, but wanted, as one told me, "to make a statement." Indeed, one of the pop-up dinners I attended—promoted through foodie social networks as a Foix Grax dinner—saw some spectacular failures in the kitchen.

Second, what does it mean to "sell" something? Here, some chefs complied with the letter but not the spirit of the law. A few told me that they took foie gras off their menus but would still send pieces out as part of a tasting menu or as an amuse-bouche. Some put it in unnamed sauces on other dishes. And some restaurants began giving it to diners "for free" when they ordered a $16 slice of bread or a particular $20 salad. One downtown restaurant, Bin36, was cited by the city for exploiting this loophole. Its owners successfully challenged the citation in city court, saying they were technically not selling the banned substance. After that, this strategy was fair game for other restaurants.

Finally, what, in and of itself, is "foie gras"? To circumvent the ban, some chefs renamed it or started using code words. At one restaurant, the savvy diner could order the "special lobster dish." Some menus were less creative, offering "liver mousse" or "fancy duck liver terrine." At Michael Tsonton's restaurant, the menu listed an appetizer called "It Isn't Foie Gras Any Moore," referencing the role of Alderman Joe Moore in spearheading the ordinance. Of course, Hot Doug's featured the Joe Moore special. As it turned out, not all code words worked equally well. One chef I interviewed recounted a confusing phone call he received one afternoon, where the female caller asked insistently if they had huckleberries that night. He explained to her that huckleberries were not in season, before realizing she was trying to ask about foie gras. To me, he rolled his eyes and asked, "Huckleberries? Really? Who came up with that one?"

The Chicago Chefs for Choice also put together a series of "underground" foie gras dinners at their restaurants in the winter of 2006–07. They were held on nights the restaurants were otherwise closed. These events were coined "duckeasies," harkening to the speakeasy scene that permeated Chicago nightlife during Prohibition and showing a type of what sociologists David Matza and Gresham Sykes once called "subterranean values"—deviant activities organized for the search for excitement by otherwise "respectable" people who know that a particular behavior is illicit or "wrong."[30] These dinners brought together a small number of chefs from different restaurants and diners who took pleasure in feeling transgressive and could afford the $100-a-plate meals.

These dinners were also not exactly "underground." Protestors knew about them, news outlets knew about them, even the police knew about them. Several served as fundraisers for Don Gordon, Joe Moore's main opponent in the upcoming aldermanic campaign. (Moore won in a close election where he would otherwise have been a shoo-in; the foie gras ban came to play a large role in the race.) They were protested by animal rights activists who showed up on frigid winter nights with placards, video screens, and bullhorns to march around, chant about foie gras's cruelty, and attempt to shame attendees (see Figure 4.5). As such, these dinners were public spectacles and double protests (with diners protesting the ban and activists protesting the diners), separated by the restaurant door.

More generally, for the ordinance to be enforced, city health inspectors had to be able to recognize foie gras if they saw it. They also had to care to look for it. Michael Tsonton told me, "My inspector came by and laughed at the notion that we may have had some. He didn't really care. He told me he was more interested in finding listeria than he was in finding foie gras. You know, something that might kill someone." Indeed, a Department of Public Health spokesman told the Associated Press and others that, given his office's limited staff and resources, foie gras was one of their lowest priorities.[31] Their seeking out foie gras was

4.5 Protesters outside of Durand's restaurant during Chefs for Choice dinner in February 2007.

wholly reactive to citizen complaints. And chefs sometimes knew from their networks when a visit from the city might happen. I was at one ban-defying restaurant one morning, conducting an interview with the chef-owner, when a call came in from another chef with word that an inspector was visiting a third restaurant looking for foie gras, and that my interviewee might want to hide what he had in case the inspector was making the rounds. Altogether, nineteen restaurants received cease-and-desist warning letters from the city, but only one—Hot Doug's, which opened this chapter—was also fined.

Foie gras's gastropolitics were also spreading to other cities during this time, where activists heralded the Chicago ban as an agenda-setting "victory" and a "milestone." The ban became a testament to what could happen in the world of food politics when different animal activist groups coordinated their efforts. Bans were introduced and debated in New York City, Philadelphia, Maryland, and Hawaii. Chefs around the country reported receiving hate mail and threatening phone calls; some saw their restaurants protested against and vandalized. People on both sides of the issue found it easier to envision a day when such a ban might apply more widely. A few Philadelphia restaurants saw raucous protests by a small anti–foie gras group cheekily named Hugs for Puppies. In the summer of 2007 in Austin, Texas, a group called Central Texas Animal Defense protested twice a week outside of Jezebel, a restaurant whose owner refused to take foie gras off the menu. In September, an activist who had cut the restaurant's main power breaker and etched the words "spit it out" with acid onto Jezebel's main window was identified through surveillance videos, arrested, held on a $20,000 bond, and charged with criminal mischief.[32]

Throughout this time, the tenor of discussions about Chicago's decision to ban foie gras shifted. Whispers fearing a potential slippery slope of food regulations became shouts. One award-winning and ban-defying chef, in telling me about his reasoning for flouting the ordinance, interpreted it as political grandstanding by the City Council. "What's most important to me about the foie thing," this fit man in his fifties huffed indignantly, "is fat white men telling me what I should and shouldn't do, more so than any misplaced or dishonest concern for the humane treatment of livestock." A sous-chef at a prominent suburban restaurant mirrored others' remarks, saying, "What gives them the right to say what we're allowed to cook or not cook, or eat, for that matter? What's next, after that?" Others argued that the city's focus on foie gras deflected attention from agricultural practices that negatively affect many more animals and eaters. From this perspective, a ban on foie gras was problematic for Chicagoans *because* it was ungrounded in their everyday realities.

Talk of repeal swirled around the news media and the City Council. Aldermanic offices continued to see waves of emails and phone calls from animal rights activists around the country. The Humane Society of the United States bought a full-page ad in the *Chicago Tribune* asking in large text, "Will Chicago Flip-Flop on Animal Cruelty?" (see Figure 4.6) and imploring readers to call their alderman or 311 (the non-emergency police line) to tell them that "repealing this humane law would be just as tough to swallow as the cruel force-feeding of birds." One alderwoman told a local journalist that she favored repeal. "It's not an issue for people in my ward," she said, "gangs and drugs and crime are more important to them [my constituents] than foie gras."[33] Another withdrew his prior support, saying, "Anybody who has traveled any-

4.6 Advertisement in the Chicago Tribune by the Humane Society of the United States. May 21, 2007 (courtesy of HSUS).

where in this country knows that people are just laughing their heads off at us."[34] A few media voices began calling the ban an "embarrassment" to Chicago, which was also then vying to host the Olympics. Chefs for Choice cofounder Didier Durand was so certain that the ordinance would be repealed that he borrowed a live duck from an Indiana farm, which he named Nicolas (after then-French president Nicolas Sarkozy) and kept in his van, to "include in the celebration of foie gras's eventual return to Chicago."

Repeal

Then, in May 2008, a Chicago alderman named Tom Tunney crafted a way to pull the ordinance onto the floor of the City Council's monthly meeting for a repeal vote.[35] Like many others, I only learned that this would happen at ten o'clock the night before, when I got a phone call from Mark Caro telling me I had better join him in the Council's press box the next morning. The City Council's intention to vote on rescinding the ban was announced as "Miscellaneous Business" on their website by its ordinance number, rather than name, only forty-eight hours before the meeting. Someone at the *Chicago Tribune* had spotted it, realized what it was, and quickly made a few calls and published a short announcement on the *Tribune's* website.

Unlike previous council meetings I had attended, all was quiet when I arrived at 9:00 a.m. There were no protestors or rallies either outside City Hall or in the lobby outside the Council chambers. Like me, local animal rights leaders had only learned of the potential repeal of this amendment to Chapter 7-39 of the Municipal Code the night before, and they had not had time to rally their troops. The guard at the metal detector sent me to see the Sergeant-at-Arms for a pass to sit in the press box. I told her I was doing research on controversies about food, and she chuckled, "Well, you've certainly come to the right place! Today is going to be . . . interesting."

The meeting began at 10:00 and dragged on for over four hours. From my seat in the press box, I watched both Tunney and Joe Moore work the floor, lobbying their colleagues. As various resolutions were announced and approved, aldermen shuffled through their papers and wandered between their seats and the antechamber where there were boxes of doughnuts and large coffee urns. A small rally in the lobby for more cops in neighborhoods sounded like a dull roar from inside the chamber. As gray-suited committee heads began taking turns standing to offer their monthly reports, a few people in the press box were literally dozing off. It was almost too easy to see how an issue—any issue— could slip through undetected.

Then, at the tail end of the meeting, "Miscellaneous Business" was announced. The room became silent as people took their seats. One of the aldermen with whom I'd been talking about his opinions on foie gras looked straight at me, raised his eyebrows, and whispered loudly, "Here we go!" Tunney stood up and announced a move to "discharge the ordinance from the Rules Committee."[36] Moore stood to object; then ranking Alderman Bernard Stone stood and ruled the motion "not debatable." A roll call vote of 38–6 pulled it onto the floor. Several aldermen abstained. As the "aye" and "nay" votes began, Joe Moore stood and protested loudly that the issue should be debated "on the floor, on its merits," although it had also not been debated two years earlier. From his perch, a red-faced Daley used his gavel several times and instructed the aldermen to continue through Moore's shouts. A second roll call vote of 37–6 repealed the ordinance. The whole process lasted eight minutes.

In the press room after the meeting, Daley stood at a podium and told the assembled reporters that he didn't allow a discussion on the Council floor because the issue had "already been debated ad nauseam." He then blustered:

> You could buy it in retail. You can bring it with you. They can put it on your salad and increase your salad by $20. They can put it on a piece of toast and charge you $10 for a piece of toast. Does that make sense? I mean, this is what government should be doing? Telling you what you should be putting on toast?

People later said they thought the mayor had pushed the repeal through because he was personally sick of having to deal with questions and complaints about the ban. Moore called it an "outrageous display of old-time Boss politics" and denounced the meeting as a new low point for the city.[37]

Doug Sohn took the news in good stride. "The one thing I'm hoping," he told the *Chicago Tribune* later that day, "is that this issue finally gets put to bed, and the city can spend its time on real issues." Once he got around to ordering some more foie gras, he told the newspaper's dining editor, the foie gras hot dog would be back on the menu. "Of course," he added, "now we have to call it the Tom Tunney."[38]

Two evenings later, seventy anti–foie gras activists gathered outside City Hall for a candlelight vigil. Mercy for Animals (MFA) publicized the event through email lists and on Chicago's vegan meetup.com group, saying that they would provide signs and banners "and will be quietly mourning the true victims of the aldermen's decision: the ducks." I arrived at the publicized start-time of 7:00 p.m., joining television reporters from Fox News and WGN. One of the reporters was interviewing MFA's executive director, a slender man in his mid-twenties named Nathan Runkle, who emphatically told the camera that "this issue stands for animal abuse" and "We were very proud of Chicago for this." But the vigil also had an odd feel. The area around City Hall is empty at seven o'clock on Friday evenings. And the vigil was being held over an hour before sunset, making the candles seem out of place. When I asked Nathan about the choice of timing and venue, he ignored the early evening sun and lack of passersby and instead replied, "We wanted to react quickly to the news with a candlelight vigil. It was a strategic timing issue, and City Hall is symbolic for the place to hold it. We wanted to refocus the issue back on the birds. It's about the animals tonight." Nevertheless, for everyone involved, human and animal alike, Chicago's "foiehibition" was over.

Taste, Control, and Culinary Transgression

The storyline and legacy of foie gras's gastropolitics in Chicago command our attention for several reasons. As a relatively narrow dispute that came to vex the city's leaders, it lets us see how the logics surrounding an issue can mutate in unexpected ways as sound bites reverberate with different audiences, especially when some of those audiences do not take it seriously. Scholars who study the ongoing dynamics between social movements and countermovements have shown that a success (or potential success) for one side can readily mobilize the other.[39] In other words, saying something akin to "We can make you do this" may well provoke people to respond with, "Oh no, you can't. Just watch me." In this case, the passage of the Chicago ordinance triggered certain responses from cultural and public opinion leaders, responses that trod the line between confidence and cockiness. These responses tapped into powerful tropes of individual rights and having the "freedom" to choose what one consumes—ideas that matter deeply (yet are not unproblematic) in the cultural narrative of being a modern-day American.[40]

When foie gras first hit the front page, it was an oddity for most Chicagoans. For foodies, it was a marker of exotic culinary desirability, highlighted on menus alongside other specialty ingredients such as heirloom lettuces, truffle oil, and diver scallops.[41] For animal rights supporters around the country, it offered a golden opportunity to insert themselves into the city's legislative apparatus. Once talk of a ban materialized in the City Council, the words "foie gras" began to bundle complex questions of agricultural and marketplace ethics, the politics of food and lifestyles, and the acceptable purview of city government over its constituents. For the most part, of course, this was not a debate that drew in large swaths of the city's population. Instead, it was a debate among relatively small interest groups: college-educated, tech-savvy activists professing moral righteousness versus upscale chefs and privileged consumers promoting the language of individual choice and autonomy. In spite of the fact that the issue was fairly low-stakes in the grand scheme of things, each group was tenacious.

What also makes this case a curious one for students of food and consumer movements is that it happened first at the level of formal politics, not through grassroots awareness-raising campaigns, boycotts, or protests—illustrating, in part, the sometimes fateful role of chance in politics. The issue entrepreneur in this case was a single official, not a groundswell of citizens. It was rather serendipitous that Chicago was the first place in the country to pass such a law. And not all new laws endure. The effectiveness of a new law or policy generally depends on how strict enforcers choose to be and how well it traverses or reflects the cultural landscape in which it is enacted.[42] Polarizing moral mandates are especially difficult to institute effectively.[43] In Chicago, the foie gras ordinance came to signify less a victory for animal rights than a struggle over a city's cultural authority to define ethical food choices. The ordinance became a comedic diversion rather than an issue for solemn consideration. Its passage, contestation, and repeal can only be understood within this context.

This case also injects ideas about the social power of cultural tastes into the domains of localized politics and markets.[44] Regulations with public health rationales are commonplace for some consumer items, such as alcohol, automobiles, and cigarettes. And in the past decade, many city and state governments across the United States have taken on projects that the federal government would or could not, playing prominent roles in issues including same-sex marriage (at least before the 2015 US Supreme Court ruling), gun control standards, and tightening environmental regulations for building codes and automobile emissions. City governments are both targeted and employed as resources by activist groups seeking to implement change. Foie gras's prohibition in Chicago was no exception.

A related issue here is how, and by whom, new directives to regulate consumption and consumers are enforced. Administering the foie gras ban was tasked to the Food Protection division of Chicago's Department of Public Health, the office responsible for inspecting restaurants for food safety violations. Given the sheer number of people potentially affected, food safety is perhaps one of the more important consumer protection jobs for the state to oversee.[45] Cities primarily police restaurants to protect workers from unsafe conditions and consumers from contaminated foods. Anxiety and concerns about food-borne illnesses have become increasingly common throughout the country, making this job a considerable one.[46] When I asked chefs whether there were any reasons they saw regulation by the city as a positive thing, the majority said they viewed regular safety and sanitation inspections as necessary and welcome. But when it came to deciding which ingredients they could or could not use for moral reasons, more than a few bluntly declared, "Stay out of my kitchen!"

The flip side of this relationship between consumption and regulation is control—namely, a government body's right to prohibit its citizens from using objects in ways that it deems unlawful. Just before foie gras entered the Chicago arena, for example, the City Council had controversially flexed its muscles over the Illinois Restaurant Association in passing the law that now prohibits smoking in restaurants and bars. It is somewhat rare, though, for a city government to involve itself in culinary matters of taste, especially when those tastes belong to people at—or catering to—the higher end of the socioeconomic spectrum. The foie gras ban was a jolt to this group's social and gastropolitical power. Couched in the language of "choice," their dissent signaled that this attempt at control was highly unwelcome. And because it was sale and not consumption (or even distribution) that was prohibited by the Chicago foie gras ordinance, the city eventually recognized that it lacked control over this domain.

Moral Taste and Social Class

References to social class, both overt and opaque, showed up throughout the trajectory of the Chicago foie gras ban. Due to its high price and limited availability in the United States, foie gras resides at the particular intersection points of class and consumption that require rarified cultural knowledge—what French scholar Pierre Bourdieu famously called "cultural capital."[47] Sensitizing accusations against "gourmet gluttons" and "food snobs" helped make foie gras a righteous target for animal rights activists in Chicago and elsewhere. The irony here, however, is that animal rights groups are often themselves caricatured as wealthy folks who are out of touch with regular people's needs. Foie gras's enthusiasts and opponents were mostly fighting for the support of the same social niche—well-educated, reasonably well-off people who profess to care about the moral politics of food.

Of course, theorizing about the connections among foods and cuisines, social class, and moralized "othering" is far from new for sociologists and food studies scholars.[48] We know that food choices are not fully individual decisions, but are circumscribed by a combination of social drivers: cultural beliefs, cost, availability, publicly accepted images, and norms, as well as personal preferences. Tastes—and, by extension, distastes and disgust—are necessarily bound up in the ways that food and eating connect with the intersecting logics of people's lives, identities, and experiences. According to Bourdieu, taste is a "practical operator" in this regard, transforming objects such as foods and culinary styles into distinct signs of class position. For the sociologist, then, contested tastes necessarily manifest, develop, and reproduce within the settings of classed social relations.

This had ramifications for how Chicagoans (and others) came to understand what foie gras was and what it meant, particularly for those who were unfamiliar with it beforehand. What makes one interpretation more compelling than another often depends on how, and by whom, it is introduced.[49] Activists used the public's lack of familiarity with foie gras as a resource in this regard. As a somewhat telling example, between the Health Committee meetings and the Council's passage of the ban, I shadowed a pair of animal rights activists who were out one afternoon gathering signatures for a "ban foie gras" petition . . . at a fast food restaurant in a working-class neighborhood on Chicago's South Side. They would approach people, show them their photos of foie gras production, and explain that foie gras was force-fed duck liver and that it was a cruel and painful process that produced food for rich people. Almost without fail, people would look appalled, make remarks that they were disgusted, and reach for the proffered pen—often while still chewing their burgers.

However, attempts to stigmatize foie gras's eaters were mediated by the fact that they (and the restaurateurs who serve them) could resist without fear of recrimination. In essence, thinking of lawbreaking as a fun night out is especially applicable where elites are involved. Any punishment would have been negligible—there was no risk of arrest or even of fines for these counter tactics. A field note from one of the "duckeasy" dinners I observed offers a prime example of this lack of risk or fear:

It is a frigid, wintery night after an afternoon of freezing rain. The restaurant's warm dining room, on the other hand, is energetic and lively. A self-selected group of well-dressed Chicagoans are snacking on olives, drinking wine, and chatting about the ban. I hear one express a sense of "glee at being bad"; another says he feels "like a teenager having a beer at a party." A third tells his table-mates that he places more faith in these chefs than in "showboat-ing aldermen." Servers dressed in crisp white shirts and ties carry trays out of the kitchen and set them down. The restaurant owner's twelve year old daughter, petite and wearing her own toque and white chef's jacket, is handed a microphone to announce the first course—"foie gras torchon with fruit gelée and toast points." A few minutes later, another chef, one of several cooking that night's meal, comes out from the kitchen and loudly asks the diners, "Did you eat it?" Diners respond with cheers and a resounding "yes!" Outside the restaurant, two police officers are monitoring the twenty-odd protestors who are holding signs and chanting "fancy feast for fat cats!" and "cruelty isn't a delicacy!" The officers have told the activists that they cannot stand still but rather have to keep walking in circles on the narrow sidewalk. Also present and talking with activists are a journalist from the *Chicago Reader* and a two-person news crew from a local television station. The officers do not enter the restaurant.

Those *inside* the restaurant were the ones breaking the law, but the police were concerned with the peaceful protest *outside*. Even though violations of the ban fell under the purview of the Health Department, the actions of these cops were one example of many that demonstrated the city's ambivalence about enforcing the ordinance.

Gastropolitics and "Choice"

As cultural historians such as Liz Cohen and Meg Jacobs have detailed, being a good citizen and being a good consumer became intertwined ideas over the course of the twentieth century, in large part via the aegis of government programs and policymakers interested in safeguarding the American economy.[50] The idea of "citizens" evokes a universalistic category, based on assumptions of reason, judgment, and collective belonging of persons who participate in constituent politics. Even though many of the challenges created by a consumption-driven society are largely systemic in nature, this notion of the "citizen-consumer" puts the onus for social change in the hands—and the choices—of individuals operating in the market. It individualizes social responsibility, and it works to persuade people to believe that they can make a difference in the world by consuming the right products.

The idea here is that consumption choices are "votes." This rhetorical trope follows several decades of American consumers discovering that their dollars can buy political pressure as well as things,[51] and it characterizes American gastropolitics at its finest. The core idea is that competitive markets respond to consumer demand, which in turn attracts new suppliers to the market. With enough "votes," marketplace structures will evolve accordingly. In other words, people can exercise their agency, and their citizenship, through choices in the moral economy of the marketplace.[52] Especially as public opinion polls show that Americans are increasingly disillusioned with the ideas that they make any difference in electoral or regulatory politics or might have legal successes against the multi-billion dollar food industry, "votes" with one's dollar—or one's fork—count in a different way.[53]

In this mindset, personal and social identities, as well as consumer movements, are realized through commodities and solidified through consumer behavior. This lends a political dimension to the act of choosing, or refusing, certain foods. It calls upon the ordinary consumer to mindfully and purposefully spend his or her money in order to eat certain things and at certain places (such as farmers markets) while avoiding others (such as fast-food restaurants or companies whose owners hold certain religious stances). Animal welfare and rights advocates similarly encourage people to "vote" (albeit by abstention) on the issue of eating meat. But yet, one can only "vote" as an eater among the choices made available by the business and regulatory communities. Many other factors besides consumer choice play a role in structuring markets. And who has the ability and resources to "vote with their forks" remains a salient issue of social class.[54] This analogy casually affirms the liberal rhetoric of personal choice, bypassing the myriad ways in which one's choices are influenced by others and their own life circumstances. This is the gastropolitical model that surrounded events in Chicago, meshing the language of taste and of choice with that of overt stakeholder politics.

While animal activists hoped that Chicago's fine diners would "vote" by avoiding foie gras, they also saw a legal ban as morally just and necessary. If foie gras is indeed a "product of egregious cruelty," they had an ethical obligation to do more than leave the decision to the whims of consumers. It is also important to note that in Chicago and around the country, chefs and restaurateurs have been far from unified in their stances on foie gras. For instance, in one of the City Council Health Committee hearings leading up to the ban, Michael Altenberg—then chef-owner of Bistro Campagne and a long-time proponent of the local food movement in the Chicago area—described taking foie gras off his menu after watching the GourmetCruelty.com video and being horrified by what he saw.[55] Discussions on online chef forums such as eGullet have been both heated and contemplative, and are rife with contrasting arguments about foie gras's social and culinary value. In cities around the United States that have seen foie gras become a political issue, local elites and opinion leaders have been divided as well.

The chefs I interviewed in Chicago fell mainly into one of three camps: those who agreed with the activists, those who felt obliged to comply with the ordinance whether or not they considered it wrong or unfair, and those who acted on their dissent. A number of these chefs (including those who rarely or only sporadically served foie gras) expressed indifference to fattened liver itself. Their main objection was that the City Council was telling them what they could or could not cook. Some called the ban "prohibitionist nonsense," its supporters "the food police," and Chicago "a nanny city" that was "one election shy of city-wide bedtime." Many were also openly skeptical of the testimonies of the experts that had come to Chicago to represent animal rights groups.

As such, foie gras became a heavier gastropolitical symbol through the course of its presence on Chicago's docket, but not in the ways that activists had hoped. The ban's imprecise writing and lax enforcement gave people the room to respond creatively. A new and competing definition of the situation emerged. Those who skirted the ban began to justify their actions as motivated by the desire to safeguard "choice," which quickly became a master frame and converted a marginal issue to a seemingly significant one. As Michael Tsonton, cofounder of the determinedly named Chicago Chefs for Choice, told me without a sense of hyperbole, "We want to protect our choices and our interests as restaurateurs, retailers, and suppliers from personal moral campaigns on products that are legally produced in this country." At risk, he insisted, were values at the core of American ideals. This is a culturally affirming claim in that it frames choice as a virtuous and even sacred principle. Its individualist orientation echoes an American cultural narrative of freedom, independence, and personal responsibility.[56] The dining critic for the *Chicago Tribune*, Phil Vettel, made a related point after the repeal: "You don't get rid of something you don't like by banning it. You tax it."[57]

Most of the chefs I interviewed were careful to explain that their stance did not mean they were in favor of the cruel treatment of animals. Far from it. Like animal rights advocates, many of these chefs want people to know where the food on their plates is coming from and are passionate about ethical and sustainable eating. Like animal activists, many are thoughtful and critical about how people morally value their food. Unlike activists, however, they see animals as acceptable to eat. Some truly believed the activists were wrong about foie gras's "inherent cruelty"; they trusted the expertise of producers, both American and French, in this regard. Others thought this food was being singled out unfairly by the city as a way to "get some publicity" or "stick it to foodie snobs," and they criticized the surreptitious way the ordinance was passed. In discussions with me and each other (to which I was privy), they frequently brought up negative social and environmental impacts of industrialized chicken, turkey, pork, and beef production—as well as the ways those livestock are treated—as points of comparison. "I'd certainly rather be a foie gras duck than a Butterball turkey," one chef told me. For these other animals, the moral suasion was there, but the law was not. In the words of more than one interviewee, foie gras was a "pseudo-problem."

For activists, this rhetorical countering pushed buttons as well as boundaries. Several argued that the "choice" and the "pseudo-problem" arguments should not hold water. An activist at one protest exclaimed, "They keep saying 'freedom of choice.' But, animal cruelty *isn't* a choice! It is institutionally sanctioned cruelty. It sullies our entire society and promotes violence against all vulnerable groups." She saw her role as generating social awareness and foie gras as a moral crusade.[58] Defending the validity of the ordinance and protesting its scofflaws was, for her and others, a point of civic responsibility and moral necessity. For people on both sides of the issue, then, foie gras's moral valuation and devaluation was filtered by these contested tastes.

Conclusion: Dinner Theater on the City Stage

The trajectory of Chicago's foie gras ban is an assay that helps us see how gastropolitical contests around foie gras's moral and legal status evolved in the US context, and how they shaped disputes over what actually happened once selling foie gras became a "crime." Even if foie gras was indeed a "pseudo-problem," the events orchestrated throughout the city—both for and against the ban—showed that a number of people cared enough about what it represented to get involved (albeit without fear of serious sanction). People embraced conflicting definitions of the situation. Foie gras became bigger than liver.

These events and their settings were significant symbols themselves. Restaurants—as physical and symbolic spaces "in which culture is fought over and licked into shape"[59]—operate at the interstices of markets, communities, and law. The text of the Chicago foie gras ordinance explicitly mentioned the importance of offering "the best in dining experiences" in the city's "legendary restaurants." Policymakers care about reputation—not just for winning reelections, but for the ways that the place and people they represent are perceived. While Chicago was able, at least temporarily, to prohibit foie gras in restaurants' kitchens and dining rooms, it did so without solid planning for what the act might come to mean for social observers. I found that participants in the debates sought to position "Chicago" itself as a meaning-laden symbol to organize around. What kind of city is Chicago? What kind of people are Chicagoans? What kind of city *should* it be?

Ultimately, the crucial understanding that came to dominate the discursive landscape, and eventually influenced the ban's repeal, was that of Chicago as laughingstock. The ban was derided as a joke by unsympathetic elites, including Chicago's own mayor. It became a running punch line on Comedy Central's *The Colbert Report*. An article in *The Economist* mused about how much lawsuits and appeals over the ordinance might be costing the city.[60] The manager of Chicago landmark restaurant Harry Caray's told the *New York Times* that they participated in selling foie gras the day the ban took effect because "this ban is embarrassing Chicago."[61] High-profile chefs around the country, including Anthony Bourdain, David Chang, and Thomas Keller, decried it using language of embarrassment and shame. Bourdain called Chicago "a stupid cow town" and, as dining critic Phil Vettel noted in the *Chicago Tribune* just after the ban's reversal, "a city trying to become an Olympic destination [as it was at that time] doesn't want to look like a stupid cow town."[62]

While a pioneering and entrepreneurial law may attract followers, it can also endanger reputations. The aura of negative attention received—and perceived—by the City Council was what ultimately convinced its members to reverse the ban, rather than just permit its semilegal skirting by restaurateurs and petulant foodies. Positive responses from the national animal rights community did not outweigh the derision that Chicago seemed to care "more about ducks" than problems affecting the city's human residents, including homelessness, failing public schools, street violence, and unemployment. Moreover, after-the-fact accusations from animal rights leaders that the City Council "flip-flopped" on animal cruelty do not accurately reflect the events that occurred. The Council did not take a moralized stand to begin with: the ordinance had not seen an open debate on the Council floor, and many aldermen even admitted they failed to realize it was in the April 2005 omnibus until after the fact. From there, the city did not invest real time or money in enforcing it. Ambivalence was more the rule than the exception.

Chicago's "foiehibition" shows that the gastropolitical value of a substance such as foie gras is a result of connected interactions among the people who symbolically use it. The issues woven through these particular interactions elicited questions of the institutional purview of city government, what it means to be a moral consumer, and how much "choice" one should be permitted to have. The ordinance actually served the interests of *all* people involved in some meaningful ways. Lax enforcement and ready availability of the product only slightly inconvenienced the chefs who wanted to serve it and the consumers who wanted to eat it. After the ordinance was repealed in 2008, many more people in the city knew about foie gras, and now they could order it just about everywhere. Many restaurants saw this new demand and began offering it on their menus. As of 2014, even with the financial crisis and recession fresh in recent memory, foie gras was on more menus in Chicago than it was prior to the ban.[63] For animal rights activists in the city, the ordinance brought public visibility to their organizations and to other issues they had been championing. In some ways, the campaign also connected them with like-minded people and organizations working on complementary issues. But it also had a significant unintended consequence: foie gras became a wedge issue for a number of high-profile, progressive chefs who might have otherwise been allies on other animal welfare campaigns but who came, instead, to see animal activists as an enemy.

Additionally, the symbolic politics surrounding these disputes show that emotion is a great sales device—whether what is being sold is a story, a moral judgment, or an appetizer. This is especially relevant when it comes to the politics of food. Food is central to our identities and our connections to the places we inhabit and the communities to which we belong. People feel passionately about it. Yet, twenty-first-century consumers swim in a nebulous sea of information about what is right or wrong to eat. Politicizing foods, even those that most people do not eat, hits close to home. Unlike policy issues that can be arcane, debates about food draw people in. In Chicago, both the idea and reality of foie gras's physical presence on the plate gave it acute saliency, pitting different groups against each other for cultural authority and for public sympathies.

CHAPTER 5

The Paradox of Perspective

On a breezy spring day a few years ago, I drove upstate from New York City to visit Hudson Valley Foie Gras (HVFG)—the United States's largest foie gras producer. I knew from my prior experiences in Southwest France that foie gras operations came in different shapes and sizes, and that production logistics and producer mentalities varied. I understood, for instance, that different farms used a range of force-feeding techniques, as well as distribution and sales venues. I knew that animals on every farm sometimes got sick or died prematurely, but that mortality and illness rates varied considerably. I knew that seeing ducks held in individual wire cages during gavage made me feel queasier than seeing birds held in group pens. Yet, in France, no matter what, most people I encountered in foie gras's production chain portrayed it as an important symbol of their food culture and their national identity—a material product embedded in cultural and historical legacies. Further, family considerations and local community histories had shaped the occupational choices of many of the French producers I met. Foie gras's main region of production—the rolling hills of the Southwestern départements—similarly appealed to French consumer mindsets as a unique landscape steeped in antiquity and needing protection from the strong winds of globalization.

I was eager to see firsthand how the largest producer of foie gras in the United States compared. What was it like there? I had interviewed Michael Ginor, one of Hudson Valley Foie Gras's co-owners, near his home on Long Island a few months before. Now I wanted to hear directly from the people in charge of the farm's operations. HVFG, which produces about three hundred and fifty thousand foie gras ducks a year, had recently found itself at the epicenter of American outrage about the ethics of foie gras production. Disputes about foie gras's legality had become incendiary in places around the country. Chicago had banned its sale at restaurants the previous year, California's ban on production and sale was looming large, and protests and potential legislation were making news headlines in other cities, including nearby New York City.

Unlike the motivations that have spurred a number of journalists to visit HVFG over the last decade, my primary interest in this visit was not in reporting the ethical "truth" of foie gras production.[1] Rather, I was interested in better understanding their operations and future plans in relation to changing market and political conditions, as well as their interpretations of foie gras's recent and combative disputes. More generally, I hoped that this visit would help me to understand why foie gras has traveled such different cultural pathways in the United States and France. As market institutions proved to be such an important but hidden force behind the culture of foie gras in France, I was also curious to learn firsthand how producers in the United States framed their work in the absence of both institutional support and deep-seated cultural valence.

The directions given to me by Izzy Yanay—the farm's other cofounder/owner and general manager—took me through the Catskill Mountains' rolling hills, blanketed with early summer foliage. I came to a large metal gate marked only by two small signs, one with the company's name and the other reading "Private Property." I drove through and parked my car next to several others in an unpaved, gravelly area, and looked around. Unlike the surrounding landscape, the farm was not a pretty place. The buildings were long and squat, with rust-tinged roofs and shabby-looking metallic siding, and none was marked.[2] A number of small wooden houses on cement foundations, which looked hastily built, sat off to one side of the property. As I learned later, about 150 people—workers and their families, all Mexican immigrants—lived on site. (I also learned later of labor investigations at this farm. Because farm work is exempt from many labor laws, including overtime pay, it can be a site of worker exploitation, especially for migrant workers, albeit with a good deal of variability across farms.[3]) Hudson Valley Foie Gras was remarkably different—and much larger—than any of the farms I had seen in France.

Izzy came out to meet me, shook my hand with a meaty grip, and said he needed to drop off a notebook in his office "before we go to see the ducks, from the beginning to the end." He was getting right down to business. We headed to a nondescript cement building and walked down a hallway lined with heavy-duty carpeting, framed vintage French foie gras posters, and menus from renowned restaurants nationwide—often personally autographed by their chefs—that featured Hudson Valley Foie Gras on their menus. Izzy pointed proudly to a few signatures and remarked, "But when people make small talk and ask what I do for a living, I say 'duck farmer' because ninety-nine percent of people here in the US don't know what foie gras is."

After dropping off the notebook, we got in Izzy's car to drive to the other side of the property. As we jostled in our seats along the unpaved path, Izzy's loud, gravelly, and Israeli-accented voice was accompanied by extensive hand gestures. Almost immediately, without my even asking directly about foie gras production, he went on the defense.

Indignantly, Izzy told me that he had at least two or three visitors per week—chefs, journalists, and others who want to see foie gras production for themselves after being exposed to activists' condemnations. He explained the pivotal question asked of him is one about cruelty, and declared that he was "trying to be as open as possible" by allowing visitors to come, even though it took up a lot of his time, "because there are so many wrong ideas out there." Later that week, a group of extremely high-profile restaurateurs and chefs was going to come up from New York City, and Izzy worried out loud that they might "go the way of Puck." Three months prior, Austrian-born and California-based superchef Wolfgang Puck—the first chef to make the Forbes Celebrity 100 list—had renounced foie gras as part of his new culinary philosophy. Puck's numerous restaurants, from quick-service to fine dining, would promote the use of organically raised vegetables and meat and would not permit eggs from battery-caged hens, pork from gestation-crated pigs, veal from calves raised in confinement crates, or foie gras. However, this plan did not arise autonomously; rather, it followed a targeted online and in-person campaign against Puck and his "egregious practices" by animal rights groups Farm Sanctuary and the Humane Society of the United States.

This statement about "wrong ideas" implied that Izzy believed his own standpoint was the right one. He continued, explaining that he thought the sample of people who had visited the farm was biased toward skeptics:

> The main questions of everyone who comes to the farm are based on the information they are getting from the animal rights people. It is this: are these ducks suffering? Are they in pain? Are they being tortured? Well, you look and see how they act. See if you see struggling, or hear screaming. You don't have to be a scientist to know how they are feeling, if they are suffering. You just look.

On the surface, Izzy was saying the same thing that foie gras's most determined enemies had also told me—that simply by observing the ducks, anyone would know if they are suffering and if the force-feeding process is indeed cruel. Do the birds look scared? Sound upset? Seem sickly? Do they fight back against the metal tube or the feeder? Are you, the observer, physically uncomfortable because of the cramped space, the temperature, the humidity, the smell? All thought that this simple act of observation, of experiencing through one's senses, would resolve the conflict between opposing mindsets. But how could an appeal to empirical observation resolve matters if both sides relied so heavily on the very same "look for yourself" and "if only the other side had the correct information" tropes?[4] That particular morning, this paradox of perception had indeed dominated my thoughts as I drove to the farm: how would I—or anyone else, for that matter—know what I was seeing? How do we know what an uncomfortable duck looks like? The argument I heard from both camps—about personal, "natural," and sensory experiences—however, cuts both ways. If one should not anthropomorphize pain or discomfort, one should also not anthropomorphize calmness. With a nod to philosopher Thomas Nagel's oft-cited question, how can we know "what it is like to be" a different kind of animal?[5]

Izzy and I then arrived at our destination. He opened the door, and two thousand fuzzy, yellow, chirping two-day-old ducklings—delivered just that morning from the farm's partner hatchery in Quebec—came barreling toward us. They were all male, Izzy explained, because male ducks' livers are better suited for foie gras.[6] We then went up a flight of stairs to see the next step of the ducks' growing process. Izzy opened a door to a large room, several hundred yards long, full of juvenile gray ducks whose feathers had yet to turn black and white. Similar to industrial foie gras operations throughout France, Hudson Valley uses mulards, the hybrid and sterile duck crossbreed used for the good and consistent quality of their livers. The room was bright with morning light coming in through large windows and was kept cool with large, humming air conditioners. Food and water stations were installed at intervals throughout the cavernous space, and the floor was covered with straw. The ducks were standing close to each other, but still had room to move about. It was the largest number of ducks I had seen in one place. This was a distinct scalar contrast to anything I had experienced in France, where the industry is vertically differentiated. While operations like the Rougié factory I visited are large ventures, processing thousands of livers a day, the raising and force-feeding of ducks for foie gras there is dispersed over several thousand farms around the country. Hudson Valley, on the other hand, does it all on site.

We stood there for a few minutes, just observing the young ducks. They did not run toward us, as the ducklings had, but they did not run away either. I asked about the ducks' lack of access to outdoor spaces, which was another activist criticism of how HVFG ducks were treated. Izzy responded, a bit defensively, that they used to put the ducks outside in fenced enclosures in warmer months. But ducks are vulnerable to predators when they are outside, even in fenced enclosures. In the recent past, they had lost ducks to foxes, dogs, raccoons, and hawks. Additionally, the previous year, the New York Department of Environmental Conservation had recommended keeping the ducks inside due to fears they might contract avian flu from passing wild birds. A final rationale, also reacting to state regulators' concerns, was about environmental impacts from the ducks' waste. The farm had just installed a new $600,000 system to treat manure collected in the barns, but they could not operate it outside. For these reasons, he and the farm's operations manager, Marcus Henley, had decided for the time being against outdoor access.

We returned to the car and drove to a different building—the one from which Izzy had originally emerged when I arrived—to see the ducks in gavage. On the drive over, he explained that HVFG's ducks were fed three times daily, rather than the two times typical in France, in order to help them adjust to the process by increasing the amount of feed they receive in smaller increments. Almost every time he said "feeding tube," Izzy also said "not cruel." I wondered if stringing those words together was a conscious decision or whether it had become second nature for him with his steady stream of visitors and requests for media interviews. "But don't believe me," he said in what I also assumed was a common refrain, "believe the ducks." In other words, he invited me yet again to judge with my own eyes.

The room was dark and noisy, as several men fussed over a broken pneumatic feeding machine that looked analogous to those used at many industrial farms in France. Izzy asked them if they had made any progress. To me, he explained that their ducks were fed "the old-fashioned, grandma way with a funnel and auger" but that they were "trying out" this machine on a few hundred ducks to see how their livers turned out. (Not mentioned was the fact that this machine was the type heavily critiqued by foie gras's adversaries, as well as by chefs and consumers who claimed to value more "traditional" foie gras produced by "artisanal" methods.[7])

We ambled down the long, echoing barn. The lighting was low inside, and the air smelled a bit gamey, but not of ammonia. (The lack of an ammonia odor meant the air was clean and circulating well.) What I saw all around me was a very large number of white and black ducks that mostly ignored us, neither moving toward nor away from us (see Figures 5.1 and 5.2). These ducks were eighteen days into gavage (out of twenty-eight) and were housed nine to a pen in three long rows of raised pens. They did not run away from me when I approached. Brigita, a "poster child feeder" as Izzy described her, sat on a stool in one of the pens feeding ducks. Pausing momentarily to nod a quick greeting, Brigita picked up a duck, placed it between her legs, and inserted the funnel that dangled above her left arm into its beak and down its esophagus.

5.1 Hudson Valley Foie Gras ducks in gavage, June 2007.

The duck remained still. With her other hand, she poured a measured scoop of ground grain (a mix of eighty-nine percent corn, eleven percent soy, and a vitamin supplement) into the funnel and massaged the duck's neck for a minute, pushing the feed down—what Izzy markedly called "hand feeding," and not "force feeding." She then slid the tube up and

5.2 A close view of Hudson Valley Foie Gras ducks in gavage.

out its beak and moved the duck to her left side, where it shook its head and got a drink from the trough of running water through the bars of the pen.

Izzy then led me downstairs to a different part of the barn and toward a group of ducks that were only two days into gavage. He narrated the scene for me, directing me to notice that these ducks were "more nervous and panicky," saying:

> Gavage is a process. They are frightened the first day, when they aren't used to being handled. You have to train them, like training a dog to walk on a leash. Do you torture a horse by sitting on him, putting your weight on him? The first couple of times it is tough, but then they get the hang of it quickly. Look at these ducks compared to the ones upstairs . . . I'm asking you not because I want you to agree with me. I'm asking you. Do they act different?

They did. In fact, these ducks were clamoring over each other to squeeze into the side of the pen furthest away from us. "What about the ones you saw before?" Izzy almost shouted. "In your eyes, did they look frightened? Do they look under torture?" he insisted. Indirectly referencing actress Loretta Swit's testimony to the Chicago City Council, "Do they look like the Iraqis at Abu Ghraib?" Izzy nodded gamely when I answered, "To my eyes, no," although I couldn't help but think of the learned helplessness of refugees or prisoners of war whose wills have been broken and who yet seem complacent on the surface.

Back in Izzy's office a bit later, the conversation turned to foie gras's opposition. We were joined by Marcus Henley, a soft-spoken veteran of poultry farming. Izzy began venting his frustrations, slamming his fist on his desk as he spoke:

> The scientific evidence is very obvious. It is completely, one hundred percent, opposing activists. All [scientists] agree that there is no cruelty involved. Anyone who knows about agriculture knows that the birds are *not* suffering. But their agenda is *much* bigger than the ducks. You saw the ducks, and you saw they're not afraid. So my question is if that is so, what is going on? If they know that

I'm not torturing the ducks, why are they doing what they're doing? Why are they costing me a million dollars in a year in damages? We have a USDA [United States Department of Agriculture] inspector here every day. Are they saying the USDA is not doing their job? And we've had all the scientists, people from the AVMA [American Veterinary Medical Association], impartial people who come with us to the slaughterhouse and look at the esophagus, and say "we don't see anything wrong."[8]

Izzy continued that he and Marcus were "busy all the time" not with raising ducks but dealing with lawsuits filed against the farm. The animal rights contingency has not based its legal objections to Hudson Valley Foie Gras solely on the claim of cruelty, but rather has challenged the farm on a number of secondary fronts. A few examples of the operation's numerous legal entanglements includes a $30,000 fine levied against them by the New York State Department of Environmental Conservation over an unauthorized waste lagoon, a dismissed 2006–07 HSUS lawsuit claiming that they were selling an adulterated and diseased product,[9] and a 2010 federal charge of violating the Clean Water Act. Izzy explained that some complaints, especially about the state of their property and the need for repairs, were valid, but that he had little time or money to remedy them. Once a charge filed against them was held, settled, or dismissed, activist groups would file another suit or legal complaint almost right away. In New York State, recovering legal expenses from dismissed charges for civil cases can only happen under certain circumstances, meaning recouping monies was practically impossible.

They are trying to bury us. We spend $30,000 a month on legal costs, minimum! Lawyers, lawyers, letters, and lawyers. And then we don't have the money to improve our facilities and fix the buildings. So more violations. It's a cycle.

Izzy abruptly changed the subject, pulling a newspaper article out of a desk drawer, with a photograph of Wolfgang Puck signing a document declaring his new philosophy. "Then they go to the chefs! Look," he commanded, referencing our earlier conversation:

You can see that he's sweating. And you can see that the guy from the Humane Society is underneath the table, holding Wolfgang's balls. Now, why did he decide to sign on that? Why did he decide to stay away from foie gras and veal and whatever else? He's the animal defender, but he's never been to my farm or to Guillermo's, and he was promoting foie gras left and right, like a month before!

Without pausing, he answered his own question with a resigned overtone. "Politically, it's good for him. They attacked him for a long time. And his clients are very exposed people."

As Izzy stopped to catch his breath, Marcus quickly added, "Farmers don't like to hurt animals." He told me, as a case in point, that several years before, they had briefly experimented with using the individual confinement cages that were ubiquitous in France but stopped doing so fairly quickly because the ducks "did not fare well," the results were "disastrous," and the cages made him "personally very uncomfortable." Marcus then agreed with Izzy that The Humane Society of the United States was "out for our blood, even if a drop at a time," and explained that veterinary studies supported their position, that yes, there was a funnel and a tube being put down the ducks' throats and their livers were being enlarged, but what they were doing is not painful, damaging, or cruel when done responsibly.[10] The process, he articulated, replicates what ducks and geese do in the wild: overeat before migration to store fat.[11] In an email follow-up a week later, Marcus told me that Dr. Lawrence Bartholf (a former president of the New York Veterinary Medical Association who is also quoted at length on HVFG's website) had attended the tour with their high-profile New York City visitors to explain the science behind gavage and foie gras production—that waterfowls' esophagi lack a gag reflex and sensory nerves, such that they can eat "whole live fish and, thus, not have any difficulty with the tube"—as well as recent animal behavioral research studying aversion behavior in ducks. Marcus wrote:

> What we saw was a lot of ducks that mostly didn't mind people being there. Of course, the ducks were a little put off by the tour

group of seven big men. . . . Then, we went to the processing plant. We opened and cut up a duck for them, and showed them the raw product and the packaged product, foie gras to legs. This gave Dr. Bartholf the opportunity to really show how the inside of a duck works. A very real tour.

Conversely, and also based on the idea that seeing is believing, the answer to "are they suffering?" is an absolute and unequivocal "yes" for foie gras's foes. This elicits a related question—for an animal destined to be eaten, what level of discomfort is unacceptably cruel? I do not have a yes-or-no answer to these epistemological questions of suffering. Both science and human judgment offer particular kinds of expertise, and both require interpretation. We know from a large and multidisciplinary body of research that what one believes—and even what one sees or claims to see with one's own eyes—is highly correlated with social location, status, politics, and prior beliefs.[12] Both Izzy and his opponents—and each faction's followers—were engaging in what some scholars call "confirmation bias" and some others call "inferred justification." This means that people on one side of an emotionally charged issue will cherry-pick some pieces of information and discount others to bolster their argument.[13] When my most partisan informants expressed their sentiments about foie gras's ethics, they were subjectively invoking some of its salient features and bypassing others. Uncertainty tended to be ignored.

Moreover, people—in this case, even specialized veterinarians and avian biologists—can and do interpret the same information in radically different ways.[14] Dogmatic people often remain adamant that their opinions are the correct ones, even in the face of strong evidence to the contrary. Interpretations of "facts" and rejections of disconfirming evidence (whether arguments, scientific data, and even sensory impressions) are also informed by people's underlying cultural assumptions about who else is, or is not, being truthful.[15] Giving extreme partisans corrective information can, at times, even have what some political scientists call a "backfire effect" by strengthening misperceptions and thus proving counterproductive for changing their minds (such as in beliefs about the risks of childhood vaccination).[16] Of course, foie gras is far from the only contested issue—food-related or otherwise—where evidence is searched, interpreted, and assimilated into moral discourses in discordant and biased ways. One of many other examples is the contemporary global debate over genetically modified plants and animals.

For foie gras, in responding to what he felt was the purposeful misinformation offered by animal rights activists in their work to garner public approval, Izzy answered his own question of "why are they doing what they're doing?" In an irate tone, he said, "We are a very easy target. Very vulnerable. The animal rights people, they have an agenda to stop animal agriculture. We are a low apple on that tree. So, we are the key, the holding in the door. Because once they get rid of foie gras, then it's going to be on to the other things."

This metaphor of the low-hanging fruit is apt not only because of its edible imagery. This is a question about strategy, one that evokes ideas about the choice and consequences of targeting foie gras. Indeed, when selecting a target, animal rights activists do not just ask "is it cruel?" They also ask, "is this the best place to take a stand?" Observers might call the focus on cruelty an appeal to emotion and the focus of strategy an appeal to reason. But this is a false dichotomy. Emotions, especially, can be manipulated strategically. And the answers to each question likely inform the answer to the other. Among the many and sizeable issues affecting animals in our modern food system, why mobilize around foie gras, something that has little to no impact on the nation's diet or commerce, and *not* around chicken, beef, pork, or turkey (or homelessness or crime, for that matter)? And how has this focus played out among those whom activist groups intend to sway?

In the case of foie gras, the answer depends on who those groups are and where their interests lie. What these questions imply is a more intricate set of relationships among what we value, what we *say* we value, the vulnerability of various targets, and what we, as individuals and as members of society, are actually willing to fight for. Foie gras has turned out to be both a pragmatic and a problematic target for those who have challenged its legality and its existence. Drawing from a key idea in cultural sociology that meanings and values are both relational and normative,[17] this chapter shows that contested issues of food and taste poli-

THE PARADOX OF PERSPECTIVE 159

tics are understood—in some cases quite literally—by what they are conceptualized *in relation to*. For many, gastropolitics are also about the circumstances and perspectives and moralized tastes—of allies and adversaries. Such an argument also involves querying how we come to morally categorize and (de)value some singular food item or practice.

The remainder of this chapter unpacks the social antagonisms that anchor the contemporary gastropolitics of foie gras in the United States.[18] It is these relational contexts that make symbolic boundaries between "us" and "them"—and the social antagonisms that they spur—continue to matter tremendously within the contemporary politics of food.

A Pragmatic Target

If there is one thing on which animal activists and foie gras devotees have agreed, it is that foie gras is an easy gastropolitical target in the United States. It is produced by a small industry with limited resources, little political capital, and a small (if wealthy) consumer base. Moreover, the very idea of an animal being forced to eat through a metal tube put down its throat elicits squeamishness, even among committed meat-eaters. For groups interested in vilifying animal agriculture and setting the agenda on the ethical rights of animals in the public and political imaginations, these facts make foie gras a pragmatic target.

Taking on Meat and Poultry

At its most fundamental level, foie gras is a pragmatic target from the perspective of the objectives, costs, and constraints that any social movement faces when it mounts any sort of mobilization effort. Most social movements share the goals of rallying public support and changing policy, law, and, where appropriate, market structures. Thus, victories of any scale lend cultural legitimacy to the interests that the group represents. In certain instances, a symbolic victory can be as important as victories that directly affect tangible, material interests—especially when the real costs are minimal compared to perceptions of success.[19]

By acting strategically, social movements in Western nations have played powerful roles in introducing new values, beliefs, and ideas that are fostering political and cultural changes related to consumption.

Beginning in the 1980s, animal rights groups in the United States began fixing their attention on agriculture and the food system following successful campaigns against fur and vivisection (the use of live animals in medical and consumer product manufacturing experiments).[20] The campaign against veal is an archetypal example. In the late 1980s, several animal rights groups bought ad space in newspapers and on television to circulate graphic images and descriptions of how veal calves are raised (the use of small confinement crates to deliberately limit muscle development and produce more tender meat).[21] Veal consumption rates declined significantly, the US Congress held hearings for a Veal Calf Protection Act, and consumer and restaurant demand for "free-range" veal increased.[22] Because of the ways that its production methods generate shock and disgust, activists and journalists today sometimes call foie gras "the new veal."

Since then, alongside rapid gains in membership and financial contributions, national animal rights organizations have professionalized and bureaucratized their infrastructures. By adopting tactics such as lobbying lawmakers and holding stock in food companies, these groups have created new spaces and ways to negotiate and attain their goals of reducing or eliminating people's consumption of animals and shifting public opinion about the "best practices" of large-scale farm animal husbandry.[23] The 1990s saw a number of state-level, movement-led ballot initiatives and court actions directed at bettering the welfare of animals used in agriculture, typically using language of empathy and compassion, because farm animals are not safeguarded under anti-cruelty statutes that protect pets.[24] Thus far in the twenty-first century, animal activist organizations such as The Humane Society of the United States, Farm Sanctuary, People for the Ethical Treatment of Animals, and Mercy for Animals have striven to expose the workings of the modern industrial food system and to generate robust debate about the conditions in which animals are raised and slaughtered to become our food. They declare the plight of these animals—and their sentience, inherent dignity, and mistreatment—to be squarely within the public's interests, aided in part by a growing awareness of broader inadequacies and fail-ures in governmental regulation of the food industry.

Rather than vilifying meat eaters point-blank, however, some of these groups have recognized a more restrained goal of improving standards for animal husbandry practices. While most committed animal activists and leaders are themselves vegan (meaning zero consumption of animal products), almost no one in these campaigns is talking about banning bacon. For instance, Gene Bauer, the head of Farm Sanctuary, told the *New York Times* in 2007, "We're learning to present things in a more moderate way. Would I love everyone to be vegan? Yes. But we want to be respectful and not judgmental."[25] This goal of improving animal wel-fare standards is a logical sell to the broader public, in many ways. Aca-demic and industry studies alike have shown that growing numbers of Americans and Europeans say they are troubled or concerned about the well-being of farm animals[26] and that pro-animal attitudes have spread across age, race, income, and education levels.[27]

One important tool that has been used in these efforts is litigation. New legal restrictions can often catalyze cultural change in fairly rapid ways. Law also sends an important symbolic message about what we, as a society, value.[28] The largest animal rights organizations in the country currently retain teams of staff lawyers and file lawsuits directly against the state, as well as against individual companies, to force them to re-form their practices. In 2008, The HSUS threw its weight behind the passage of Proposition 2 in California, a ballot initiative that passed with sixty-three percent of the vote and turned into the state's Prevention of Farm Animal Cruelty Act—one of the most progressive American ani-mal welfare laws to date. In 2011, the group was hailed in the news media for cutting a deal with United Egg Producers (which represents eighty percent of egg farms in the United States) to support a new set of federal regulations for improving the cage conditions of egg-laying hens. But, again, these actions were about providing chickens with more spacious living quarters, not eliminating eggs from breakfast menus.

Savvy activists have also learned well how to use the video camera to stimulate public ire,[29] collecting and disseminating grisly footage on the Internet of rampant abuse at agri-giant factory farms and slaughter-houses. Seeing brutalities captured on film by these groups can be upsetting—what social movement scholar James Jasper describes as a "moral shock," or something that can compel people to see themselves as having a stake in an issue and move them to action.[30] Indeed, these exposés have repulsed consumers and even triggered arrests and massive food recalls, such as the 2008 recall (the largest in US history) of 143 million pounds of beef processed at the Westland/Hallmark plant in California. Undercover video taken by someone working for The HSUS showed workers kicking and using machines to shove wounded and distressed cows that were too injured and sick to even walk. This video went viral on social media and was reported by prime time news, putting the footage directly into living rooms around the country and causing a major public outcry.

While shocking videos and successful exposés do make national headlines, public outrage over them is often fleeting. While a growing number of Americans self-identify as vegetarian, vegan, or only consume sustainably raised meats, these numbers remain relatively small within the national population. (About five percent of American adults identified as vegetarian and two percent as vegan in 2012, according to the Gallup polling organization.[31]) Most people have not stopped eating cheeseburgers or fried chicken. This consumer pull toward meat is one that is deeply social and is culturally embedded; while many people say they want to "do the right thing" by animals, they are often simultaneously reluctant or unable to overhaul their or their families' culinary tastes or dietary habits. This makes animal activists' efforts to change hearts and minds about eating meat and animal products, and fight against their producers, that much more difficult.

From a structural perspective, launching campaigns against established and politically entrenched industries activates powerful countervailing forces. Far from capitulating to or even ignoring their critics, large-scale meat producers and processors have counterattacked. In 2008, agribusiness operations around the country donated millions of dollars to fight California's Proposition 2. More generally, these producers' ties with policymakers at federal and state levels suggest their interdependency and shared interests.[32] In response to meat producers' concerns about animal rights activists' tactics of producing undercover exposés, Congress in 2006 passed the Animal Enterprise Terrorism Act, making it illegal to "engage in behavior that results in the economic disruption of an animal enterprise." Since then, several states have also proposed and passed measures, nicknamed "ag-gag" laws by activists and progressive media, that make it illegal to take a farm or food processing job under false pretenses to gather evidence such as unapproved photographs or video on behalf of an animal welfare group. These politically embedded producers are proving daunting foes for animal rights activists.

Foie gras, alternatively, offers the possibility of an achievable and symbolically powerful victory because it gets to the root of desires to dismantle an animal-producing industry. To be sure, shunning foie gras was and is a narrow pursuit in the vast food and meat-eating landscape. But the small size and scope of the US industry made it possible to envision and pursue its total elimination, not moderation or reform (and one reason why similar campaigns have faced significantly more trouble in France). Foie gras is a relatively insignificant part of the US food system—it comprises about four hundred thousand ducks a year and four comparatively small farms (until 2012, when Sonoma Foie Gras shut its doors).[33] Compare this to the US Department of Agriculture's National Agricultural Service estimate of nearly ten *billion* animals (thirty million cattle, one hundred million hogs, and nine billion chickens) that were slaughtered for human consumption in the year 2006 alone. The scale is difficult to fully fathom. It means that each minute of every day, nineteen thousand animals in the United States are killed, destined for the plate.

Not only is the US foie gras industry small, but it is also socially and politically isolated from bigger agricultural players, often by choice. Ariane Daguin, owner of D'Artagnan, a New York City area gourmet meat and game distributor, said she found herself "in a dilemma" trying to raise funds for foie gras's legal defense first in California and then Chicago. Although large meat companies and agricultural industry and trade associations have significant resources—including armies of lawyers and lobbyists—that could potentially assist them, she and her compatriots did not consider them allies. Daguin, who sees herself as a champion of small-scale, specialty, and artisanal food production, told me, "Those are not our people. They don't support small farms. We—I—don't want to compromise our quality for their help."

American foie gras producers were also somewhat disconnected from each other. For most of their existences, the two main producers in the United States—Sonoma in California and Hudson Valley in New York—saw each other as friendly competition in the consumer market rather than as political allies. Hudson Valley did not volunteer any resources to help Sonoma Foie Gras fight against the 2004 ban passed in California. By the time they attempted to cooperate (first alongside a few Québécois foie gras farms under the auspices of the North American Foie Gras Association, and then as the Artisan Farmers Alliance), the California and Chicago bans had already been passed. With foie gras, then, activist groups could deliver a symbolically powerful win for their constituents and other aspiring activists, making inroads into dining rooms and legal chambers at a fraction of the cost relative to pursuing more powerful and politically entrenched industries.

The Social Construction of Cruelty

Most of the activists I interviewed recognized foie gras as an easy target in some way. But this did not dilute their passions. Many hoped that a win with foie gras could "wake people up" and be a "stepping stone"—in the eyes of consumers and of the law—to a broader campaign against meat consumption and industrial animal production. As PETA's website declares, consumers "can take a stand by choosing never to eat foie gras or any kind of meat." Once people felt empowered by knocking this low-hanging fruit off its branch, activists genuinely hoped, they might be further tempted to reach higher and take on other issues. One grass-roots activist in Chicago, for instance, felt that focusing resources on fighting against foie gras's legality was a "baby step" toward his group's ultimate goal of promoting veganism. Another said she hoped the anti-foie gras campaign in which she was involved would "help build momentum towards the construction of new rights for animals." Similarly, animal rights groups' press releases celebrated the passage of the California ban in 2004 as "one of the greatest victories for farm animals to date" and "a triumph for farm animals everywhere and the individuals who advocate on their behalf." Foie gras could, in this construal, become a symbol that inspired real public reflection on the moral obligation to do right by animals, and they would be the ones leading the charge.

How to build such momentum? Activists' focus on a single uncomfortable act (gavage) and single uncomfortable process (extreme liver fattening) fits easily within their broader strategy of discomforting people. They regularly use emotionally charged language of good versus evil for this undertaking. In this framework, foie gras is not just "bad." Instead, it becomes the most despicable, abusive, and inhumane food practice conceivable. It is cruel, and the people behind it are torturers and psychopaths.[34] The activists use dramatic pictures of filthy, injured, and dead birds with metal tubes in their beaks. These images, which are pasted on protest signs, emphasized on websites, and mailed to chefs and lawmakers, are designed to trigger people's strong visceral emotions—surprise, anger, and, most importantly, disgust—to make them physically recoil at first glance. One of the pictures commonly used by anti–foie gras groups around the country shows disembodied human hands—one holding the duck's head or neck and the other on the tube—to indicate the inhumane nature of the force-feeding process and to leave the expression on the face of the worker engaged in these cruel acts up to the viewer's imagination. When I asked one New York–based activist how to raise awareness for an issue like this, that most people do not know much about, she replied, "You just show them the cruelty."

It is not uncommon for social movement campaigns to use lurid images to attract attention and alter public perceptions of an issue. The pro-life movement, for example, attempts to shock and repulse bystanders with enlarged pictures of dismembered fetuses. The antiwar movement uses photographs of injured civilians. They want observers to feel physically uncomfortable, even nauseated. Such images aim to cue emotion-laden grievances and prompt accusations of wrongdoing, what behavioral economists call "associative coherence" in that the mind quickly manages to construct a story out of the pieces of information proffered by an image.[35] Images thus embolden novice activists and mobilize sympathizers by amplifying moral analyses and judgments. In other words, they help activists and members of the media—who must weigh what is in the public interest against what the public is interested in—to tell audiences why they should care.

Furthermore, ducks—the victims in the images—resonate with American audiences as cute and friendly wildlife and symbols of childhood innocence. People take their children to feed the ducks at the pond, give them rubber duckies for bath time, and read them classic stories such as Robert McCloskey's *Make Way for Ducklings*. Disney character Donald Duck was invoked frequently by anti–foie gras advocates in their appeals for bans, including the state senator who introduced the California ban, John Burton, who told the *San Francisco Chronicle*, "You don't need to be cramming food down Donald Duck's throat."[36] Both camps recognized the power of this depiction. One Chicago chef, for instance, explained his hypothesis that people root for ducks because of their "cuteness factor." Cuteness, in this way, reclassifies these animals from food to human-like creatures in need of kindness and protection. Animal rights activists I interviewed similarly emphasized ducks' cuteness, as well as their intelligence and friendliness. The image of a metal tube shoved down the beaks of "our feathered friends" can pack an emotional wallop. It makes these ducks a perfect symbol of the callousness and cruelty of animal agriculture.[37]

These associations gave anti–foie gras activists an even weightier sense of moral purpose. "How could anyone with a heart look at this video and think this is a good thing?" one activist resolutely asked the assembled group at a Chicago restaurant protest. At another restaurant protest I observed, activists holding large signs displaying pictures of dead ducks shouted, "Where are your hearts?" at arriving diners. When I asked activists why they were there, one man responded, "For moral reasons. The bad guys are inside. There aren't really two sides to the issue. They are bad guys who don't care about anything." Most activists I spoke with at these protests had not seen foie gras production firsthand, but many said that seeing the photos and videos was enough to enrage them to engage in protest. The messages of cruelty and animal abuse these images communicated were closely tied to their ideas about animal sentience and societal indifference to animal exploitation. They felt strongly that foie gras was an unqualified case of animal cruelty. In an interview, one activist emphatically told me, "This is not the way God designed animals to be treated."[38]

The category of "cruelty" is asked to bear a great deal of weight here. Framing foie gras in this manner generates a moralized binary logic, where the language of "evil" and "torture" attaches values to particular things and particular people and tailors people's attempts to create crisp, coherent categories out of complex and messy realities. Online vitriol further escalates activists' devotion to the cause. Attempts by foie gras's defenders to offer reasoned arguments were frequently shut down by threats such as "I will come and shove a tube down your throat and see how you like it" and declarations such as "I hope that you disgusting people are reincarnated as suffering and abused animals." These denunciations tie directly to other characteristics of foie gras's US consumer base.

Critiquing Foie Gras's Consumer Base

The language of moral intolerance for foie gras has been linked to critiques of foie gras's consumer base in the United States: the well-off. Throughout the twentieth century, American elites considered French gastronomy—of which foie gras is a part—to be the culinary epitome of good taste.[39] Since the early 1990s, when it was first available as a fresh ingredient, foie gras dishes have graced the menus of some of the country's most celebrated restaurants. Mentions of foie gras in the *New York Times* peaked in 1999 and 2000, almost exclusively via restaurant reviews, "good eating" features, and international travel columns.[40] This success was dependent on the ability of culinary experts to convince restaurant-goers that this item—which many did not know previously—was a distinctive specialty ingredient steeped in authentic French culinary traditions.[41] Over the next decade, due to the creativity of a number of well-regarded American chefs, foie gras jumped from upscale and old-school "white tablecloth" restaurants to "smart casual" bistros, gourmet burger joints, and farm-to-table concept restaurants. These are the same establishments favored by the American foodie-elite: hip, affluent, often urban trendsetters and the media outlets that review and publicize them.[42] These restaurants are also key players in the "good food movement"—a large and recent trend in the world of American cuisine that links ideas about deliciousness, pleasure, and consuming products from alternative food systems together with cultural and political disquiet about what food activists call "the agri-industrial food complex."[43]

As such, foie gras took up residence in the world of chefs and foodies—people who see eating as a passion, a pastime, a particular form of self-expression and even, for those with the time, money, and desire to partake, a competitive sport—as well as of "good food" supporters. In this new food world, restaurants are a constant topic of conversation, farmers and chefs can become media celebrities, and books with titles like *What to Eat, Real Food*, and *In Defense of Food* populate bestseller lists. Foodie culture values the exotic, rare, and decadent; anti-mass production; and, for some, forbidden or bizarre tastes. In many ways, foie gras is the quintessential foodie ingredient—shamelessly fatty, with an indulgent flavor and unique texture, and relatively inaccessible due to its price and limited availability.[44] Like other edible elements of the "nose to tail" culinary style popularized at "good food" and locavore restaurants in the early 2000s, such as pork jowl and beef heart (what one chef only half-jokingly called the "ingredients of the farm-to-hipster movement"), "fat liver" plays with boundaries of "good taste" by negotiating between culturally desirable and undesirable parts of animals. For restaurants in New York City and San Francisco, two foodie and "good food" epicenters, foie gras was also considered a locally sourced item from a small-scale farm.

Hyper-successful chefs and restaurateurs in New York, San Francisco, Chicago, and elsewhere are increasingly central figures, even cultural icons, in today's politics of food.[45] David Beriss and David E. Sutton write that today's chefs, in being awarded dual mantles of expertise and acclaim, "are viewed as artists, which lends cachet to the dining experience, but also as artisans, whose craft and knowledge allow them to stand as legitimate interpreters of . . . ingredients and as expert guides in the creation of taste."[46] On top of the hard work that comes with running restaurants and developing new high-quality dishes, many top chefs are being asked to be public intellectuals who comment on everything from national agricultural policy to biodiversity and fracking.[47] Some see themselves as issue entrepreneurs or educators and have become involved in charitable organizations, urban farming initiatives, and healthy eating campaigns (what food studies scholar Signe Rousseau calls a "politics of everyday interference"[48]). This makes highly visible and esteemed chefs cultural intermediaries, or brokers, for audiences who increasingly care about food. It also makes them good targets. Chefs feel vulnerable to social scrutiny because of the ways "reputation matters" in an industry in which "the economics are ferocious, even crippling," as one New York chef and cookbook author told me.[49]

Targeting foie gras also taps into conventional ideas of French cuisine as high culture. For ordinary consumers, "French cuisine" has often served as a signal for the culinary things we are told we should hold in high regard. Yet in the United States, "French" has also long been a stand-in term for snooty otherness.[50] Due to its long gastronomic history and characterization across various media, foie gras occupies both symbolic positions. Its difficult-to-pronounce, untranslated French name makes it sound strange as well as hoity-toity. It's impossible to argue that people will go hungry if foie gras is abolished. Disparaging it, then, becomes a way to take snobs, hipsters, and the privileged class all down a notch.

Such class-laden critiques have been especially relevant in an era marked by growing income inequality. Mitchell Davis, a coauthor of *Foie Gras: A Passion* and vice-president of the James Beard Foundation (a culinary organization in New York City), told me he thinks it is a "brilliant strategy" on the part of animal rights groups, "because if you can demonize something having to do with class, that hits a nerve." Populist rhetoric of "gourmet cruelty" saturated Chicago's foie gras politics, for instance. One example of many is the full-page HSUS newspaper advertisement reproduced in the previous chapter, which linked attempts to overturn the foie gras ban to the palates of snooty elites, asking, "Doesn't Mayor Daley have more important things to do for the city than try to revive an inhumane fancy feast for rich fat cats?"

This relationship among social class, consumption, and the cultural construction of "good taste" is one to which sociologists have long been attuned. As early as Thorstein Veblen's late-nineteenth-century critique of "conspicuous consumption," sociologists and social critics have shown that tastes for particular foods and cuisines (as for art, music, and fashion) are heavily mediated by status-seeking and the ability to display one's identity through consumption.[51] In this framework, there is a degree of consensus about what foods or culinary trends are socially respected. Yet we also know that anti-elite sentiments also matter for social perceptions of consumption, that tastes can be idiosyncratic and flexible, and that neither producers nor consumers are automatons blindly following cultural trends laid out for them by others.[52]

Moreover, when it comes to labeling certain foods as social problems to be solved through law and collective action, foie gras presents an interesting paradox. Historically, it has been the lower classes, or deviants from the middle and upper classes, who have been stigmatized for their food practices and choices. Indeed, the current discourse around fast food and obesity rates—as well as recent political moves to ban trans fats and "supersized" portions from chain restaurant menus—usually focuses on sanctioning the consumption habits of lower income populations.[53] In this sense, mobilization for anti–foie gras legislation may even be viewed as support for reverse sumptuary law.[54] A major problem here is that it has proven very difficult for foie gras's opponents to get the support of working- and middle-class citizens, of whose eating habits they heartily disapprove.

Foie gras's status as a dish of the wealthy thus cannot be the only variable in this equation. We haven't seen the same level of hostility directed toward pricey steakhouses or $40-a-pound artisanal cheeses. Caviar, the salted eggs of various fish, most notably Beluga sturgeon, similarly connotes luxury and gastronomic opulence due to its high price and limited availability (following decades of overfishing), but criticism derives from the threat to the species, not humane grounds.[55] Foie gras is rarely contested on similar grounds.

Additionally, both its protagonists and antagonists draw from similar backgrounds. When conducting my fieldwork in Chicago, I was surprised to discover that some even resembled each other. For example, I conducted two lengthy interviews on consecutive days, one with an executive sous chef at an upscale restaurant on the Magnificent Mile and one with a local animal rights leader. Both were skinny, heavily tattooed

white men in their late twenties. Both had grown up in politically liberal, lower-middle-class suburban families, and both had had trouble
with grades, alcohol, and self-discipline in school. Both lived in roughly
the same gentrifying neighborhood, one with his wife and one with a
longtime girlfriend, and both had pets that they adored. Both understood the power of harnessing new social media tools in their work.
Each had a frankness and humility in his demeanor that made him
wholly likeable. But one was a vegan activist who had been previously
involved in laboratory break-ins and "leaned toward animal liberation,"
while the other proudly showed me a walk-in refrigerator full of hung
whole quail and full sides of pork that had been delivered that morning.
Their similar backgrounds, yet wholly disparate taste politics, are important for understanding that factors other than class status and cultural
background engender lifestyle, career, and personal moral choices
around food.

Educating the Public

Foie gras is also a pragmatic target for activists because of its lack of
culinary embeddedness among American eaters. First off, foie gras is
liver, which in itself is something many Americans avoid eating. Sec-
ondly, public opinion polls show that most Americans have never heard
of or eaten foie gras (although awareness has grown due to its presence
in the news and on popular television shows such as *Top Chef*). Among
other indicators, "foie gras" is regularly spelled wrong on Internet message boards and pronounced incorrectly in media reports by opponents
and supporters alike. It is also frequently referred to as "goose liver," but
in the United States this is factually inaccurate: all four foie gras producers are or were duck farms. Finally, it is easier to get people to es-
chew something they already feel indifferent about, rather than something important to them. For meat eaters, purposefully forgoing foie
gras is a way to signify that they care about animals without having to
engage in real culinary sacrifice.

Moreover, it's not just foie gras, but also ducks that are a side-thought
in the American culinary world. Duck meat does appear on some restaurant menus, to be sure, but it is not something people regularly cook

at home or eat frequently. According to the USDA, the average American eats eighty-seven pounds of chicken, sixty-six pounds of beef, fifty-one pounds of pork, and seventeen pounds of turkey per year. But only 0.34 pounds of duck was consumed per person in 2007, down from 0.44 in 1986.[56] Goose consumption is even lower. The USDA's Economic Research Service does not even track markets for duck or goose products as it does for other poultry.[57]

The fact that the majority of Americans do not eat duck or goose meat regularly and have not even heard of foie gras has been a limitation for anti–foie gras groups looking to rally people to the cause, but it has also served as an opportunity. Important to consider here is how audiences come to understand a social issue, especially when they do not know much about the matter in question beforehand. Animal rights activists have worked hard to interpret foie gras and build it into an intelligible symbol for unknowing consumers and legislators, to educate them through their own language and imagery, in order to bring about intended emotional and behavioral results.

As one might expect, different animal activist groups have used different tactics to raise awareness, incite indignation, and push their agendas. One activist with New York–based Farm Sanctuary (who has tabled outside of New York City grocery stores for several animal rights issues, including foie gras) described her group's approach to me over lunch at a vegan restaurant:

> We're working toward the same goals, but in different ways. PETA, for instance, is much more in your face, the street theater, yelling and all that. And they've gotten an awful lot done. But that's just not Farm Sanctuary's style. We prefer to expose, to educate people, and to leave it to their conscience, really, if this is a civilized way to treat other sentient beings. And a great many of them will say no, and be willing to put their ethics above their taste buds.

The reach of these tactics can extend beyond activists' own campaign materials and websites. As an example, activists and journalists writing about foie gras have frequently cited a poll conducted by Zogby International, a well-known market research firm, in 2004 (and repeated in select states in 2005 and 2006). The pollsters found that seventy-five to eighty percent of respondents favored a ban. The text of the Chicago City Council's 2006 ordinance cited this poll as representative of public opinion on the subject.

However, the Zogby poll came to the conclusion it did by asking questions in ways that actively exploited Americans' lack of familiarity with foie gras. Not surprisingly, in response to the initial question "how often do you eat foie gras?" of the one thousand respondents asked each time, thirty-five to forty percent said "never" and four to five percent "less than once a year"; an additional fifty to fifty-two percent had "never heard of it." For those who answered "never" or "never heard of it," the Zogby interviewer then described foie gras production as follows:

> Foie gras is an expensive food item served in some upscale restaurants. It is produced by force-feeding geese and ducks large quantities of food, causing the animals' livers to swell up to twelve times their normal size. A long metal pipe is inserted into the animal's esophagus several times a day. Often, this process causes the animals' internal organs to rupture. Several European countries currently prohibit this practice as cruel. Do you agree or disagree that force-feeding geese and ducks to produce foie gras should be banned by law in the United States [or in their particular state, as the later surveys asked]? .

Given that the question focuses on charges of cruelty, illegality, and elitism for a food product that about ninety percent of respondents had either never eaten nor even heard of, it is little surprise that seventy-seven percent of the original January 2004 poll's respondents "agreed" with the statement that the process of force-feeding to produce foie gras should be banned in the United States. (Sixteen percent answered "disagree" and seven percent "not sure.") Similar numbers were reported for the state-specific Zogby polls, though the number of people claiming to have "never heard" of foie gras decreased over time.

In his reporting for *The Foie Gras Wars*, Mark Caro approached Fritz Wenzel, Zogby's communications director, and asked him who wrote the question. Wenzel told Caro that the animal rights group Farm

Sanctuary had approached his company with the idea, but Zogby was responsible for making the language "defensible from a research stand-point." The challenge, Wenzel noted, was how few people were familiar with the subject. "The only way you can get people to respond to a topic of which they know nothing is to give them some information," he said. "We're simply laying out a menu of facts for respondents and gauging their response." Playing devil's advocate, Caro rephrased the question for Wenzel, offering:

> Foie gras is a delicious food item prepared by many of the world's greatest chefs and enjoyed in many of this country's finest restaurants. It is a delicacy produced according to a tradition that dates back thousands of years. Scientific studies have shown that ducks and geese raised for this product do not experience elevated stress levels. Foie gras has become increasingly popular in the United States as American farms have made the product more freshly available. Do you agree or disagree that the production of foie gras should be banned?

"There is some subjectivity to this," Wenzel admitted. "The clients wanted to measure what people thought of the process, and that's why we came up with the question we came up with." He did not acknowledge that Farm Sanctuary might have had particular objectives in phrasing its script, but did add, "Food production is a tough field because if Americans knew what happened to food on the way to its plate, people would be eating a lot less."[58]

As the contrast between the two vignettes highlights, "how foie gras is produced" varies by who stands to gain or lose from the words used to characterize it as a social issue, and how they signpost the issue as a moral one. Language classifies, typifies, and defines. It can artfully give the subjective reality it constructs an accent of objectivity.[59] Questionnaire design matters for studying public opinion; nevertheless the shoddy Zogby poll statistics continue to be cited by activists, media reports, and legislators as proof of Americans' desire to ban foie gras.

For politicians, purported sympathy for the ducks has played a central role for prescriptions regarding what to do about foie gras. Jack Kelly, a gruff, Republican Philadelphia councilman who led the charge on an unsuccessful citywide ban soon after Chicago's passed, expounded on some of the activists' allegations in interviews with various reporters. "These poor things," he said. "They are tortured for weeks, for months, and it's not right."[60] In Chicago, at the City Council meeting in May 2008 where the city's foie gras ordinance was repealed, one alderman told me just before the vote, "I'm going to vote to discharge the committee,[61] but I still think it's still cruel to animals, so I won't vote for the repeal. I'm an animal lover; if it were me with the tube down my throat . . ." He grimaced as he grasped at his own neck. These expressive reactions show that activists' frames and techniques of moral signaling have been persuasive with public officials.

Offering evidence-based clarifications about production practices may not be a strong-enough rejoinder for public officials who are motivated to ban foie gras. For example, at the 2004 California State Legislature hearings that led to the prohibition of foie gras's production and sale in the state, State Senator Michael Machado testified against the bill, telling his colleagues that he had personally visited Sonoma Foie Gras (one of the only state senators to do so) and found that activists' descriptions "were not borne out in practice." Machado claimed that Guillermo Gonzalez's operations could be considered "exceptional" among the poultry operations he had seen, which were many as he was a farmer himself. In 2008, one month after the Chicago ordinance was repealed, New York City Council member Tony Avella of Queens proposed a resolution by the city in support of prohibiting foie gras production in the state of New York.[62] In a debate broadcast on *The Brian Lehrer Show* on National Public Radio with Michael Ginor, co-owner of Hudson Valley Foie Gras, Avella—who admitted that he had never seen foie gras production in person—reiterated animal rights arguments, declaring:

The practice of force feeding ducks and geese in order to produce foie gras is simply cruel and inhumane. You're literally blowing food into the stomach in order to artificially enlarge the liver. I mean, this is extremely painful to the animal, and really is animal cruelty. The industry should be ashamed of itself.

Ginor countered that Avella was rushing to judgment. He referenced that both the American Veterinary Medical Association and the American Association of Avian Pathologists have established that foie gras is not a product of animal cruelty and attempted to debate Avella's base understanding of the process:

> Unfortunately, so much of what the councilman has mentioned is rhetoric and is factually, completely incorrect.... I welcome him to visit the farm one day. He said the process is blowing, which is not the case. There are operations in the world that use pneumatic systems to feed in foie gras production. We do not. And so this term, blowing, is not accurate in New York State. I just wish that before people go out and try to make such drastic economic changes, and take the livelihood of two hundred employees in a New York State company, that they would at least do minimal research before just jumping on a bandwagon.

In an earlier interview with me, Ginor described his first time seeing foie gras production, saying, "I wasn't horrified, but I wasn't blasé about it either. I came into it from a love of the product. I didn't know anything—force feeding, gavage—nothing about it. So I kind of saw it for the first time with very naïve eyes." He encouraged me to visit the farm with an open mind. But, he told me, I should also know that

> after all the tests we've done, all the veterinarians who've come to the farm and checked the ducks pre- and post-mortem, all the birds we've sent to laboratories, I have yet to come across *any* [emphasis his] hard-core medical evidence that these birds are suffering in any way. Our mortality rate is lower than it is in turkey farms and chicken farms. Yes, you do put this funnel down their throats. However, the question is, is that damaging? Is it painful? Is it stressful? No. And there's a lot of evidence that says it's not.

They have a calcified esophagus. They have a natural ability to gorge and grow the liver. So, it's hard to look at ourselves as the monsters that we're being drawn to be.

The inability of *either* side of this debate to consider opposing viewpoints while concurrently seeking to champion their interpretations of reality illustrates the extreme forms that symbolic politics around food can take. Proponents on each side see themselves as rational and the other side as ideological. This is significant because it crystallizes the ways we think about consuming in rigid moral terms—good food versus bad food—and illustrates how this can polarize already complex questions about the future of food and eating. To the impartial observer, this makes both sides seem imprudent. To my knowledge, none of the legislators who introduced or supported bills to ban foie gras in different cities and states had visited a foie gras farm prior to doing so, and only a few did so after the fact. Of course, it is not uncommon for legislators to propose or vote on issues they know little about or have not personally researched. But the good chance of achieving a legislative victory while also dramatically denouncing something like animal cruelty has helped make foie gras a pragmatic target within the broader politics of food.

A Problematic Target

However, this pragmatic target has proven more difficult than activists anticipated. Their appeals to get chefs, legislators, and consumers to renounce foie gras have met with some successes, but also with more roadblocks than they expected. In fact, foie gras has proven a *problematic* target in a number of respects: sometimes the low-hanging fruit is not that appetizing after all.

Opening the Barn Door

Several factors quickly began contributing to the issue's tempo and pitch and to reactive mobilization.[63] Rather than finding a sympathetic and enthused audience, anti–foie gras activists also experienced a great deal of pushback. Most of the moral arguments against foie gras are not so clear-cut as activists would make them out to be. While its haters and enthusiasts all have rigid understandings of what foie gras is and what it symbolizes, the questions that it raises for others are more complicated and nuanced. Perhaps most importantly, these partisans have been fighting for support from the same relatively narrow field of consumers—well-educated, reasonably affluent people who care about and believe they are knowledgeable about food.

Opposition to animal rights activists' perspectives on foie gras has taken several forms. First, doubt over the reality of the cruelty claim increased as more information about the specifics of foie gras's production methods became available in the public sphere. Foie gras producers and their high-profile culinary supporters attempted to dilute the negative media attention they received by drawing out the differences between animal *use* and animal *abuse*. Primarily, they argue that foie gras production is not torturous and that animal rights activists are unjustly anthropomorphizing—giving human characteristics and emotions to—these ducks rather than recognizing the significant physiological differences between the bodies of humans and waterfowl. Viewed through this lens, producers are using animals, not abusing them. Indeed, visitors to foie gras farms (myself and others) report *not* witnessing what activists claim is obvious—the unmistakable cruelty of force-feeding.

Perhaps the most meaningful way that American foie gras producers have responded to activists' and legislators' accusations of torture and cruelty was to open their barn doors. Confident of a lack of wrongdoing, both Hudson Valley Foie Gras and Sonoma Foie Gras willingly allowed interested journalists, academics, chefs, and legislators to visit. For people who are curious or on the ethical fence, this transparency problematizes the easy target, as a number of inquisitive third parties investigating activists' claims of visible suffering have come to disagree with them. Author Mark Caro, for example, wrote of watching a feeding at Sonoma Foie Gras: "Did they [the ducks] look happy about the force-feeding that was about to take place? No. Did they look particularly fearful or agitated? No. They looked like ducks, big ducks."[64] About his visit to Hudson Valley Foie Gras, he wrote,

There was no perceptible difference between the ducks that already had been fed and those still awaiting the feeder. What I saw was the opposite of what [veterinarian and staunch foie gras opponent] Holly Cheever told the California Senate committee that she had observed at Hudson Valley regarding the ducks' "terror."[65]

Sarah DiGregorio, a writer for New York City's *Village Voice* newspaper, similarly visited HVFG for an article titled "Is Foie Gras Torture?" after talking with Holly Cheever and renowned animal welfare expert Temple Grandin. Cheever prepped DiGregorio that she would be "witnessing an elaborate cover-up, because 'they can cherry-pick out the disastrously sick ducks'" before she arrived. Grandin—whose work with understanding animal behavior through her own experience with autism has led to the redesign of about half the slaughterhouses in the United States—had not visited a foie gras farm herself but encouraged DiGregorio to see if the ducks had trouble walking and whether they actively avoided their feeders. After visiting the farm and seeing "thousands of ducks" at each stage of production, the journalist concluded that the images and rhetoric presented by anti–foie gras activists "are not representative of the reality at the nation's largest foie gras farm."[66]

Another of Hudson Valley's many visitors during this time was New York State Assemblyman Michael Benjamin, who had previously introduced a bill to ban foie gras production in the state. After his tour of the facilities, he withdrew the bill. "I've had a change of heart. To my knowledge, none of the ducks looked uncomfortable or mistreated," Benjamin told reporters at a press conference. "We shouldn't anthropomorphize animals into humans. What might look painful to us isn't painful to them."[67] But by this point, foie gras's foes were not about to reverse course. One of many comments posted on the Internet in response to the bill's withdrawal proclaimed, "Perhaps Mr. Benjamin should try the technique and see how he feels afterwards,"[68] continuing the escalation of partisan allegations over a process that would indeed damage a human's esophagus.

Foie gras's producers also respond to accusations of "obvious suffering and cruelty" by appealing to the connection between economic value and high-quality products—that such products could not be made using cruel practices. Causing the birds undue pain and stress, they have declared, "would not make a good foie gras," for the resultant liver would be "too small" or "too veiny," and thus not as economically valuable.[69] "Why," one asked me, "would anyone do that and hurt their business on purpose?" Ariane Daguin of D'Artagnan, the New York City area gourmet food distributor, took particular umbrage in this regard. She described the importance of "good" foie gras production as follows:

> You have the small farmer who takes care of his animals, who's very conscientious. You have nice happy ducks on the farm. And then you have the guy who doesn't care and he's not going to stay in business. Because it's like everything in life if you don't do it right. Especially with ducks. If you don't do it right with ducks, they're going to die on you. If they die on you, you're not doing a lot of business.

A less-successful tactic among producers has been to stress that there are "good producers" and "bad producers," and that the latter give the former a bad name. Sociologists refer to this reactionary type of identity work as "defensive othering."[70] Producers of all stripes in the United States and France told me, perhaps not surprisingly, that they were among the "good" ones. (But, of course, this elides many of the conditions under which the sizable majority of ducks in France currently raised for foie gras must abide.) The challenge of this tactic is that it admits that the practice of force-feeding can be cruel, which opens the door for further scrutiny.

This made me and a number of other interested parties wonder, can foie gras be produced without force-feeding? The possibility of gavage-free foie gras is an appealing one; however, the jury is still out on this question. This is a question that producers are asked frequently. A handful say producing foie gras without force-feeding might be possible, and it is something that a Spanish farmer named Eduardo Sousa has claimed to have achieved. La Patería de Sousa raises a small number of geese, providing them with open access to roam and forage among acres of olive, nut, and fig trees. For the most part, the birds live as wild animals—breeding, hatching, and eating without human interference. In late autumn, when wild geese fatten themselves for migration, Sousa has said that his geese become "naturally greedy" and gorge themselves,[71] and are also given extra corn (grown organically in a nearby province).[72] Sousa's "ethical foie gras" became widely known when it won the 2006 Coup de Coeur Prize for Innovation at an international food salon in Paris. After criticism from the French foie gras industry association, CIFOG, however, the prize was revoked, because French law states that foie gras by definition *must* come from a goose or duck that has been specially fattened via force-feeding.

Admirable as they might be and as sought after as his foie gras is, Sousa's methods have proven neither replicable nor commercially viable. (A goose farmer in South Dakota named Jim Schlitz has had some success producing "naturally fatty goose livers," but these are not of the same size and consistency as those produced through gavage.[73]) Also, Sousa has provided little documentation about his production methods to those who have come asking—such as members of CIFOG and Izzy Yanay from Hudson Valley Foie Gras. Award-winning chef Dan Barber of the farm-to-table restaurant Blue Hill at Stone Barns, located just north of New York City, became interested and developed a relationship with Sousa. Barber[74] has discussed Sousa's visit to Stone Barns, his own visit to northwest Spain, and his unsuccessful attempts to duplicate Sousa's techniques in a widely viewed TED talk,[75] on NPR's *This American Life*,[76] and in presentations around the country. Barber has jokingly attributed his "failed gras" to his inability to perfectly replicate the ecological conditions of Sousa's farm.[77] He thinks there would be a market for "ethical foie gras," and told me in an interview that that he believes when people are willing to pay for something, someone somewhere will eventually figure out how to make it happen.

Most Americans, of course, have not visited and will not visit a foie gras farm, or any industrial livestock operation, for that matter. A journalist who set out to write an article on the chicken industry that was published in 2007 in *Gourmet Magazine* wrote, "Spokesmen at the five biggest companies refused to show me the farms where their suppliers raise the chicken you eat. They refused to show me the slaughterhouses. Executives even refused to talk to me about how they raise and kill chickens."[78] This is, in large part, by design. Old MacDonald himself would not recognize the large majority of today's farms. Ariane Daguin, who grew up in rural Gascony and now lives in Manhattan, echoed others in telling me that she believes one of the problems in the United States more generally is that Americans are "too remote" from the world of modern farms. Farms are businesses, she emphasized, and the animals raised on them are not pets. Using the name PETA to substitute for animal rights organizations as a whole, she said, "In a real farm, it's not pretty. It smells like animals and manure. Once in a while, you have a dead chicken in the corner. When it rains, you have a leak in the barn. Stuff happens . . . So, PETA can show one picture and, for me, I need a whole page of explanation."

In other words, most Americans' remoteness, both geographically and cognitively, from contemporary livestock facilities makes them reliant on translators, whether they explicitly recognize it or not. PETA and other animal rights groups wish to be those translators. In France, where farms—foie gras and otherwise—are more accessible, this kind of animal rights strategy would not work, or at least not nearly as well.[79] The fact that visitors are welcome at all at Hudson Valley Foie Gras is significant (even though activists continue to assert that the visits are staged). The open barn door became a persuasive gastropolitical tool because of its relational context; the businesses that produce most of the meat that Americans eat will not do the same.

The Promises and Pitfalls of Single-Issue Advocacy

Foie gras is an issue-specific fight. Focusing on issue- or species-specific campaigns has long been a popular tactic of the animal rights and welfare movements (as well as the environmental and women's movements, which animal rights activists view as philosophical precursors). Not only can focused efforts yield positive legal or policy outcomes, but leaders have hoped that catering to audiences who care about specific issues will draw them into the broader movement. Sentimental appeals might just turn strangers into comrades. One often-used example is drawing on people's love for their dogs and cats to steer them into conversations about animal experimentation and veganism, with the hope of building sympathies with the broader animal rights movement.[80] In that they allow donors to feel as though they know where their money goes, issue-specific campaigns have also proved useful fundraising tools.[81] Due to issue-specific anti–foie gras campaigns, some foie gras eaters have indeed changed their minds about it. Other people have donated to an animal-related cause or participated in a protest for the first time. Some chefs have taken the dish off their menus voluntarily, and some have spoken out against it on the Internet or at legislative hearings. In these instances, anti–foie gras campaigns have been wildly successful.

Small but zealous anti–foie gras groups have formed around the country in places where fine dining is long renowned and also where it is unfamiliar. Cities from Austin to Baltimore, Pittsburgh to Minneapolis, and Portland, Maine to Honolulu have seen anti–foie gras activism take root in the last decade. One early low-level tactic of these groups was to get their supporters to make reservations and then not show up (to cost the restaurant the money they would have received from service that night). Another has been to leave fake negative reviews of the restaurants on websites such as Yelp. Between the California state ban on production and sale in July 2012 and its reversal in January 2015, some law-focused activist groups worked together to sue a few restaurants for continuing to sell foie gras, which kept the issue in the news.

But this intense and concentrated focus on foie gras also caused problems for activists. Unlike the campaign against veal in the 1980s, which resulted in significant declines in the rate of American veal consumption, foie gras controversies actually had an effect that was opposite of what activists hoped. People—especially Americans—often want what they are told they cannot have.[82] By piquing consumers' awareness of its existence, foie gras opponents created new enthusiasts. It appeared for the first time on menus from Maine to Texas and began making regular appearances in the online worlds of food bloggers and the home kitchens of amateur chefs around the country. In 2006, Michael Ginor of Hudson Valley Foie Gras told the *New York Times*, "If the animal rights goal is to save ducks, that will not be achieved. The market has grown at least 20 percent since they began their efforts. At the end of the day, they have helped increase the popularity of foie gras."[83] Izzy Yanay told me when I visited in 2007 that their sales were up seven percent from the previous year. But why would this be the case? Why would people purposefully seek out, serve, or choose to eat an arguably cruel dish?

In interviews and more informal conversations with restaurateurs and other food industry figures in Chicago, New York, and California, I found that the answer is in no small part because of *who* was pushing back against the anti–foie gras movement and what they claimed to represent. For many people who have been actively engaged in the broader "good food" movement of local, sustainable, and small-scale food production, campaigns aimed at banning foie gras come across as petty and insincere. While foie gras production presumably throws a kink into chefs' "good food" refrain of opposing the inhumane treatment of animals in agriculture, many saw themselves as the *wrong* targets in a food system with an immense number of problems that affect many more people and animals than does foie gras.

All of this is not to say that chefs are interested in providing diners with a delicious dish at the expense of ethics. In fact, I found the opposite. But what it means to be an ethical eater, for this group, is quite different than for the animal activists. Some told me that they had themselves visited foie gras farms (sometimes as part of culinary school training), either in the United States or France. Those who had not explained that they placed more trust in their fellow chefs' understandings of foie gras's production methods than in those of animal rights activists or legislators. They said they believe in supporting alternative agriculture and small-scale, independent producers that demonstrate care and respect for the animals they raise. For example, New York chef and Food Network star Alex Guarnaschelli, told me:

> There are a lot of things I don't serve. I don't need to make a list and tack it on the door. Every chef has their own line to draw. I don't like serving overfished fish. That's big on my list. I like serving local vegetables, produce grown by farmers who are covered with dirt and work ten times harder than I do. That's my gig.

A number of chefs who actively advocate for the "good food" movement consider foie gras not only acceptable, but exceptional, in this moral framework. These individuals put foie gras in the category of valued "authentic" ingredients connected with "artisanal," "Old World" food "traditions" and outside the realm of mass-produced, industrial agribusiness, which they see as oppositional to their culinary philosophies. This judgment is anchored in a gastropolitical hierarchy that privileges certain modes of food production over others. The insight here is that these code words and categories, as important parts of this culinary identity movement, can and do shape action.[84] Using this language seemed to help these chefs protect their own identities as good—and ethically minded—food citizens and moral entrepreneurs. One chef called this philosophy "giving good ingredients the respect they deserve" (a statement that rhetorically translates "cooking" to "respect" and "animals" to "ingredients"). For consumers, choosing to eat at these restaurants is also a form of identity work, seen as a way of demonstrating one's commitment to this framework and to the symbolic politics of "good taste." Animal cruelty meets the locavores.

Thus, the features that made foie gras seem like an easy target for activists—its industry's small size and lack of political influence and its low overall consumer recognition—also made it seem like the *wrong* target to this group of high-profile, politically engaged, media-savvy culinary opinion leaders. While the existence of greater social ills does not necessarily obviate the value of combatting lesser ones, even people who have lingering questions about foie gras's ethics have said that criminalizing it in the name of eliminating cruelty to animals or improving the food system is like putting a Band-Aid on a broken arm. Jenn Louis, a *Top Chef Masters* alumna, penned a column in the *Huffington Post* in 2014 encouraging consumers to compare the .00265 pounds of foie gras to the eighty-odd pounds of chicken the average American eats per year and "choose the battle that will make a greater difference."[85] Similarly, chef Dan Barber told me that while he believed "any issue that makes people think a little bit more about their food is a good thing . . . foie gras production does not affect how our land is used and how our farming communities are being decimated."

Even Michael Pollan, one of the unofficial leaders of the local food movement, published a sarcasm-laced *New York Times* editorial in 2006 about the Chicago foie gras ban. In it, he derided Chicago's political leaders for taking up a low-hanging fruit like foie gras and giving lip service to bettering animal welfare in the food system rather than tackling the practices that affect the animals most Americans eat every day.[86] In 2012, responding to a question about the imminent California ban, Pollan told a *New York Times* reporter, "I think it's really a way for people to feel like they've done something without doing anything. There's [sic] so many more serious problems we're not dealing with."[87] From his perspective, anti–foie gras forces take political momentum away from reforming the overall system and the modern American diet, and foie gras is simply a case of moral signaling that does little actual good.

Ad Hominem Attacks

For both sides of a hotly contested issue like this, finding common ground with opponents becomes increasingly difficult when competing groups are out to discredit each other, ad hominem attacks substitute for reasoned dialogue, and some actions are viewed as overly extreme. Attempting to recast well-known and admired chefs as "villains," especially, has offered activists a way to keep the levels of drama and media attention high. Justly or unjustly, these attacks alienated people who might have otherwise been allies on a number of other issues and turned them into staunch adversaries.

Even though they make up a minority of actions in the overall anti–foie gras movement, harassment, trespassing, vandalism, property damage, and even the intimation of personal violence have been real problems for the culinary community. Chefs around the country have reported (to me and to others) receiving hate mail calling them "evil," "torturers," and worse. Based on my own perusal of a few chefs' physical caches of letters and printed emails, the text of these messages has ranged from heartfelt pleas to profanity to vindictive threats of personal violence against the chefs as well as their employees and families. A number have worried aloud and online that some of foie gras's foes might forget the difference between posturing and causing real harm.

Some chefs and restaurateurs capitulate: at my last count, more than 750 restaurants across the United States have officially pledged not to serve foie gras (though a number of these establishments either didn't serve it before the hubbub or signed only after being accosted by activists). Others do not. Some chefs around the country bristled at the personalization and perceived zealotry of anti–foie gras activists' tactics, and responded by selling more foie gras. Others have told reporters that they wished they could act similarly but did not want to risk having their "windows broken" or their door locks "super-glued shut."[88]

This is not an idle fear. In the summer of 2007, several Austin, Texas restaurants that served foie gras had their façades spray-painted with obscenities. A group called Central Texas Animal Defense protested twice a week outside of one restaurant in particular, Jezebel, whose owner refused to take foie gras off the menu. Jezebel had its main power breaker cut and the words "spit it out" etched with acid onto the main window. Jezebel's owner told his local paper that, despite all of this, his business actually tripled and that people were "ordering foie gras even when they would not normally."[89] In September, the activist who committed these acts was identified through surveillance video, arrested, held on a $20,000 bond, charged with criminal mischief, and, a year later, sentenced to seven months in state prison. Similarly, after their Columbia, Maryland restaurant was vandalized and its walkway spray-painted with the words "get rid of the foie gras" in 2009, the owners told the *Baltimore Sun*, "We're going to have more foie gras. We're thinking about doing a Foie Gras Night, a progressive foie gras dinner for charity in response."[90]

In Philadelphia, several restaurants and chefs' homes were targeted by a small but highly aggressive anti–foie gras group called Hugs for Puppies (later renamed the Humane League of Philadelphia). Hugs members relied heavily on the public performance of protest. For weeks at a time, they would stand outside a chosen restaurant with bullhorns, sandwich boards, and screens that showed images and videos of force feeding.[91] Protesters would hector staff, loudly hassle diners entering the establishment saying that they were ugly and would die of cancer, chant, "For the animals, we will fight! We know where you sleep at night!" and yell through bullhorns about the restaurant owners being "murderers" and "duck rapists."[92] Invectives cut the other way, too. Some posters in the comments sections of online articles about Hugs for Puppies' protests called group members "terror-loving extremists" and "useless idiots" and told them to "get a real life."

The transcript of a restraining order filed by the Philadelphia restaurant London Grill—which served a steak dish with a foie gras sauce and whose owners took Hugs to court—details some of the group's other activities, as well. These included the targeting of restaurant workers' homes, the handing out of leaflets to workers' neighbors that gave their addresses and said they were cruel to animals, and showing up at an owner's home dressed as ninjas in order to frighten his children. Another well-known Philadelphia chef and restaurateur, Jose Garces (who later became an Iron Chef on the Food Network), told author Mark Caro, "Once they come to your home, it just becomes a lot more personal. I have two little children. For them to be exposed to that, screaming my name, saying I'm a murderer and so forth . . ." Like several other Philadelphia chefs targeted by Hugs members, Garces took foie gras off his menus grudgingly, but kept some in the kitchens in case a customer asked for it.[93]

For some chefs, putting foie gras on the menu became just as much a response to activists' demands as taking it off. "Foie gras" came to represent the notion that their cultural authority and expertise in the culinary world, as well as their own moral sensibilities, were being tested.[94] These people—chefs, food writers, and their supporters—are doing a great deal to sway opinions among the class of people who see them as moral entrepreneurs for the "good food" movement. The fact that these individuals have defended foie gras and vociferously challenged the claims of animal rights activists may be a strong enough signal for people who want to self-identify as ethical eaters but are not really sure what to do.

Doubling Down

These kinds of responses have not been well-received by animal activist leaders. According to one of the most dedicated anti–foie gras activists in the United States, Bryan Pease of the Animal Protection and Rescue League (APRL), "it's almost worse" for a business that says they care about ethical food practices to continue to serve foie gras. But their doubling down on the "good guys" has confused onlookers. For example, in 2010, when the APRL announced they would protest outside Telepan, a locavore restaurant in Manhattan, Grubstreet (a popular food website) asked, "Wait a minute—*Bill* Telepan? The chef who's trying to improve school lunches with hormone-free milk? The same chef who won a merit badge from Animal Welfare Approved for switching to a grass-fed beef burger?"[95]

In an interview I did with him a few years before these events, Bill Telepan said that he sourced his ingredients "extremely carefully" and that he was very proud that his restaurant was one of only seventeen in New York City on the Certified Humane list. He had visited Hudson Valley Foie Gras several times and had known Michael and Izzy for years. He served their foie gras, he said, because he believes that "they do a pretty honest product," unlike "penning up chickens and pigs and cattle and making them sleep in their own shit and eat their own shit." After the APRL protest outside his restaurant, he told me by email that he was quite surprised by their focus on him. He did not take foie gras off the menu.

Finally, putting a bull's eye on foie gras has contributed to broader arguments in the public sphere about where legal lines around food and culinary choices could or should be drawn—and who should wield the pen. There is no shortage of controversial farming practices drawing fire from animal welfare and rights groups, from confinement practices for veal calves and gestation-crated sows to the culling of just-born male chicks by way of euthanasia or a high-speed grinder. Because animal rights activists talk about foie gras production as a gateway into these broader issues, consumers and food industry members alike have responded by invoking the specters of the "slippery slope" and the "nanny state"—expressing fears (whether justified or not) of excessive government interference in consumer markets and people's everyday lives.[96] A large number of Internet comments and blog posts on foodie websites that I collected between 2004 and 2009 show that these libertarian-tinged frames became more prevalent over time. Prognostic worries and innuendo about the destabilizing, "floodgate" effects of "what might be next"—"Veal? Chicken? All meat?"—filled social media. While it is highly improbable that meat in general will be banned, this rhetoric of suspicion and precedence was one of the most common features of responses to contestation around foie gras.

On the other side, I found real, optimistic hope for policy advances that would build on foie gras victories. As Bruce Friedrich, then a vice president of PETA and now a senior director at Farm Sanctuary, told the *New York Times* after the Chicago ban passed, "It's only a matter of time before practices like cramming nine hens into an 18-by-20-inch wire mesh cage for their entire lives is made illegal."[97] In framing foie gras in this way, as the first domino, one of these groups' main motivations involves convincing people that if they are disgusted by foie gras, they likely espouse moral ideals that may be easily applied elsewhere. In the words of another activist, "We've hopefully made them say 'oh, well, that's kind of bad. Hmm, maybe it's all kind of bad.'" From this perspective, however incremental, controversy is essential for progress.

But whether this strategy of discussing animal welfare around foie gras as an issue of public morality opens doors to other cases is a fairly complex issue. Who is to say what is more or less wrong that something else? Does the existence of greater ills preclude the benefits of fighting lesser ones? It is one thing if campaigns against foie gras connect people with how awful much of the industrial meat system is, and quite another if banning it is pegged as having solved the problems of the existing system. Moreover, whether or not lawmakers agree that foie gras is indeed the first domino to knock over, their mere involvement has sparked passionate disagreements—played out publicly, in newspaper editorials and on the Internet, and privately, at dining room tables—about what best defines the proper role of government in people's food choices and when, if at all, to justify prohibitionist market restrictions. Lawmakers who spearheaded foie gras bans have faced criticism and even ridicule from the press, ostensibly for diverting attention and resources away from other issues. Yet, even those jurisdictions that have considered bans do not see it as a "first step" toward a vegan world. In fact, local politicians may even see foie gras as a one-shot way to appease some outspoken constituents. If chicken were to be prohibited at a city or state—or even national—level, or even if a decision were legislated to allow only free-range chickens to be raised and consumed, many more businesses and people would be unhappy.[98] While "better treatment for animals" is a concept many people claim to support, the idea of state-sponsored removal of meat from people's dietary options is generally not. Foie gras, then, may be more of a sacrificial lamb than a red herring.

CONCLUSION

Foie gras is a cultural barometer for those who claim to care about food, one that involves clashes over identities, perspectives, and moral tastes. Like other provocative symbols adopted or challenged by partisans, it bundles issues and has been used as a de facto wedge issue to further galvanize the committed and boost contestation. If we are what we eat, as the saying goes, we are also what we *think* about eating. This throws into sharp relief how people's perspectives lead them to emphasize or deemphasize different aspects of a contested issue, and even to perceive the same experience in wholly different ways. Of particular interest here is the diffuse nature of claims to cultural authority; virtuous tastes are not so easily corralled.

The simple facts of the foie gras production process alone cannot explain animal rights activists' actions or responses to their campaigns. There are a number of very good reasons why foie gras has ignited so much emotional energy on both sides of the fence, as well as why contending parties have been stubbornly resistant to each other's viewpoints. With perspective come explanation, judgment, and evaluation. Objects or ideas can be "read" in a variety of ways, and they can communicate what groups or networks deem valuable. As a scholar in the symbolic politics tradition would argue, struggles over the interpretation and institutionalization of these "readings"—over attempts to own them in the public arena—inevitably have social ramifications.[99] They are especially consequential when they reflect the lengths to which opponents and proponents of something are willing to go. We see these easily in heated, contemporary American conflicts over other cultural objects, such as flags, guns, health care, and marriage licenses. The discursive repertoires that accompany such objects and ideas serve as tools for marking social inclusion and exclusion, as well as instruments that activate the sympathies or contempt of others.[100]

Yet, the case of foie gras also makes plain that it is far from clear which ethical evaluation is correct, if any. There is a sensible set of arguments that foie gras production is something that should be prohibited, and a sensible set of counterarguments that it should not. Where the dividing line falls at different points in time has depended on differing perceptions of opportunities, how unintended consequences come to matter, and the shifting reputations of the players involved. A player's orientation toward foie gras as a powerful symbol is certainly influenced by the group identities he or she claims. So, while perspective is (structured) perception, it is also susceptible to the ways that other people define the problem. People have tended to see answers to the questions "Is foie gras cruel?" and "Is it ethical?" that they have wanted to see, or that they thought they *should* see. This is what, in large part, helped foie gras to be deployed successfully as a political symbol in certain ways and to particular ends.

For many people, the foie gras story is fleeting and relatively inconsequential. The paradox here is that people often talk about and remember things that we might consider trivial, and these topics can come to compel deeper scrutiny and expose other anxieties about social life in the process.[101] Sometimes the efforts of a committed few *do* put new concerns on broader agendas and influence mainstream public opinion. Shouting insults at restaurant-goers may be more about communicating grievances than fostering solid policy changes, but it may serve as a justification for action, or for shame. Sometimes localized battles *do* make it beyond their borders. The mobilization effort around foie gras is but one of a number of recent efforts by small but tenacious activist groups in this regard. It is important to remember, though, that due in large part to foie gras's class-based overtones in the United States, as well as to the relative class privilege of people who work for the animal rights movement, this has mainly been a story of a select few battling it out in a relatively contained cultural arena.

The French case offers a very different story, in that nationalized efforts to expand and safeguard the foie gras industry over the course of several decades created a broader base of sympathetic consumers and a much deeper sense of culinary embeddedness—one that has proven far more difficult for animal rights groups to access. In both countries, these issues—and many ideas about food and eating—are made coherent to larger publics through translators, a category that includes chefs as well as journalists, critics, activists, industry members, and even academics. Translators broker information, have interests in promoting certain objectives, and serve as points of contact between experts and the lay public.[102] Even what one sees with one's own eyes is affected. The media, especially, coproduce storylines with these opinion leaders, give voice to particular viewpoints, and offer an arena for those who seek to impart or impose their versions of reality on others.[103]

Regardless of one's dietary commitments, the moral and cultural prescriptions championed by these translators help us think through how and why values, and menus, change. Understanding these changes becomes less about how individuals change their minds, and more about a story of the interest-laden bases for organizing consumer and culinary culture. "Virtue" and "vice" are realms of active negotiation when it comes to the politics of food, taste, and consumption. It is useful, then, not only to be attuned to what activists do, but also how they are relating to the groups and communities they need to be sensitive to their grievances. People determine the credibility of new information in part through whether they trust the messenger. Today, any number of food and farming practices are drawing fire from animal rights and welfare groups, not to mention sustainable-food activists, and being discussed at policy levels ranging from local to global. Which ones will "take" with the public remains unknown, but those that do will necessarily be ensconced in game-like negotiations and fights for symbolic control found at the intersections of social movements, markets, and states.

As this chapter shows, the "problem" of foie gras is itself an artifact of how the tastes of different groups come to gain and lose particular moral footholds. This has implications for how we think about gastropolitics—how moral and ethical boundaries around taste are drawn, erased, and policed, and the effects they generate. In particular, I found that debates over foie gras's existence have occurred within two broader discourses, both of which show the paradoxes and contradictions of using "perspective" as an explanatory tool: first, over what is or is not legitimate treatment of animals that are raised for food and where those lines are drawn and, second, over cultural authority in consumer markets. Perspective, like taste, helps to explain why people emphasize or deemphasize different aspects of the foie gras issue and links these disputes to broader, unresolved tensions in the social organization of consumption.

CHAPTER 6

Conclusion

*O*n July 1, 2012, California's statewide ban (passed seven and a half years earlier) on "liver products produced as the result of force feeding a bird for the purpose of enlarging its liver"—what is better known as foie gras—took effect.[1] A few months earlier, more than one hundred of the state's best-known chefs, aided by the Golden Gate Restaurant Association, had mobilized to try to prevent the ban's realization. Their group, named the Coalition for Humane and Ethical Farming Standards (with the fitting acronym of CHEFS), petitioned the state government and wrote newspaper opinion pieces, Facebook updates, and web posts, asserting the group's hopes to create new, reformed production standards that would preserve foie gras's legality and keep open the sole foie gras farm in the state. Critics dismissed them for being late to the game, for they petitioned the state when the ban was all but imminent.[2] To CHEFS' chagrin, the ban was instated as planned, shuttering Sonoma Foie Gras's doors as well as making the sale of foie gras illegal in the state.

The following day, Hudson Valley Foie Gras, a Canadian foie gras association based in Quebec, and a Los Angeles–based restaurant group together filed an injunction against the state of California, requesting a jury trial to declare the sales ban invalid under the US Commerce Clause. The injunction argued that the law "excessively burdens" interstate commerce because foie gras is legally produced elsewhere. They also asserted that the text's vagueness violated the Due Process Clause of the US Constitution. Two weeks later, a judge refused to block the law temporarily, but allowed the lawsuit to proceed. Two months after that, the California Attorney General's office filed a motion to dismiss. During this time frame, many of the same loopholes that Chicago chefs had exploited several years earlier, such as hosting semisecret underground foie gras dinners or giving foie gras away for free with the purchase of a $20 slice of bread, were used in California.[3] One restaurant, Presidio Social Club, even claimed it had found a way around the ban because it is located in the Presidio National Park, which is on federal land and thus technically exempt from the state's jurisdiction (although the Presidio Trust demanded that foie gras be delisted from the menu).[4] Animal rights groups, which had similarly learned from the Chicago ban, protested outside noncompliant, well-known restaurants and filed several lawsuits against violators rather than leaving enforcement up to state officials. The following summer, a three-judge panel of the US 9th Circuit Court of Appeals upheld the ban, essentially dismissing the suit brought by the US-Canadian foie gras coalition.[5] Animal rights groups around the country celebrated triumphantly.[6]

But this outcome was itself a temporary one. In January 2015, a federal district judge in California's Central District invalidated the ban (now California Health & Safety Code §25982). He did so by ruling in favor of the coalition of plaintiffs mentioned above, finding that the federal Poultry Products Inspections Act—which gives regulatory power to the federal government and prohibits states from imposing certain conditions on food distribution and sales—superseded the California ban on the sale and distribution of foie gras.[7] Of course, Sonoma Foie Gras had already been forced to close. But restaurants could again buy the ingredient legally from producers located elsewhere. Reaction was swift. Animal rights spokespeople bemoaned the decision.[8] Some chefs rejoiced, promising to have foie gras back on the menu as soon as they could. Gawker, the gossip website, declared that this was "great news, for assholes."[9] The following month, the state's Attorney General filed an appeal of the ruling, which at this writing is still undecided—meaning that foie gras's legal status may change yet again (maybe even before this book is published).

The day after California's "bird feeding law" took effect in 2012, another food ban was introduced on the other side of the Pacific Ocean.

This one involved a different luxury item—shark fin soup.[10] On July 2, 2012, China's national governmental body introduced new regulations to prohibit the traditional delicacy from being served at official state banquets.[11] While not a national ban, this was a symbolic and consequential act that functioned as a tool of morally grounded social judgment.

Shark fin soup's politics and controversies are often compared to those of foie gras. It is the material nature of both items, and how they are produced, that is at the very heart of their contested symbolic statuses. Like foie gras, shark fin soup has also been socially classified as a culturally valuable and celebratory dish, one that is imbued with the symbolic power of "tradition" and "national belonging." It has long been an emblematic Chinese dish served at important occasions, often as a social requisite of wedding banquets. It denotes virility and power and signifies a host's status and generosity toward his guests. Once limited to elites, the rising income of China's middle class has led to a growing appetite for this expensive dish in China and at restaurants and banquet halls in Chinatowns worldwide. "No shark fin soup, you're cheap," a seafood distributor in San Francisco's Chinatown told the *New York Times*.[12]

Shark fin soup has also been tagged as ethically and ecologically abhorrent. The practice of shark finning—where sharks are caught, their fins cut off, and thrown back into the water alive, left to bleed to death— is considered by many to be cruel. But shark finning has been framed primarily by opponents as an ecological crisis of scarcity, not as an ethical or moral threat to humanity. Marine scientists estimate that as much as ninety percent of the global shark population has been destroyed in the last few decades, with many arguing that this decimation was due in large part to rising demand for shark fins. Today, conservationists classify more than one hundred species of shark as threatened or endangered, a detrimental shift not only for sharks but for ocean ecosystems.

In the last decade, similar to the international anti–foie gras movement, campaigns against shark finning have gained rapid momentum around the globe. As of 2013, twenty-seven countries—including the United States and the European Union—have bans on their books. However, these polities often do not have complementary laws against import, sale, possession, or consumption. Moreover, international waters are unregulated by any one institution. A group called the Shark Alliance was founded in 2006 and has partnered with environmental and marine conservation NGOs to campaign for closing loopholes in the EU ban on shark finning. In the United States, California, Washington, Oregon, Hawaii, and Illinois passed bans on the sale and possession of shark fin (thus making the soup illegal) in the last few years. Two Canadian cities passed similar bans but saw them overturned following opposition from their Chinese business communities and others' concerns about jurisdictional authority.

Even in China, the global anti–shark fin soup campaign has made speedy headway. A few respected Chinese celebrities and professional athletes began serving as spokespeople for the campaign, consumption rates declined, and a national import ban on shark fin passed. Its exclusion from state banquets—a response to both lawmakers in the National People's Congress who cited shark finning's environmental impact and the State Council's observed need to cut costs—became a reality in December 2013, two years ahead of schedule.[13]

As with foie gras, the marking of something like shark fin soup as morally reprehensible is not merely a reflection of reality; it is a force that has implications for reality. Yet, this moral marking—by way of a gastropolitical framework—means that certain foods can become more contested and more vulnerable than others. Why have opponents of shark finning succeeded in garnering such positive public and institutional support, particularly in China and Hong Kong (the global center of shark fin trade), whereas those of foie gras in France have not? Because some sharks are endangered species, rhetorics of biodiversity, vanishing national resources, and disrupted ocean ecosystems trump the rhetoric of tradition. This has broader implications for other wild species that comprise culinary practices, as well. By contrast, ducks and geese raised for foie gras are farm animals—domesticated agricultural commodities—whose production and use is controlled by humans.

To further support the idea that the protection of ecological or natural resources might serve as strong gastropolitical motivations is the case of ortolan. The ortolan is a small songbird traditionally caught, fattened, drowned in Armagnac liqueur, and then roasted and eaten whole, bones at all. It is said to be so delicious that you have to eat it with a napkin covering your head so that God will not see your greediness. Described as a culinary part of "the soul of France," ortolan was served at French President François Mitterrand's fabled "last meal" in 1995. (Foie gras was also on the menu.)[14] In 1999, following a European Union directive, France passed a ban on the trapping and killing of ortolan after over-hunting led to its official protection as an endangered species. Although some French culinary leaders argued at the time and since that ortolan hunting was part of their cultural heritage, the rhetoric of nature and biodiversity—or, the threatened ecology of vanishing species—took both social and legal precedence.[15]

Other examples of morally problematic animal/culinary practices that have raised social and political ire include eating horsemeat in parts of Europe; seal and whale hunting in Canada, Scandinavia, and Japan (highlighted by the Academy Award-winning documentary *The Cove*); and eating dog in parts of Asia. Such cases have critical analytic value when, and because, they become an axis around which many other acts and questions revolve. Each has come to connote questions and concerns about not only cruelty, but rights and responsibilities: the right to choose what to eat; the responsibility to act ethically; the rights of animals to live without pain or suffering; the responsibility of institutions to protect citizens, markets, and physical environments; and the right to ban something that is legal elsewhere.

The symbolic politics that characterize debates over these different dishes depend on strongly held, yet not immutable, beliefs and priorities. For shark fin soup, the visible support for conservationists' efforts by governments and transnational institutions—including the Chinese government—matters. It is becoming normative for younger generations of China's rising middle class to refuse to have the dish served at their weddings. Interestingly, what is being marketed as a substitute for this dish in China and Chinatowns elsewhere—as a comparable symbol of status, affluence, and a host's generosity—is expensive French wine.[16]

Considering our ideas about, and attachments to, culinary symbols such as these lays bare the fact that we have an understandably complex relationship with the billions of animals that are bred, born, and hunted each year specifically for human consumption. At one extreme, we see animals as material resources to use and consume as we see fit. At the other, we think of animals as sentient creatures that merit humane treatment, empathy, and compassion.[17] While declarations of "tradition" attempt to infuse foods such as these with positive social value, they are not always compatible with ideologies of welfare or environmentalism in an increasingly interconnected world of global commerce, culture, and politics. Foods that are instantiated as "cultural heritage" or "patrimony" become especially salient when an item or practice that one group calls "tradition" angers or morally disgusts others. Sometimes, opponents declare, traditions *should* be broken with.

Not only might certain foods be more vulnerable than others, then, but both the political environment of the specific places that claim them and the rhetorics being used to challenge their existence may moderate their vulnerability. We know that the boundaries of national cuisines are far from static and that determining what "authentically" represents a place's culinary spirit or character—and who can be included in that spirit—is in no way a straightforward process.[18] Indeed, what is considered "national" cuisine in modern consumer societies such as the United States and France is likely that which is considered essential to those who stand to profit from it, such as food industry professionals, advertisers, and politicians.

We might suspect that discourses of heritage and tradition are valued less within the political environment of a society currently undergoing rapid modernization, such as China, than in a Western nation such as France. This would help explain why it is increasingly common for the Chinese elite to look toward classic Western symbols of status such as French wine (or foie gras, for that matter—China is currently developing a homegrown industry to meet the demands of celebrity chefs' restaurants in Asian metropolises). It is also easier to envision legislators in an American city sponsoring an unlikely yet successful food ban than to imagine the same happening in more centralized political systems (such as France's), even with the American penchant for seeing "individual choice" as type of "freedom."[19] With respect to moral rhetoric, challenges to culinary heritage and tradition often include discourses about humaneness and cruelty, healthfulness and purity, and biodiversity. Each of these conceptual challenges to "the way things are" signals some combination of concerns for food ethics as well as for the symbolic boundaries marking food producers' and consumers' modern-day identities.

As such, political fights about these issues are fights about rules, values, and cultural logics—namely, which and whose values and tastes should proliferate, and who possesses the knowledge and power to define a situation in a way that suits particular ends and solidifies certain meanings into history. For people and food practices, following—or contesting—these rules and logics converts food into something more: a key facet of citizenship, a reason for policy negotiations, an indicator of humanity, or a social problem that needs political resolution.

Gastropolitics and Mercurial Morality

Food is undeniably political. Beliefs about foods and cuisines—and the people who make and consume them, the resources they use, the tastes they signify, or the markets that move them—are far from innocuous. Just like other types of politics, food politics are about power, control, and conflict. *Gastropolitics* manifest when and where social power is exerted over a food or culinary item to fashion it as a vessel of moral, cultural, or political significance. This makes the morality of food mercurial, allowing social and political circumstances to fluctuate through tangible, edible objects. Gastropolitics illuminate relationships among—and have real effects on—people, communities, markets, and states. And they show that it is never just "live and let live" when it comes to our food choices and those of others. A gastropolitical perspective compels us to ask: Who makes the rules and legitimates policy decisions? Which fights are picked, and who sets the agenda? Who benefits? Examining contested tastes through a gastropolitical lens helps us better appreciate the times and places when some food-related issue becomes classified as a moral risk[20] and comes to serve as a touchstone of cultural contention, righteous indignation, or political debate.

Few fights within today's world of food politics have proved more fraught than those over foie gras. Even after more than a decade of disputes, controversies over its existence still generate headlines around the globe. In 2014, the Directorate General of Foreign Trade of India unexpectedly changed its national policy for imported foie gras from "free" to "prohibited" after pressure from animal rights groups. In June 2015, the city of São Paulo, Brazil, one of South America's gastronomic hubs, banned foie gras production (a symbolic ban) and sale in restaurants (a material ban). After several weeks of vocal objections by a cadre of São Paulo's restaurateurs and culinary professionals, a city judge ordered the law to be suspended. At this writing, the final outcome is still pending.

Indubitably, foie gras remains an issue of contested tastes—a food that some people love, and that others love to hate. Animal rights activists denounce it as torture, with some even willing to go to extreme lengths to vilify it and its supporters. Others say that activists are ill-informed and focused on the wrong issue. Some call it a tradition worth protecting as part of French national cultural heritage, and others a vestige of the past that is unsuitable for the modern world. Some call the idea of banning it ridiculous, while others call it morally necessary. It depends, of course, on whom you ask.

But, as this book has shown, it is not *just* whom you ask, but also whose interests are at stake, who has the authority to answer, and who has the power to cement that answer in conventional wisdom, that matter tremendously. Ethics must be weighed against cost, availability against sustainability, desire against need, the flavors on our tongues and fullness in our stomachs against the beliefs in our minds. Gastropolitics situate these personally felt questions of ethics, tastes, and belonging within their cultural and place-specific contexts.

Such considerations inform the varied efforts of social movement and state actors to claim moral authority in the market-based world of consumption, to shape the commodity chains that carry items from their place of production to their retail sale. States regulate markets based on societal needs, and activist groups attempt to utilize markets as vehicles for social and cultural change, to draw new lines in the sand of consumer tastes. For instance, consumer boycotts of food items can help create communities of concern across civil society and make grievances about physically and cognitively distant food production seem close at hand. In the late eighteenth century, hundreds of thousands of British antislavery activists refused to add sugar to their tea to protest slavery on sugar plantations.[21] Almost two centuries later, the United Farm Workers similarly used national boycotts of table grapes and lettuce, publicized through localized boycott committees, to generate support from millions of middle-class and urban consumers for the reorganization of agricultural labor laws and improvement of laborers' working conditions, and to give farmworkers collective bargaining rights.[22]

But while consumer boycotts (or buycotts, which are when purchasing rather than avoiding specific goods is what is encouraged[23]) may express a person's or group's moral standpoint and place some pressure on producers, concrete effects on retail sales and spending habits are often hard to ascertain. As social movement scholar James Jasper writes, "A silent choice, made alone, in the aisle of a crowded supermarket, is a poor way to sustain a sense of injustice and indignation."[24] Similarly, choosing a dish off a menu of dining options is a decision shared only with those at the table and the restaurant staff (and sometimes social media). There may be any number of reasons why someone chooses to eat at one restaurant over another, opts for a salad instead of a steak, shops at Wal-Mart rather than Whole Foods, or purchases apples instead of grapes at their local supermarket. Moreover, scholars across the social sciences have recently underscored the limitations that this version of consumer-citizenship encompasses. "Voting" with your dollar, or your fork, is unlikely to resolve the structural, systemic problems associated with the food system: environmental degradation, labor and human rights violations, food safety and contamination risks, and increasingly concentrated corporate power within the field of transnational agribusiness.[25]

The politics of a relatively insignificant item like foie gras may not tackle the very real and important questions about the quality, fairness, transparency, or sustainability of our food system, and yet a number of people see them as a critical opening into these issues. While some observers express disdain about the vast attention foie gras has received from different parties—legislators, the popular press, the culinary elite, and the blogosphere, among others—this concentrated awareness demonstrates that claims for or against some divisive culinary practice can resonate from the micro-level of individual beliefs up through the macro-level of the state.

We are extremely aware of the ongoing politics of difference that play out in debates over objects and practices such as guns, vaccines, flags, and oil pipelines, and yet we can be easily lulled into thinking that such contentiousness does not apply to food. Food is safe, simple, benign. It is something that satisfies the body and the mind, and that brings people together in a corporeal way to "break bread" and strengthen social ties over shared meals. Everyone participates in one way or another on a regular basis. And food is fun. When a food-related problem, scare, or dispute makes headlines, the title and lead are often written as cutesy puns, obliquely relegating these issues to a softer, nonserious status. This puts news about food politics in a different conceptual silo than the status of the Confederate flag. Discourse analysts, however, consider the use of humor a lens into the strength of social norms and as indicative of nervousness with the web of social values invoked.[26] A gastropolitical lens reminds us that the world of food politics is not only highly charged, but not exempt from "real" politics.

Foie Gras and Symbolic Power

Highly charged questions about foie gras's existence and ethics have ranged in scale from the level of international institutions such as the European Union and transnational social movements to state and municipal regulation of geographically bounded markets, as well as sensationalized personal battles among activists, chefs, media figures, and consumers. Comparing its symbolic power across these levels highlights the messy ways in which people mix and match ideas about what is good or bad within their constantly evolving worldviews.

The questions foie gras raises are thus not just about cruelty or culinary delight; they are also about what we know about what we eat, how foods are selected to represent whole cultures, and the ways that contested markets end up creating certain types of consumers. They are also about the ways that disgust, as a classifying dimension of taste, is implicit in the upkeep of symbolic boundaries around different foods, cuisines, and tastes. Is eating foie gras a sign of national pride? Of individual liberty? Of cruelty? Of being the best kind of foodie? The worst? Is the labor involved in producing this food (both human and avian) to be celebrated or reviled? Is foie gras depicted as the showpiece of a carefully crafted plate or as an accompaniment to the glutton who sits beside it?

Foie gras's symbolic politics exemplify how the twenty-first-century marketplace for food operates as a complex site of moral conflict over consumption. While a historical view shows us that industrial food production has leveled a number of practices and tastes once reserved for the wealthy,[27] the idea that our modern food system is dysfunctional is garnering mainstream traction. It has become commonplace for the professional middle class—disproportionately white, highly educated, and relatively young—to reject mass-market industrial food and turn to alternatives, from grocery cooperatives to urban rooftop gardens and backyard chickens. Similarly, the field of gourmet restaurants in the United States and elsewhere has pushed tastes for non-industrial food products—local, seasonal, grass-fed, foraged, and Slow—as a fine-dining blueprint.[28] Picking sides in fights over foie gras raises questions about the strategies that culinary opinion leaders and change agents choose, as well as about their resources and capacities to act.

For ongoing debates about foie gras's production ethics, it is hardly surprising that the definition of "cruelty" is hotly contested and that different social actors committed to distinct ethical principles and worldviews claim that their position is the properly moral one. Conceptually, the central issue here turns from a plea for the humane treatment of particular animals to a discussion of *how* to reasonably define humane treatment, and to a parallel discussion of *who* should be doing the defining. Who has, or should have, the expertise and authority to define cruelty: Artisanal farmers? Industry professionals? Activists? Avian biologists? Chefs? Politicians? It is in this context that the values we attach to contested foods become moral tastes. This matters for how foie gras is depicted in the popular media, which has bearing for how it is understood by those with lawmaking power.

For all parties involved in the fights over foie gras, some cherished value is felt to be deeply threatened. In France, while foie gras is not unanimously treasured (as the existence of opposition groups shows), its positive moral valence depends on its function as a sign of shared national identity in the face of industrial change, limits on French sovereignty in regional and global politics, and immigration. French foie gras producers and consumers rely on sentiments of national value, first labeling it as unique and authentic "patrimony" and then reifying that label through law, which in turn has further stimulated market growth. I call this gastronationalism. Members of the French foie gras industry—large and small—articulate their gastronational commitments to foie gras as an essential part of France's "brand" in the contemporary world.[29] Yet, other countries in the European Union, arguing that its production is unethical, want to see foie gras production cease. In the French mindset, then, threats against foie gras come to be interpreted as a threat against Frenchness itself.[30] Safeguarding foie gras production from animal rights activists and EU officials becomes metaphorically akin to protecting monuments or historic sites or to saving an endangered language or species from extinction. Yet national endorsement of foie gras's "authenticity" remains a thorny topic, as these carefully articulated claims of tradition mask the industry's capital-intensive modernization and conglomeration. New interpretations of moral tastes may very well emerge.

In the United States, where there were only four (and are now three) small farms in the entire country, savvy and tenacious animal rights activists successfully brought foie gras into the critical public and legislative eye, vilifying it as "gourmet cruelty." "Is it really worth it," a New York-based Farm Sanctuary activist asked me, "to create that much suffering for a luxury item?" Potential city and state bans on producing and selling the fattened liver were pitched to constituents as prohibiting something that threatened a place's ethical reputation. Since then, foie gras's opponents and supporters alike have found ways to account for the events that have happened, or not happened, and to make sense of contradictory evidence that has arisen.

But clarifying what is actually imperiled by foie gras is far from a straightforward task. Foie gras is a drop in the bucket when it comes to the scale of the American industrial food system, much of which is arguably cruel to billions of animals. Moreover, any species—animal or plant—raised for human consumption is manipulated to some degree in the process. Foie gras's defenders also employ the language of threatened rights: the freedom to choose what we eat, the rights of chefs and restaurateurs to have autonomy over their menus, and the rights of democratic governments to ban something that is legal elsewhere. For example, in a court filing charging that he was breaking the California law by giving foie gras away for "free," one chef defended himself somewhat hyperbolically, saying, "what I do give away to customers is my way of dumping tea in the harbor, so to speak."[31] The fear here is that a minority group's moral ideas about food could be imposed on the majority (even if the fear is unfounded given that consumers of foie gras are themselves a minority), and further disruptions of their ways of cooking, eating, and doing business could be imminent. While activists hope that chefs and consumers will refuse to serve and eat foie gras, heightened awareness of the controversies in the United States has also paradoxically created new foie gras devotees.

As such, evolving assumptions or claims about ostensible threats and risks circulating around foie gras become tightly woven into the debates themselves. The challenge for foie gras's defenders and opponents in both France and the United States is a cultural one, that of symbolic control in noisy cultural landscapes. It is also one of legitimate influence over how markets work and over public understandings of social problems. Importantly, most of those who became involved in foie gras's politics chose to do so because they saw foie gras as a symbol of what *could* happen in regard to cultural change around food, for better or worse. This is not necessarily a negative thing. Rather, it permits us to become more sensitive to the numerous ways that different social actors produce, use, and dispute symbols and stories about desirable "solutions" to social problems.

After all of this, it is my hunch that few minds were actually changed. Chefs may have taken foie gras off their menus, voluntarily or not, but they continue to serve meat. People who didn't eat meat before continue not to eat it. People who love foie gras continue to wax poetic about it on their food blogs or visit artisanal farms in the French countryside. Factory farms continue to cram billions of pigs, chickens, and cows into crowded feedlots and confined spaces. Fewer ducks are force-fed in the United States, but more are worldwide.[32] The animal rights movement continues to challenge institutions it characterizes as abusive. Societies continue to manipulate and manage the world's creatures to reflect normative ideas about what is right and wrong, about what is "natural" and what is an abomination. Loathed or loved, foie gras remains locked in an unsettled classificatory struggle. And the fights over it plainly show that emotions, politics, and the culture of markets go hand in hand.

As historians and anthropologists remind us, eating has never been simple. Yet, as food systems and the interests that propel them continue to expand and globalize, choosing what to eat becomes ever more sociologically complex. Twenty-first-century consumers in both the United States and France are not only encouraged, but often admonished to think about the moral and political ramifications of what they are eating. It is, in many ways, a good thing if consumers are reflecting more on the ethical implications of their consumption choices. But one of the main problems with the fights over foie gras is that we're debating whether or not a particular food practice should exist, and not examining the broader politics of and potential alternatives in our brave new food world.

A culturally informed theory of how gastropolitics reflects and shapes moral choices, then, shows that it can be hard to think straight about food. Such a theory needs to parse the deep relations between changes in communities and markets as well as foods as both physical and symbolic objects. Food is, of course, fair game for moral posturing. Many of us would like to eat ethically, if only we could figure out what that entails. Everyone has an idea about what is or is not good to eat. Everyone has to decide what "good" means—at least people who care about food *hope* that everyone else will take the time to do so. People who care about food will do their best to redefine what is or should be counted as "good," engendering ongoing and contentious debates about what to eat and the exigencies of power and social influence that shape food and taste. The one thing that does seem easy to predict, however, is that the global fight over foie gras is far from over.

NOTES

Preface

1. Griswold, 1987.
2. The history of the Wikipedia pages for "foie gras" and "foie gras controversy," for example, clearly shows this evolution of available information. Contributions only took off (with the latter gaining a distinct entry) after 2007.
3. Journalists have also been chastised, bullied, and threatened online for writing about foie gras in ways that are not wholly sympathetic to the activist point of view. In 2013, for example, a freelance food writer in Texas received a number of threatening emails and even had a Change.org petition created against her after publishing a short article about five restaurants in Houston that served foie gras. Comments on the petition called her "an excellent example of human arrogance and ignorance" and a "selfish egoist." She told me she was nervous about the intimation of violence in the emails she received. She averred that she did respect the fact that people feel so passionately about foie gras, but was also "a bit depressed by the quick turn to ad hominem attacks and a seeming lack of desire for more informed debate."

Chapter 1. What Can We Learn From Liver?

1. Gonzalez later and separately told Mark Caro and me that this accusation shows activists' lack of understanding of farm life versus wildlife. "Ponds are a source of disease of animal husbandry," he told Caro (2009, 90), and said to me, "Ponds on farms are a main source of bacteria and can spread infection."

2. Kim Severson, "Plagued by Activists, Foie Gras Chef Changes Tune," *San Francisco Chronicle*/SFGate, September 27, 2003.

3. Grace Walden, "Sonoma Saveurs Foie Gras Shop Closes," *San Francisco Chronicle*/SFGate, February 9, 2005.

4. Marcelo Rodriguez, "Foie Gras Flap Leads to Vandalism," *Los Angeles Times*, August 25, 2003.

5. Patricia Henley, "Vandals Flood Historic Building," *Sonoma News*, August 15, 2003. Jaubert also told a UK paper that Sonoma Foie Gras was the wrong target, as their ducks had "extremely good treatment, certainly compared to the way the big chicken producers behave with their animals." (Andrew Gumbel, "'Meat is Murder' Militants Target California's New Taste for Foie Gras," *The Independent*, August 23, 2003.)

6. Serventi, 2005.

7. This statement was made on a special holiday episode of Bourdain's television show *No Reservations* in 2007, which is available on YouTube. Gastronomy is typically defined in English as the science and art of cooking, preparing, and eating good food. In French, the term also refers to culinary styles, for example in reference to the cooking customs of a place or region (what in English would more likely be called "cuisine").

8. Hugues, 1982; Serventi, 1993; Toussaint-Samat, 1994.

9. Daguin and de Ravel, 1988; Guérard, 1998; Ginor, Davis, Coe, and Ziegelman, 1999; Perrier-Robert, 2007.

10. Around nine hundred specific food products from countries throughout Europe currently have these legal protections for production and marketing, with more under consideration.

11. Some French chefs in the United States, nevertheless, began smuggling fresh livers into the country in the early 1970s. Jean Banchet, the longtime chef of Le Français, outside of Chicago (which closed its doors in 2006), is quoted in Ginor, Davis, Coe, and Ziegelman (1999, 63), as saying: "Every time I returned from France I would hide some in my suitcase. A few times I made the mistake of packing it in Styrofoam boxes; when the inspector saw it, he knew that there was food inside. He would just throw the whole box of foie gras in the garbage, right in front of me." During my research, I also heard a few scattered stories of small-scale home production dating back to the 1840s.

12. Kamp, 2006.

13. http://chronicle.nytlabs.com/?keyword=foie%20gras.

14. Only one French producer—Rougié, which is part of a transnational

firm named Euralis—currently exports foie gras products to the United States, although several Canadian farms in Quebec (affiliates of French companies, including Rougié) also distribute to the US market.

15. In an interview, one Chicago chef exclaimed, "Twenty-five million dollars! That's nothing. That's what the Cheesecake Factory location on Michigan Avenue pulls in in a year. Not the whole chain. One location."

16. The United States produces about six billion broiler chickens annually. See the USDA's Poultry Slaughter Annual Summaries, available from the National Agricultural Statistical Service. Also see Ollinger, MacDonald, and Madison, 2000.

17. The CEO of Whole Foods Market, John Mackey, actively prohibits its stores from carrying foie gras products.

18. Johnston and Goodman, 2015.

19. Heldke, 2003.

20. In fact, the two main US foie gras farms came into existence just after the term "foodie" was coined by Ann Barr and Paul Levy in *The Official Foodie Handbook* in 1984. See also Johnston and Baumann, 2010.

21. Some producers have experimented with less rigid tubes, in part to appease critics. Hungarian foie gras producers use specially designed plastic tubes in goose foie gras production. In California, a goose farmer named Tom Brock was featured in a 2007 *New York Times* article for using shorter flexible plastic feeding tubes. (He closed his doors a few years later.) But Izzy Yanay of Hudson Valley, while claiming to be "intrigued" by Brock's technique, told me, "Look, you need to have a metal pipe. Because the plastic pipe is accumulating bacteria. The plastic pipes are terrible for them. They get fungus in the esophagus. Metal pipes you can clean, you can disinfect. Ours are stainless steel."

22. I use "animal rights" as an umbrella term to characterize people and groups who advocate for an ethical obligation to animals through not using them for human purposes. Animal rights groups encompass a spectrum of issues, tactics, and ideological factions, from promoters of vegan diets to liberationists, some of whom even reject some "rights"-based approaches in favor of direct action tactics. Philosophical tomes including Peter Singer's *Animal Liberation* and Tom Regan's *The Case for Animal Rights* undergird this movement. Every animal activist I interviewed owned a copy of Singer's book; many quoted directly from it in our conversations.

23. Irvin Molotsky, "Foie Gras Event Is Killed by Protests," *New York Times*, August 24, 1999.

24. New York–based GourmetCruelty.com was founded by Sarahjane Blum and Ryan Shapiro (brother of Paul Shapiro, the founder of animal rights group Compassion Over Killing and the current vice-president of The Humane Society of the United States). A detailed, journalistic account of these activists' lives and professed motivations can be found in Mark Caro's excellent book *The Foie Gras Wars*.

25. As a relevant side note, Ryan Shapiro told Mark Caro that all but one of the ducks they took were able to be "rehabilitated" and that "their livers just naturally shrank back down almost all of the way" (Caro 2009, 73–74). This idea, that the fattened liver *could* return to normal, is actually one of foie gras's proponents' main arguments that the process is "natural" and not a "disease."

26. Marcelo Rodriguez, "Activists Take Ducks from Foie Gras Shed," *Los Angeles Times*, September 18, 2003.

27. Several celebrities (including Bea Arthur of TV's *The Golden Girls*), who were called "true friends of animals" in one press release, either testified or submitted supportive statements.

28. The website www.nofoiegras.org, from Farm Sanctuary, titled their press release "Schwarzenegger Terminates Animal Cruelty."

29. A large literature on agenda-setting has well documented the role and power of mass media in influencing what citizens deem important, as well as policy agendas, because politicians use the news media as a source of information of what constitutes an issue. In other words, issues matter precisely because they appear as news. See: Baumgartner and Jones, 2009; McCombs and Shaw, 1993.

30. Patricia Leigh Brown, "Foie Gras Fracas: Haute Cuisine Meets the Duck Liberators," *New York Times*, September 24, 2003.

31. Rollin, 1990; Lowe, 2006.

32. Jasper and Nelkin, 1992.

33. See, for example, Farm Sanctuary's nofoiegras.org website, which, at the time of this writing, said: "In medical terms, the liver is in a state of dysfunction called hepatic lipidosis or hepatic steatosis, meaning it can no longer perform its intended function." Hepatic lipidosis is known in humans as "fatty liver disease," stereotypically caused by overconsumption of alcohol. Lawsuits filed against Hudson Valley Foie Gras and the United States Department of Agriculture claiming the company was

producing and distributing a "diseased and adulterated product" have been rejected by state and federal courts.

34. For an analysis of the American public understanding about animal sentience, pain, and foie gras production through the lens of blog comments, see Youatt, 2012.

35. "Statement of Dr. Holly Cheever." Chicago City Council Health Committee, October 2005.

36. The overwhelming majority of agricultural animal research in the United States has been about beef, pork, dairy, and chicken—not ducks or geese. French scientists, on the other hand, have conducted an array of experiments and studies to consider everything from the chemical composition of the liver during feeding practices, to techniques that minimize stress, to the effects of force-feeding on the birds' hormones. Many of these studies were conducted in conjunction with INRA (the French National Institute for Agricultural Research); others are detailed in the 1998 European Union report on the welfare of foie gras ducks and geese.

37. See, among others, Bennett, Anderson, and Blaney, 2002; Harper and Makatouni, 2002; *Consumer Attitudes about Animal Welfare: 2004 National Public Opinion Survey*, Boston: Market Directions, 2004.

38. While Pierre Bourdieu's (1984) influential sociological model of taste and food consumption guides my questions and analyses, he mostly neglects the roles of morality and ethics in how people form their cultural preferences and strategies of social judgment of others.

39. Curtis, 2013.

40. Though, as Mary Douglas has shown us, formal and informal distinctions between pure and impure foods reveal that many tastes are highly nuanced. (Gourmet hamburgers served at an upscale restaurant are still hamburgers.)

41. Gabaccia, 1998; Wallach, 2013.

42. Biltekoff, 2013; DuPuis, 2002.

43. Gopnik, 2011.

44. Appadurai, 1981.

45. Brown and Mussell, 1984.

46. Ferguson, 1998; Ferguson, 2004.

47. See, for example, Gusfield, 1986; Beisel, 1997; Tepper, 2011.

48. Douglas, 1984, 30.

49. Douglas and Isherwood, 1979.

50. Gusfield, 1986, 11.

51. Jacobs, 2005.
52. Inglis, 2005.
53. Goodman, 2002.
54. Gusfield, 1981.
55. Lamont and Fournier , 1992.
56. Lamont, 1992; Bourdieu, 1984.
57. Biltekoff, 2013. Also see Guthman, 2007.
58. Lamont and Molnar, 2002; Beisel, 1992.
59. DiMaggio, 1987.
60. Zelizer, 1983; Zelizer, 1985; Zelizer, 2011.
61. Healy, 2006; Almeling, 2011; Chan, 2012.
62. Beisel, 1993; Fourcade and Healy, 2007.
63. A historical example is alcohol and the temperance movement. (See Gusfield, 1986.) As a relevant side note, for a great deal of human history, access to alcohol was a fundamental aspect of public health because it was safer to drink than water. See Standage, 2006.
64. Steinmetz, 1999.
65. Tarrow, 1998.
66. Revenue numbers come from the organizations' annual financial reports.
67. Organizational budgets reported in Kim Severson, "Bringing Moos and Oinks into the Food Debate," *New York Times*, July 25, 2007. As of 2007, PETA claimed more than one million members. PETA began buying stock in McDonald's and attending shareholder meetings in 1998. The Humane Society of the United States owns enough stock in Tyson chicken, Wal-Mart, McDonald's, and Smithfield Foods to have the power to introduce shareholder resolutions.

Chapter 2. Vive le Foie Gras!

1. A year later, Schwebel became the inaugural president of Euro Foie Gras, a group created to represent the foie gras interests of France, Spain, Bulgaria, Hungary, and Belgium in the European Union. Among other initiatives, the group put out press releases decrying the 2012 California ban in the United States.
2. Trubek, 2008.
3. Which areas are encompassed by the term "Southwest France," or "Sud-Ouest," is often disagreed upon due to overlapping place names. One of the best and clearest explanations of these names I have found

comes from a cookbook by Paula Wolfert, *The Cuisine of Southwest France*. Wolfert writes (2005, xxiii), "The entire area is sometimes thought of as two distinct regions: the Aquitaine, whose most important city is Bordeaux, and the Midi-Pyrenees, whose 'capital' is Toulouse. Additionally, cutting across these two regions are the two old duchies of Gascony and Guyenne, Gascony consisting of the Landes, Gers, and some other parts; Guyenne consisting of the Bordelais, the Dordogne, parts of the Quercy, and the Rouergue. But now the real confusion begins: There are names for the old provinces and names for the new departments, and the borders do not always precisely coincide. Thus traditionally one can speak of the Perigord, Quercy, and Rouergue while also speaking of the Dordogne, the Lot, and the Aveyron."

4. Barham, 2003; Bowen, 2015.

5. Dubarry, 2004; Vannier, 2002.

6. "Gavage" is the tube-feeding process through which ducks and geese are fattened.

7. Amendment to the *Code Rural* Article L645–27–1: "Le foie gras fait partie du patrimoine culturel et gastronomique protégé en France. On entend par foie gras, le foie d'un canard ou d'une oie spécialement engraissé par gavage."

8. Stop Gavage is now a campaign of L214, an animal protection and rights group with a broader purpose and goals.

9. Bendix, 1997; Grazian, 2003; Peterson, 2005; Fine, 2006.

10. Wherry, 2008; Potter, 2010; Cavanaugh and Shankar, 2014.

11. Terrio, 2000; Herzfeld, 2004.

12. DeSoucey, 2010.

13. This follows what Prasad (2005) and Fourcade-Gourinchas and Babb (2002) call the French state's turn toward "pragmatic neoliberalism," where state-led industrialization helped create an industrial economy out of an agricultural one in order to participate in the new international economy.

14. Hoffman, 2006.

15. In 2008, UNESCO began keeping an official list of practices—today almost three hundred distinct items from countries around the globe—of "Intangible Cultural Heritage in Need of Urgent Safeguarding." The list includes ritual dances, fiber and fabric arts, musical instrument playing, festivals, and architectural crafts. It helps to position and brand countries for economic development and tourism. In 2010, three food-related "traditions" were inscribed on this list (following separate debates over

the appropriateness of each): the "Mediterranean Diet," "traditional Mexican cuisine" of "the Michoacán paradigm," and "the gastronomic meal of the French." It is crucial here to remain cognizant of the politics of UNESCO's database construction, as not all countries have equivalent resources or are equally motivated to register their stocks of cultural heritage with organizations like UNESCO.

16. Controversies about traditions intrude on what some communities take for granted. Simon Bronner's book *Killing Tradition: Inside Hunting and Animal Rights Controversies* (2008) is exemplary in this regard.

17. Definition adapted from Grazian, 2003 and Fine, 2003. As the former argues, the commodification of authentic cultural products can grow the scope of consumers' desire to seek out authenticity with oft-surprising results.

18. See, among others, Held, McGrew, Goldblatt, and Perraton, 1999.

19. Chapter 3 of Held and McGrew, 2007.

20. Mabel Berezin, co-editor with Martin Schain of *Europe Without Borders: Remapping Territory, Citizenship, and Identity in a Transnational Age* (2003) succinctly defines territory as "congealed identity that embeds relations of social, political, cultural, and cognitive power in physical space" (10) and identity as "the cognitive form that lends transparency to the emotional dimension of territory" (11).

21. McMichael, Philip, 2012; Stiglitz, 2002.

22. Fourcade-Gourinchas and Babb, 2002; Sklair, 2002.

23. Brubaker, 1996.

24. Anderson, 1991.

25. Hobsbawm and Ranger, 1983.

26. Billig, 1995. In the United States, state governments also claim some commonplace symbols, such as trees, flowers, and birds, as official representations. See Dobransky and Fine, 2006.

27. Anderson, 1991. Also extends Richard Peterson's well-known 1997 work, *Creating Country Music: Fabricating Authenticity*.

28. Bandelj and Wherry, 2011; Croucher, 2003.

29. Wilk, 2006.

30. For example, the former French Cultural Minister, Jack Lang, was quoted in the *Washington Post* in 1993 as saying that free trade in cultural goods originating in the United States would lead to the "mental colonization of Europe, and the progressive destruction of its imagination" (October 16).

31. Foie gras is popular in places with tastes for luxury consumer products,

including the United States and elsewhere in Europe. Its popularity is also rising in wealthy urban hubs in Asia and the Middle East.

32. Toussaint-Samat, 1994; Combret, 2004.

33. I also found in my fieldwork and interviews in the United States that people who had spent time in France or learning about French cuisine (at culinary schools or in restaurant kitchens, for example) told many of the same stories and evoked some of the same imagery.

34. For me, FGFT was a mnemonic tool that provided descriptive value of what was being explained and allowed me to note additional details or variations (of which there were few) in its telling.

35. The term "fairytale" can also be used semantically to denote a happy, problem-free story. It is this usage to which my alliterative phrase refers.

36. Wuthnow, 1987.

37. Conceptual uses of nature, as Lévi-Strauss and others have taught us, are culturally embedded phenomena, and many distinctions between nature and culture are the products of ideological choices. See also Heath and Meneley, 2007.

38. http://www.rougie.us/Foie%20Gras.html.

39. Historians of Egyptian art and material culture note that Egypt's aura still has a commanding presence today. See Meskell, 2004.

40. Giacosa, 1992.

41. Toussaint-Samat, 1994; Wechsberg, 1972.

42. Bits of physical evidence of this pathway linger among Gallo-Roman edifices and ruins in France's Southwestern regions. For example, geese are represented on the arch of the church Sainte-Foy de Morlaàs, built at the end of the eleventh century in the town of Béarn. See, among others, Perrier-Robert, 2007, and Daguin and Ravel, 1988.

43. Davidson, 1999.

44. One of Judaism's fundamental tenets is to appreciate the world God has given humankind, including the utility and benefits provided by religiously permitted domestic animals, which reciprocally necessitate humane treatment. See Schapiro, 2011, 119.

45. This connection to Jewish populations offers evidence for the contemporary prominence of a foie gras industry in Hungary. Throughout Eastern European shetls, Jews were not allowed to own land or to farm, yet could raise a few geese in or close to their homes. When demand for foie gras in France exceeded supply during the pinnacle of haute cuisine, importers turned to Eastern Europe, particularly Hungary, where a small cottage industry had developed. By 1938, Hungary was exporting

about five hundred metric tons of foie gras by refrigerated railway cars to France each year.

46. While culinary historians agree that Jews played a role in diffusing foie gras throughout Europe, they debate the extent to which Jewish populations contributed to creating its modern industry. Some note that surviving sixteenth- and seventeenth-century cookbooks produced in the Alsace region credit Jews with creating a foie gras business (see Davidson, 1999). Others disagree. Silvano Serventi, for example, writes (2005, 13) that "the reputation of the Jews as producers of foie gras was not fully established until the 16th century, whereas similarly French agronomes described the process for obtaining this foodstuff."

47. Anderson, 1991; Bell, 2003.

48. Allen Weiss (2012, 75) argues convincingly, "The typical is only a cross section of possibilities at a given moment of time and not a historical account."

49. Ferguson, 2004, 7. See also Trubek, 2000.

50. Spang, 2000.

51. As food historian Megan Elias writes (2011), the qualities attached to the character of the gourmet (i.e., connoisseurship, authenticity, and knowledge about wine) were first described in the 1800s as theoretical in an approach to food, as compared to the gourmand, who combined theory and practice (i.e., eating).

52. Gopnik, 2011, 36.

53. People generally ate somewhat better in the cities, but many foods (for example, milk, fish, and vegetables) were unreliably fresh until the twentieth century. See Scholliers, 2001.

54. Ferguson, 2004.

55. See also Mennell, 1985.

56. Furlough, 1998.

57. As feminist anthropologist Micaela Di Leonardo shows (1984), the image of the grandmother as a carrier of ethnic or national identity is far from unique to France. In the late twentieth-century United States, the grandmother became a powerful image in advertising and television programming of white ethnic selfhood, characterized by nurturing, family loyalty, neighborhood ties, and home cooking. Sociologist Mary Waters (1990) offers a similar analysis of this trope's cultural importance.

58. For example, the figure of the cowboy—a rugged, masculine, indepen-

dent ideal—is regularly presented as a hero in folk understandings of the American West. See Savage, 1979.

59. Gary Alan Fine (2001) called these individuals and groups "reputational entrepreneurs" in his research program on historical figures with "difficult reputations."

60. Hall, 1992.

61. Fieldnotes, May 2006. Importantly, due to the French state's official secularism, or *laïcité*, Christmas is celebrated as a French national holiday, rather than a purely religious one. This is similar to classifying medieval cathedrals in the domain of French national *patrimoine*.

62. For additional details regarding the industrialization of French foie gras production and the historical role of the National Institute for Agricultural Research (INRA) in creating and diffusing these new technologies, see Jullien and Smith, 2008.

63. Today, only three producers of significant size remain in Alsace, down from about sixty in the early 1900s. Smaller operations disappeared during World War II, were forced to merge, or were acquired. Moreover, land there is more expensive, meaning that farming is a more capital-intensive practice than in the Southwest. None of my respondents mentioned negative implications of this shift for Alsace, only that it happened.

64. Throughout the 2000s, the number of ducks processed in France increased by about five percent each year. Sometimes, however, the industry slows down production to prevent foie gras from being overproduced and to keep it as a prestige item (personal communications with industry representatives).

65. At the time (between 1982 and 1987, after which it was once again privatized), Compagnie Financière de Suez was a nationalized entity.

66. Reported in Coquart and Pilleboue, 2000.

67. Numbers from CIFOG's *Rapport économique, marché du foie gras*.

68. This has changed in recent years, as demand for higher-quality foie gras products reemerged.

69. I accessed CIFOG newsletters from 1996–2002, the entire collection housed at the Bibliothèque Nationale in Paris, in the summer of 2006. *Magret* is the breast meat of a fattened foie gras duck.

70. Ginor, Davis, Coe, and Ziegelman, 1999.

71. Hungary produces about two thousand tons of foie gras annually, making it the second largest producer in the world after France. Their goose

farms typically use flexible rubber tubes attached to machines that rapidly dispense measured amounts of feed. Zsuzsa Gille (2011) has written about the present-day politics of the Hungarian foie gras industry, particularly about a 2008 boycott that received media attention and government response.

72. See Guémené, et al. (2004) for a (now-contested) review of research on physiological indicators. But see also the Stop Gavage rebuttal, available in English at http://www.stopgavage.com/en/inra.

73. Female ducklings are either raised for meat or euthanized. In the United States, all foie gras production is from male ducks. Hudson Valley Foie Gras has said it ships its female ducks to growers in the Caribbean to be raised for meat. Goose foie gras is produced from both male and female birds.

74. In France, Rougié and Feyel-Artzner both sell foie gras ice cream. In 2007, Rougie's was awarded a prize for innovation at the Sirha/Bocuse D'Or Festival in Lyon. In the United States, foie gras ice cream was part of the winning meal prepared by Richard Blais on the 2011 season of *Top Chef All-Stars* on the Bravo cable network.

75. This also leads to poor reporting on foie gras controversies by journalists and scholars. For example, even though duck foie gras accounts for ninety-five percent of the foie gras produced in France and all of the foie gras produced in the United States, many news reports, op-eds, and even some academic articles continue to call it goose liver.

76. According to France's General Association of Maize Growers (Association Générale des Producteurs de Maïs*)*, as of 2008 France produces about fifteen million tons of corn (*maïs*) each year, forty percent of which is grown in the Southwest. Its main use, as in the United States, is as animal feed. Corn was domesticated in Mesoamerica and was first introduced in Europe in the late fifteenth or early sixteenth century, meaning that it is not part of a duck's "natural" diet.

77. I observed both types of gavage during my fieldwork in 2006 and 2007.

78. These numbers also show how "industrial" is a relative concept. Eight hundred to two thousand ducks at a time is a much smaller number than Hudson Valley Foie Gras in upstate New York, which produces twenty thousand livers at a time in a vertically integrated operation. But these gaveurs are considered part of the "industrial" chain in France, because of the way labor is divided and spaced in the supply chain.

79. See https://wcd.coe.int/wcd/ViewDoc.jsp?id=261425 for the full English text of the Standing Committee of the European Convention's

1999 "Recommendation concerning domestic ducks," and https://wcd
.coe.int/wcd/ViewDoc.jsp?id=261543 for the full French text.

80. Worldwide production numbers for 1996, according to the CIFOG report, were France: eighty percent; Hungary: twelve percent; Bulgaria:
four percent; Israel: one percent; Poland: one percent; Others: two percent. In 2005, the French contribution to total worldwide production
was 78.5 percent, dropping to seventy-five percent in 2009.

81. This ratio is up from about sixty-five to seventy percent in the 1960s and
is still growing. Moreover, French consumer demand exceeds what the
nation produces. Processors, wholesalers, and restaurants rely on farms
in Eastern Europe to supplement. Several producers have begun building or financing foie gras farms in China to meet new demand in Asian
markets.

82. Euralis, which owns the Rougié, Bizac, and Montefort labels, is the
largest conglomerate of foie gras and luxury food companies in France
(see www.euralis.fr). It also owns Palmex, a foie gras farm located in
Quebec, and is one of the firms starting foie gras farming in China.

83. For example, manufacturing firms in the Southwest would allegedly
import cheaper, lower-quality livers from Eastern Europe and sell them
as their own, or producers would mix pork fat into foie gras pâtés as a
less-expensive supplement (author interviews).

84. The regulations decree that a product cannot be called solely "foie gras"
if it contains less than ninety-six percent fattened duck or goose liver.
(The other four percent can include flavorings and spices.) Whole fattened duck livers must weigh at least three hundred grams, and fattened
goose livers four hundred grams. The regulations differentiate products
such as "foie gras entier," "bloc de foie gras," "pâté de foie gras," and
"produits au foie gras" (with higher prices for those that include more
whole liver).

85. France has a complicated and variable history of trade-based associations and *filière* networks for skilled workers in various industries, with
associations in the agricultural sector being the most historically prominent. It is also among the least unionized countries in Western Europe.
Schmidt, 1996.

86. Over the last few decades, France has ratified or signed many (but not
all) transnational conventions on mistreatment and cruelty to animals,
including European-level conventions on animal protection. France also
has a large number of animal welfare organizations and charities, in-

cluding the Société Protectrice des Animaux, which has existed for one hundred and fifty years.

87. Religious exemptions are made for ritual kosher and halal animal slaughter practices.

88. See DeSoucey, 2010.

89. Polls conducted by Sofres (a French polling organization) and reported in *Le Monde*. *The Economist* observed that same year, "French politicians have been queuing up to support the right to cultural protectionism" ("France and World Trade: Except Us," *The Economist*, October 16, 1999, 53).

90. Téchoueyres, 2007.

91. Benedict XVI and Seewald, 2002, 79.

92. Mark Caro notes in his book *The Foie Gras Wars* that some Israeli producers moved to Hungary and now export foie gras back to Israel. He quotes Izzy Yanay, the Israeli co-owner of Hudson Valley Foie Gras, decrying this fact: "Who is benefiting? The same operators as before, and labor from Hungary. They didn't save one goddamn duck or goose!" (2009, 38–39).

93. Gille, 2011.

94. This has forced activists to focus on different targets, namely on retail markets. Stores and restaurants in other countries, for example, have removed foie gras after direct pressure from animal rights supporters.

95. Joint answer to Written Questions E-2284/01, E-2285/01, and E-2286/01 given by Mr. Byrne on behalf of the Commission, September 18, 2001. Published in the *Official Journal of the European Communities*, May 16, 2002.

96. Calhoun, 2007.

97. Lévi-Strauss, 1966.

98. Somers, 1994; Holt, 2004.

99. In an arresting study of the theaterlike atmosphere at the open-air produce market in Carpentras, a village in Provence, French sociologist Michelle de la Pradelle (2006) identifies contemporary fictions that build on *terroir* claims as marketing devices at the point of sale.

100. Wagner-Pacifici and Schwartz, 1991.

101. Kowalski, 2011.

102. Nora, 1996.

103. Sutton, 2007.

104. This is especially true given the context of the recent financial crisis, EU-level debates over debt reduction strategies, and the forced imple-

mentation of austerity programs in certain nations. The May 2014 election for seats in the European Parliament offers additional confirmation, as far-right political groups in numerous countries saw victories.

CHAPTER 3. GASTRONATIONALISM ON THE GROUND

1. Lamont, 1992.
2. Appadurai, 1986.
3. Ferguson, 2004.
4. I conducted this research before the 2008–09 economic crisis began making headlines. Since then, national and transnational European politics have realigned the continent's priorities. Still, this story remains relevant because of food and agriculture's continued economic and political importance, and because food politics continue to resonate symbolically for groups engaged in drawing boundary lines around themselves. The 2012 French election, for example, brought out a few other cases of foods being used to indicate belonging and otherness in the country—namely around the existence of halal meat (meat that is suitable for consumption by Muslims) by members and supporters of the right-wing political group Le Front National.
5. My sample was non-random and snowball-based.
6. Barham, 2003; DeSoucey 2010.
7. Pilcher, 1998.
8. Bowen, 2015. See the WTO's explanation of the TRIPS provisions at https://www.wto.org/english/tratop_e/trips_e/gi_background_e.htm.
9. Goody, 1982.
10. Leitch, 2003.
11. Terrio, 2000.
12. Serventi, 2005.
13. Mennell, 1985; Ferguson, 2004.
14. In 1994, for example, French Cultural Minister Jacques Toubon declared the film *Jurassic Park*—which had appeared on almost twenty-five percent of French movie screens the previous year—"a threat to French identity."
15. A *gaveur* at a farm in the Gers region only half-jokingly called duck feces "the petrol of Gers," explaining that they are spread on fields several times a year as fertilizer.
16. A *ferme auberge* is the official classification for a working farm that serves meals, has guest rooms, or both. At the time I was there, the Jau-

mards' *ferme auberge* served afternoon meals on the weekends and did not have accommodations for paid overnight stays.

17. However, use of the term "artisan" is evolving in commercial, even absurd ways. The word graces the marketing materials of nationally and internationally distributed retail products and the menus of restaurants of all shapes and sizes. There are artisan food consulting groups. The meaning is being stretched to an eye-rolling extent. Domino's Pizza now carries an Artisan Pizza line. Starbucks uses the term to brand its breakfast sandwiches, as does the Panera chain for its breads.

18. Trubek, 2008.

19. Anthropologist Michael Herzfeld (2004) criticizes artisans' simultaneous marginality and exemplification as national "tradition"—or commodified folklore in a "global hierarchy of value"—that serves as a double-edged sword for artisans' daily lives and aspirations.

20. For an excellent analysis of how this worked similarly for the case of champagne in the early twentieth century, see Guy, 2003. See also Sahlins, 1989.

21. Heath and Meneley (2007) differentiate these methods as "neo-artisanal" or techne, which they define as legitimated by embodied artisanal skill and craftsmanship, and industrial production, which they call "technoscience."

22. Herzfeld, 2004.

23. Two such films are *Jean de Florette* and *Manon des Sources*, both made by Claude Berri in 1986.

24. Held and McGrew, 2007.

25. Bishop, 1996.

26. Since then, the Confédération Paysanne has worked to represent the interests of small farms on the postindustrial, international stage and has been especially active in European anti–genetic modification campaigns. See Heller, 2013.

27. The action also provoked McDonald's to revamp its operations and rebrand itself as catering to the French public. French McDonald's restaurants source most ingredients from French farmers and hire mainly French employees at every level of management. Takeout restaurants are subject to a 5.5 percent value-added tax as compared to 19.6 percent at sit-down "gastronomic" restaurants, making them appealing to students, pensioners, and other lower income consumers. As of 2007, France was McDonald's second most profitable market after the United States. See Steinberger, 2010.

28. Hewison, 1987.
29. The "invention of tradition" here does not mean that the new meanings and values created by this industry are illegitimate, nor that they do not do real cultural and political work.
30. http://agriculture.gouv.fr/signes-de-qualite-le-label-rouge. For poultry, see http://www.volaillelabelrouge.com/en/home.
31. Both artisanal and industrial foie gras producers in the Southwest can apply for foie gras's PGI designation.
32. Eurobarometer 2014. Available at http://ec.europa.eu/agriculture/survey /index_en.htm. In France as well as the United States, growing concerns about social and environmental sustainability also contribute to the market for artisanal foods. See Dubuisson-Quellier, 2009.
33. See, among others: Terrio, 2000; Boisard, 2003; Paxson, 2012.
34. Shields-Argelès, 2004.
35. Larger foie gras producers also use the language of terroir and tradition to market their products. But in using livers from hundreds to thousands of farms, they need their brands to have a distinct and *unvarying* taste.
36. Without knowing it, this declaration sounded similar to words written in 1998 by Alexandre Lazareff, then-director of the National Council of Culinary Arts: "In France, it has been a long time since we have eaten solely for nourishment; we give to the plate a portion of our souls."
37. This heritage discourse is somewhat paradoxical given that France is a leading player in international bulk agro-food trading and is one of the main beneficiaries of the EU's Common Agricultural Policy (CAP) for agricultural subsidies. Some of the largest food chain corporations in the world are headquartered there.
38. Bessiere, 1996; Long, 2003.
39. In the early twentieth century, reputable presses began publishing gastronomic inventories of regional dishes and guidebooks exalting the foods and restaurants of French regions. The tire company Michelin produced some of these guides, which quickly became famous for their grading system of restaurants and hotels and mold culinary reputations to this day. As Ferguson aptly notes, these texts widened the ranks of the French gastronomic public, or "taste community," and helped turn the culinary field into a world-renowned cultural field.
40. Heller, 1999.
41. Personal interview with French anthropologist Isabelle Téchoueyres, November 2007.

42. Trubek, 2007.
43. Aurier, Fort, and Sirieux, 2005.
44. MacCannell, 1973; Smith, 2006.
45. Kirshenblatt-Gimblett, 1998.
46. In 1991, the French Ministry of Culture registered "le patrimoine culinaire" in *L'Inventaire des monuments de la France*, giving it the same level of recognition as churches and castles and charging its guardianship to the Conseil National des Arts Culinaires (created in 1989 and composed of representatives from five ministries—Culture, Agriculture, Education, Tourism, and Health). After conducting a pilot study of "patrimoine culinaire," CNAC selected one hundred Sites of Taste "which make up our gastronomic history" to encourage tourism to these sites, making them accessible to the public.
47. Wherry, 2008.
48. To an American sensibility, it seems a bit odd that observing slaughter and butchery is considered a desirable vacation activity.
49. Heath and Meneley, 2010.
50. Barham, 2003.
51. Bowen and De Master, 2011.
52. Potter, 2010.
53. This phrase is actually a pun. Going to the market makes it literally "a fat morning," but it also plays with the idiomatic expression to "faire la grasse matinée," meaning to be lazy and sleep in.
54. As of 2011, animal rights groups alleged that only fifteen percent of French foie gras producers had implemented the new rule. The new deadline for removing the cages completely was 2015, after producers petitioned CIFOG for a more gradual implementation.
55. See Meunier, 2005. A popular television show during my tenure in France was a sketch comedy program featuring "conversations" between hand puppets portraying George W. Bush and Rocky Balboa.
56. I was unable to track down the source of these references to Americans pouring French wine in the street. My educated guess is that a popular national French evening news program televised someone doing so to represent the American indignant response to the French government's decision to remove their troops stationed in Iraq.
57. See Mintz, 2003, 27.
58. Winter, 2008; Laachir, 2007.
59. Ducks and geese used for halal foie gras are slaughtered according to the precepts of Islam, with their heads facing Mecca. The Muslim com-

munity in France is estimated at six to seven million people and is seen by consumer product firms as an emerging and profitable market demographic.

60. http://www.actionsita.com/article-14096886.html.

61. http://www.occidentalis.com/blog/index.php/foie-gras-hallal-labeyrie -non-merci.

62. http://www.al-kanz.org/2010/12/06/labeyrie-halal-communique/; http://www.al-kanz.org/2007/11/24/foies-gras-halal-ce-quaffirme -labeyrie/.

63. http://www.actionsita.com/article-14096886.html.

64. It is hard to say whether these boycotts, and threats of boycotts, have significantly affected Labeyrie's sales, due in no small part to the company's size, new shareholding structure, and multiple labels.

65. http://resistancerepublicaine.eu/2013/foie-gras-labeyrie-halal-sinon -rien-par-daniel/.

66. http://www.theguardian.com/world/2010/apr/05/france-muslims-halal -boom.

67. http://www.theweek.co.uk/17471/france-today-tale-halal-foie-gras-and -burkas; http://islamineurope.blogspot.com/2010/01/france-halal-foie -gras-hit.html.

68. http://www.guardian.co.uk/world/2011/jul/19/france-outrage-germany -foie-gras-ban.

69. http://www.just-food.com/news/le-maire-threatens-anuga-boycott -over-foie-gras-ban_id115995.aspx.

70. Bruno Le Maire, letter to Ilse Aigner, Ministry of Agriculture, July 11, 2011.

71. Quoted in Cécile Boutelet and Laetitia Van Eeckhout, "Le foie gras français 'non grata' en Allemagne," *Le Monde*, July 16, 2011.

72. Henry Samuel, "Foie Gras Diplomatic Spat between France and Germany Intensifies," *The Telegraph*, July 28, 2011.

73. Antoine Comiti, letter to Reinhard Schäfers, Ambassador of Germany, Bron Cedex, France, July 11, 2011.

Chapter 4. Foiehibition

1. By pure and funny coincidence, Doug's inspiration for cooking fries in duck fat was a visit to the restaurant in Bordeaux that served as the opening scene to Chapter 3 of this book.

2. Ostensibly the most devoted of fans, those who tattooed Hot Doug's

logo on their bodies, were promised free hot dogs for the life of the business.

3. In 2010, well after the ban had been repealed, Doug and Joe Moore held a reconciliation meeting and, along with an Illinois State Senator, signed a document attesting that the "once menacing hatchet" was "duly and lastingly buried."

4. Johnston and Baumann, 2010.

5. To the surprise and sorrow of fans, Doug Sohn closed Hot Doug's in the fall of 2014 to take a break and go, as he said, "on a sabbatical." Since then, he has been hosting pop-up restaurant events and co-wrote a coffee table book, *Hot Doug's: The Book*, with Kate DeVivo in 2014.

6. Weber, Heinze, and DeSoucey, 2008.

7. Bob, 2002; Berry and Sobieraj, 2013.

8. Kristine Hansen, "And the Ban Goes On: California Still Says No to Foie Gras," *FSR Magazine*, January 28, 2013.

9. Heath and Meneley, 2010.

10. California's statewide ban, passed in 2004, went into effect in 2012 and was repealed in January 2015 by a federal district judge, just three months after the Supreme Court decided not to review the 9th Circuit's decision not to reverse the ban. Several states that did not have foie gras producers had previously passed production—but not consumption—bans.

11. The article's publication was actually delayed a few weeks because of then-fresh coverage of the legal struggle over taking Terri Schiavo, a comatose Florida woman, off life support. According to Mark Caro, his editors wanted to keep the two feeding tube stories separate in readers' minds.

12. In the summer of 2012, after twenty-five years, Chicago chef Charlie Trotter shut the doors of his famed restaurant. The closing announcement, made several months earlier, was reported by national news outlets as bittersweet but not entirely surprising. While Trotter had helped define new American cuisine and make Chicago a city where people cared about food, many claimed he had not kept pace with the edgy culinary world. Perhaps it was a twist of fate that many other now-famous Chicago chefs, his competitors, had once worked in Trotter's kitchen. Nevertheless, rarely does a fine dining restaurant last twenty-five years in a fast-changing and competitive business, and accolades were heaped upon him. Then, to the shock of the culinary community, Charlie Trotter passed away at the age of fifty-four in early November 2013. See his

obituary in the *Chicago Tribune* for a compendium of his myriad accomplishments and significant influence over modern American haute cuisine: Mark Caro, "Charlie Trotter 1959–2013: Chicago's Revolutionary Chef," *Chicago Tribune*, November 5, 2013.

13. "The Chef's Table: Someone's in the Kitchen with the Cooks," *New York Times*, October 27, 1993.

14. Ariane Daguin of D'Artagnan made it her job to find out which farms had given Trotter this impression. Even though he used Hudson Valley Foie Gras at his restaurant, Trotter had declined every invitation from Michael Ginor and Izzy Yanay to visit. He had visited Sonoma Foie Gras in the early 1990s. The photos of Trotter in the *Meat & Game* cookbook were taken at a Canadian foie gras farm. Trotter told Mark Caro that the final farm he had visited used individual confinement cages, indicating it was either in Canada or France because none of the US farms used that cage system.

15. When told about Trotter's response, Tramonto's response was first stunned silence and then "Charlie's in my prayers—that's what you can put in for my comment." See Chapter 1 of *The Foie Gras Wars* (2009) for additional details on this celebrity-chef smackdown and Caro's 2012 five-part biographical series about Charlie Trotter's career in the *Chicago Tribune*. Trotter would not return my phone calls and requests for an interview. I did get to speak with Tramonto and at length with other people who had worked for both chefs.

16. Mark Caro, "Trotter Won't Turn Down the Heat in Foie Gras Flap," *Chicago Tribune*, April 7, 2005.

17. Moore has long been known in the City Council for championing progressive causes, including a 2003 ordinance to oppose a US preemptive strike on Iraq. Rogers Park, his ward, prides itself on residents' diversity, though the neighborhood has also long struggled with crime and poverty.

18. This came on the heels of a citywide ban on smoking at restaurants and bars, also passed by the Health Committee.

19. After the ban was repealed, Trotter told the dining editor for the *Chicago Tribune*, "I was never in favor of the ban to begin with. I was appalled when Joe Moore decided to list my name as an advocate of this point of view. He wanted me to come out and support this thing. I have my own reasons for not serving this product, but don't get me involved in his mess" (reported by Phil Vettel in 2008). He told author Mark Caro, referring to animal rights activists pushing for the ban, "These

people are idiots. Understand my position: I have nothing to do with a group like that" (Caro, 2009, 12).

20. One alderman later switched his vote, making the final count 48–1.

21. Zukin, 1995. It is telling that hip new restaurant districts are often located in former urban industrial zones, such as the meatpacking district in Manhattan, former tobacco warehouses in Durham, North Carolina, and the Near West Side in Chicago.

22. Phil Vettel, "Foie Gras Ban, We Hardly Knew Ye," *Chicago Tribune*, May 16, 2008.

23. Beisel, 1993.

24. Similarly, chef Carrie Nahabedian of independently-owned Naha testified before the Chicago Health Committee that she knew a "considerable (*sic*) amount of chefs" who opposed a ban but were "afraid of the repercussions that their feelings, their views, their opinions will have on their corporations' restaurants." She also entreated the Committee to do more research, asking, "How can you intelligently vote for something if you don't know enough about it?"

25. Monica Davey, "Psst, Want Some Foie Gras?" *New York Times*, August 23, 2006.

26. The owner of one defiant restaurant even said he served lunch to a table of uniformed police officers that day.

27. Illinois Restaurant Association, et al. v. City of Chicago, No. 07–2605 2006. See contrasting law review articles on the constitutionality of the ban: Grant, 2009, and Harrington, 2007.

28. Merry, 1998.

29. I found no evidence about immunity from the state by bribing or otherwise influencing public officials, as is sometimes the case in other illegal markets. Sarat, Constable, Engel, Hans, and Lawrence, 1998.

30. Matza and Sykes, 1961.

31. Don Babwin, "Chefs Duck Ban on Foie Gras in Chicago," syndicated Associated Press story, January 14, 2007.

32. A year later, this activist was sentenced to seven months in state prison. Jezebel's owner told the local newspaper at the time that despite continued protests, his business actually tripled and that people were "ordering foie gras even when they would not normally." See Amy Smith, "Foie Gras Foe Foiled!" *Austin Chronicle*, September 14, 2007. In July 2010, the restaurant was destroyed in an early-morning fire that caused $200,000 in damages. (No one was injured, and investigators were not able to determine the cause.)

33. Reported in Mick Dumke, "Council Follies: When Activists Attack," *Chicago Reader*, June 22, 2007.
34. Vettel, "Foie Gras Ban, We Hardly Knew Ye."
35. Tunney was himself a restaurant owner (of the city's Ann Sather chain) and one of two openly gay aldermen on the City Council.
36. It had been moved there from the Health Committee in May 2007 through an obscure parliamentary procedure by alderman Ed Burke, the Council's longest-serving and most powerful member.
37. Vettel, "Foie Gras Ban, We Hardly Knew Ye"; Fran Spielman, "City Repeals Foie Gras Ban," *Chicago Sun-Times*, May 15, 2008.
38. Phil Vettel, "Foie Gras Ban 'Victim' Doug Sohn Happy the 'Absurd' Law is History," *Chicago Tribune*, May 14, 2008.
39. Rohlinger, 2002.
40. Lakoff, 2006.
41. Kamp, 2006; Naccarato and LeBesco. 2012.
42. Wilde, 2004.
43. Politicians and regulators at all levels of government limit consumer choices all the time; without rules and standards, consumption would be risky and potentially even dangerous.
44. Of course, many conservative politicians defend deregulation as better serving the consumer interest.
45. It is important to note that overall coordination and enforcement efforts for safety regulation in the United States—at national, state, city, and local levels—are lacking at almost every stage of the food system, from licensing and certification to regularized health, sanitation, and labor inspections. See Nestle, 2010.
46. Lavin, 2013.
47. Bourdieu, 1984.
48. Veblen, 1899; Goody, 1982; Warde, 1997; Belasco and Scranton, 2002.
49. Beisel, 1993.
50. Cohen, 2003; Jacobs, 2005.
51. Socially responsible investing, for example, is now a multi-trillion-dollar business.
52. Johnston, 2008. Some scholars, such as Julie Guthman (2011), argue that labels such as "organic" and "Fair Trade" are actually harmful because they make consumers, and not governments, responsible for policing corporations and agricultural practices. In the growing arena of sustainability research, analysts tend to view this emphasis on consumer re-

sponsibility as too soft a path to have a meaningful impact or lead to transformative outcomes.

53. Nestle, 2010.

54. Guthman, 2011; Biltekoff, 2013.

55. In his expansive testimony before the City Council's Health Committee, Altenberg also pushed for the Council to "take on—and the state should take on—at an even larger level, the whole concept of the factory farm and the inhumanity that's happening with other animals beyond ducks and foie gras." He later told me that this was "not just for show" but represented his "true feelings."

56. Callero, 2009.

57. Vettel, "Foie Gras Ban, We Hardly Knew Ye."

58. Gusfield, 1986.

59. Douglas and Isherwood, 1979, 37.

60. "Fat Geese, Fatter Lawyers," *The Economist*, May 20, 2006, 37.

61. Monica Davey, "Defying Law, a Foie Gras Feast in Chicago," *New York Times*, August 23, 2006.

62. Vettel, "Foie Gras Ban, We Hardly Knew Ye."

63. In August 2013, the reviewing website Yelp.com mentioned 122 different restaurants in Chicago (not including the suburbs) where users had eaten foie gras. For avant-garde foodies and cooks interested in new trends such as fermentation, foraging, and snout-to-tail charcuterie, however, foie gras is already considered passé. Sociological thinkers back to Georg Simmel have explained how elites reject fashions that have been adapted by the masses and search for something new, so that the evolution of style and what is considered hip never ends.

CHAPTER 5. THE PARADOX OF PERSPECTIVE

1. See, for example, Sarah DiGregorio, "Is Foie Gras Torture?" *The Village Voice*, February 17, 2009; J. Kenji López-Alt, "The Physiology of Foie Gras: Why Foie Gras is Not Unethical," Serious Eats, http://www .seriouseats.com/2010/12/the-physiology-of-foie-why-foie-gras-is-not -u.html, December 16, 2010.

2. The property was previously a chicken farm; HVFG had yet to fully renovate some of the buildings.

3. See Gray, 2013, 49–50; Bob Herbert, "State of Shame," *New York Times*, June 8, 2009; Steven Greenhouse, "No Days Off at Foie Gras Farm;

Workers Complain, but Owner Cites Stress on Ducks," *New York Times*, April 2, 2001.

4. This similarity in advice also elicits provocative points raised in the last decade by behavioral psychologists, who have suggested that our moral judgments derive as much, if not more, from gut feelings as from deliberative reasoning. See Haidt, 2001; Greene, 2013.

5. Nagel, 1974.

6. When I asked, Izzy told me that after being sexed, Hudson Valley's female ducklings are exported to another country, typically Trinidad, where they are raised for meat. He told me that visitors often ask this question. This contradicts animal rights activists' claims that the females are euthanized after the birds are sexed (which is what happens at French hatcheries).

7. Whether they got the machine working or not, it is my understanding that as of this writing, in 2015, HVFG continues to use the more "artisanal" production methods and not pneumatic feeding machines.

8. The American Veterinary Medical Association, an ostensibly objective source, refused to take a position on foie gras, which problematizes the idea of scientific validation for both sides. This lack of side-taking may be related to caution about endorsing any anti-agricultural position. Producers, however, interpreted this decision in their favor.

9. The American Legal Defense Fund filed a thematically similar lawsuit against the United States Department of Agriculture in 2012, seeking a declaration that foie gras is an adulterated, diseased food product that is dangerous to consumer health. This lawsuit was dismissed in 2013 by a California federal judge for lack of standing, a decision that was upheld in a New York appellate court in 2014.

10. Stress levels in foie gras ducks have been assessed by measuring levels of an adrenal hormone called corticosterone. French studies on the physiological effects of gavage, regularly cited by foie gras producers, suggest that wild ducks with babies are under more stress than the ducks in gavage and that the ducks become less stressed as they become more familiar with a human feeder. This is the main reason that only one feeder is assigned to a number of ducks for the entire length of the gavage period at Hudson Valley Foie Gras and elsewhere. Guémené and Guy, 2004; Guémené, Guy, Noirault, Garreau-Mills, Gouraud, and Faure, 2001.

11. Some hunters have reported identifying "wild foie gras"—occasional larger and fattier livers among wild ducks and geese. See http://www

.theatlantic.com/health/archive/2010/11/ethical-foie-gras-no-force
-feeding-necessary/66261/

12. See for example, Mannheim, 1985; Haraway, 1988.

13. Prasad, Perrin, Bezila, Hoffman, Kindleberger, Manturuk, and Smith Powers, 2009.

14. American biological research on foie gras is quite limited; the enormous majority of studies pertaining to farm animals in the United States deal with cows, pigs, sheep, chickens, and turkeys—not ducks or geese. In France, agricultural research is conducted through the French National Institute for Agricultural Research, or INRA, which has a compelling interest in safeguarding the French foie gras market and has been called an "industry accomplice" by French animal rights group Stop Gavage (renamed L214).

15. Prasad et al. 2009; Nyhan, Reifler, Richey, and Freed, 2014.

16. Nyhan and Reifler, 2010.

17. Griswold, 1994; Emirbayer, 1997.

18. Broadly speaking, this framework held sway, I found, in France as well as the United States. While a detailed comparison to France is not this chapter's central focus, I point out a few places that I think make these paradoxes all the more compelling.

19. Gusfield, 1986.

20. Rollin, 1990.

21. Jasper and Nelkin, 1992.

22. Marian Burros, "Veal to Love, without the Guilt," *New York Times*, April 18, 2007.

23. PETA began buying stock in McDonald's and attending shareholder meetings in 1998. The HSUS currently owns enough stock in Tyson chicken, Wal-Mart, McDonald's, and Smithfield's to have the power to introduce shareholder resolutions.

24. Garner, 2005.

25. Kim Severson, "Bringing Moos and Oinks into the Food Debate," *New York Times*, July 25, 2007.

26. See, among others, Bennett, Anderson, and Blaney, 2002; Harper and Makatouni, 2002; *Consumer Attitudes About Animal Welfare: 2004 National Public Opinion Survey*. Boston: Market Directions, 2004.

27. Franklin, Tranter, and White, 2001.

28. Saguy and Stuart, 2008.

29. Video camera manufacturers such as Sony and Panasonic first launched

their lines of digital video recorders in 1995. These recorders became standard in low-budget filmmaking, activism, and citizen journalism.

30. Jasper, 1998.

31. http://www.gallup.com/poll/156215/consider-themselves-vegetarians .aspx.

32. Robert Kenner, Elise Pearlstein, Kim Roberts, Eric Schlosser, Michael Pollan, and Mark Adler, *Food, Inc.* (Los Angeles: Magnolia Home Entertainment, 2009).

33. An economic development report for New York State valued the foie gras industry in 2004 at $17.5 million, chump change in the multi-trillion-dollar food industry. See Shepstone Management Company, "The Economic Importance of the New York State Foie Gras Industry," prepared for Sullivan County Foie Gras Producers, 2004.

34. According to Ascione (1993, 228), animal cruelty is "socially unacceptable behavior that intentionally causes unnecessary pain, suffering, or distress to and/or death of an animal." Another sympathetic movement analyst defines cruelty as "any act that contributes to the pain or death of an animal or that otherwise threatens the welfare of an animal" (Agnew, 1998, 179). Others suggest that most animal suffering is not the result of intentional cruelty but by regular practices in the food, fashion, and scientific industries. See Rollin, 1981.

35. Kahneman, 2011.

36. John Hubbell, "Foie Gras Flap Spreads—Bill Would Ban Duck Dish," *San Francisco Chronicle*, February 10, 2004.

37. For additional examples, see Chapter 2, "The Importance of Being Cute," of Herzog, 2010.

38. When I asked activists in interviews if they thought there was a humane way to produce a chicken for food, every one of them said no.

39. Kuh, 2001.

40. http://chronicle.nytlabs.com/?keyword=foie%20gras.

41. Daguin and de Ravel, 1988; Ginor, Davis, Coe and Ziegelman, 1999.

42. Kamp, 2006, xv.

43. Schlosser, 2001; Pollan, 2006; Kingsolver, Hopp, and Kingsolver, 2007; Foer, 2009.

44. Also see B. R. Myers's diatribe against gourmet food culture, "The Moral Crusade Against Foodies," *The Atlantic*, March 2011.

45. Johnston and Goodman, 2015.

46. Beriss and Sutton, 2007.

47. Ruhlman, 2007; Rousseau, 2012. See also Mario Batali and Bill Telepan, "Fracking vs. Food: N.Y.'s Choice," *New York Daily News*, May 30, 2013.

48. Rousseau, 2012. See also Hollows and Jones, 2010.

49. It is a popular misconception that white kitchen jackets are lined with gold. Most restaurant cooking pays relatively little, and it is physically demanding work that requires long hours, stress, and personal sacrifice. See Fine, 1996.

50. Shields-Argeles, 2004.

51. Veblen, 1899; Schor, 1998.

52. Benzecry, 2011.

53. Saguy, 2013.

54. A comparison to this in France is a prohibition, established in 1999, on eating ortolan, the tiny songbird whose popularity among gastronomes—who traditionally drowned it in Armagnac, plucked, roasted, and ate it whole with napkins covering their heads—led to its near extinction.

55. Fletcher, 2010.

56. United States Department of Agriculture 2007 Census of Agriculture.

57. See the Agricultural Marketing Resource Center at www.agmrc.org for additional information.

58. Caro, 2009, 115–16.

59. Bourdieu and Thompson, 1991.

60. See Caro, 2009, for the entirety of this quote. See also Lindsay Hicks, "Stuck on Duck," *Philadelphia City Paper*, June 1–7, 2006.

61. For the ordinance to be repealed, it first had to be removed from the Means Committee and brought to the Council floor for a general vote. This is what was meant by "discharge."

62. The legislation has been stalled in part because Michael Benjamin, the New York State assemblyman who had originally proposed the bill banning foie gras production, withdrew his name from it a year before Avella's proposition. Benjamin was quoted by Bloomberg News at the time as saying "I've had a change of heart" after visiting Hudson Valley Foie Gras and seeing the production process firsthand.

63. This is related to social movement scholarship on political opportunity structures, which has demonstrated how factors such as the presence or absence of political allies, or shifts in the balance of political power, are significant in shaping social movement activity. See Gamson and Meyer, 1996.

64. Caro, 2009, 91.

65. Caro, 2009, 103–04.
66. Sarah DiGregorio, "Is Foie Gras Torture?" *The Village Voice*, February 17, 2009.
67. Henry Goldman, "Sponsor of New York Foie Gras Ban Changes His Mind," Bloomberg.com, June 11, 2008.
68. http://www.brownstoner.com/brownstoner/archives/2008/06 /wednesday_food_78.php.
69. Livers are graded and sold as A-grade, B-grade, and C-grade, with A-grade fetching higher prices. Hudson Valley Foie Gras pays feeders bonuses for the relative number of A-grade livers they produce in each force-feeding cycle.
70. Schwalbe, Holden, Schrock, Godwin, Thompson, and Wolkomir, 2000.
71. Jasper Copping and Graham Keeley, "'Ethical' Foie Gras from Naturally Greedy Geese," *The Telegraph*, February 18, 2007.
72. http://www.gourmettraveller.com.au/recipes/food-news-features/2010/7 /a-good-feed-ethical-foie-gras/.
73. Juliet Glass, "Foie Gras Makers Struggle to Please Critics and Chefs," *New York Times*, April 25, 2007.
74. Among other odd coincidences I found while researching this book, Dan Barber's father and Hot Doug Sohn's father were college roommates, and Dan and Doug knew each other growing up.
75. http://www.ted.com/talks/dan_barber_s_surprising_foie_gras_parable .html.
76. http://www.thisamericanlife.org/radio-archives/episode/452/poultry -slam-2011.
77. Anna Lipin, "The Gras is Always Greener," *Lucky Peach* 16 (2015), 18–19.
78. Daniel Zwerdling, "A View to a Kill." *Gourmet Magazine* June 2007, http://www.gourmet.com/magazine/2000s/2007/06/aviewtoakill.html.
79. This is perhaps why the French fight against McDonald's was so reactionary at first, when there were only a few restaurants scattered throughout the country, and why such a fight would be laughable now. In fact, as of 2011, France is McDonald's second-largest market after the United States.
80. Jasper and Nelkin, 1992; Jasper, 1999.
81. Francione and Garner, 2010.
82. Social psychologists refer to this as "reactance."
83. Marian Burros, "Organizing for an Indelicate Fight," *New York Times*, May 3, 2006.
84. Rao, Monin, and Durand, 2003.

85. Jenn Louis, "Foie Gras vs. Factory-Farmed Chicken: Which Will Make a Greater Difference?," *Huffington Post*, February 27, 2014.

86. Michael Pollan, "Profiles in Courage on Animal Welfare," *New York Times*, May 29, 2006.

87. Jesse McKinley, "Waddling Into the Sunset," *New York Times*, June 4, 2012.

88. Mackenzie Carpenter, "Foie Gras Controversy Ruffles Local Chefs' Feathers," *Pittsburgh Post-Gazette*, June 22, 2006.

89. Amy Smith, "Foie Gras Foe Foiled!," *Austin Chronicle*, September 14. 2007.

90. Don Markus, "In a Lather over Liver," *Baltimore Sun*, March 24, 2009.

91. Most of the videos shown at US protests use footage that was shot in France. This is apparent because they show ducks in individual cages, but all the farms in the United States use group pens.

92. http://articles.philly.com/2007–07–13/news/24995117_1_foie-gras -bastille-day-puppies. See also Lisa McLaughlin, "Fight for Your Right to Pâté," *Time Magazine*, October 9, 2007; http://content.time.com /time/arts/article/0,8599,1669732,00.html.

93. Caro, 2009, 185.

94. There are fascinating parallels here regarding claims of expertise, authority, and legitimacy to scientists and medical researchers targeted by anti-vivisection activist groups.

95. http://www.grubstreet.com/2010/03/ducking_controversy_telepan_re .html.

96. This is not limited, of course, to foie gras, nor does it affect Americans alone. In May 2014, the World Trade Organization upheld a European ban on importing seal fur, blubber, and meat, originally imposed to uphold "public morals." Critics of the ban from seal-hunting countries, namely Canada and Norway, immediately tried to raise a slippery-slope argument, that the ban could set an unwelcome precedent to similar prohibitions on other animal products that are argued to be raised in inhumane conditions.

97. Burros. "Organizing for an Indelicate Fight."

98. California is experiencing this in regard to its new state standards for egg production and pushback from egg producers in other states who must abide by these standards to sell in California. See www.nytimes .com/2014/03/09/opinion/sunday/californias-smart-egg-rules.html.

99. Gusfield, 1996; Nelson, 1984.

100. Lamont, 1992.

101. Bearman and Parigi, 2004.
102. Miller, 2006.
103. Koopmans, 2004.

Chapter 6. Conclusion

1. Sections §25980–§25984 of the Health & Safety Code (the "Bird Feeding Law").
2. Jesse McKinley, "California Chefs to Wield Their Spatulas in Fight over Foie Gras Ban," *New York Times*, April 30, 2012.
3. http://www.eater.com/2012/7/10/6566489/california-restaurants-find-loopholes-in-foie-gras-ban.
4. http://sfist.com/2012/07/26/presidio_social_club_pulls_foie_gra.php.
5. Maura Dolan, "California's Foie Gras Ban is Upheld by Appeals Court," *Los Angeles Times*, August 30, 2013.
6. Two months prior, even though the ban was on its way to implementation, the Animal Legal Defense Fund and several other animal rights organizations filed suit against the United States Department of Agriculture (USDA) in United States District Court in the Central District of California to attempt to have foie gras declared an "adulterated product" and "pathologically diseased" and thus "unfit for human consumption"—something the USDA has the authority to regulate. This was not a new argument, nor was it a distinctly new legal move. In 2009, the USDA denied a similar petition that the same plaintiffs had filed two years before. Here, the Animal Legal Defense Fund claimed the previous two-page denial was "insufficient" because it "did not cite" studies to support its determination and "failed to explain" the ruling. The newer lawsuit did not prove successful either.
7. Association des Éleveurs de Canards et d'Oies du Quebec, HVFG LLC, and Hot's Restaurant Group v. Kamala D. Harris, Attorney General. Case No. 2:12-cv-5735-SVW-RZ. Filed January 7, 2015.
8. Kurtis Alexander and Paolo Lucchesi, "California Foie Gras Ban Struck down by Judge, Delighting Chefs," *San Francisco Chronicle*, January 7, 2015.
9. http://gawker.com/foie-gras-is-for-assholes-1678213499.
10. In 2012, for instance, People for the Ethical Treatment of Animals (PETA) wrote a public letter to the publisher of the Michelin Guide, asking the organization to cease giving stars to restaurants that serve either dish.

11. Bettina Wassener, "China Says No More Shark Fin Soup at State Banquets," *New York Times*, July 3, 2012.

12. Patricia Leigh Brown, "Soup Without Fins? Some Californians Simmer," *New York Times*, March 5, 2011.

13. Michael Evans, "Shark Fin Soup Sales Plunge in China," Al Jazeera English, April 10, 2014.

14. Michael Paterniti, The Last Meal," *Esquire*, May 1998; http://www.esquire.com/news-politics/a4642/the-last-meal-0598/.

15. Critics say the ban has been flouted and poorly enforced. In all my time in France, however, I never once saw ortolan served or offered. When I inquired about it, most everyone said that it was a dead tradition. Kim Willsher, "Ortolan's Slaughter Ignored by French Authorities, Claim Conservationists," *The Guardian*, September 9, 2013.

16. Bonnie Tsui, "Souring on Shark Fin Soup," *New York Times*, June 29, 2013.

17. Arluke and Sanders, 1996.

18. Counihan and Van Esterik, 2013; Wilk, 1999.

19. Boltanski and Thévenot. 2006; Lakoff, 2006.

20. Douglas and Wildavsky (1982), for instance, write that people in every culture have to be fearful of something. For some, it is gods and monsters. For others, it is air pollution and pesticides. Neither fear is wrong, but neither is strictly rational either. And in both cases, the risks and the capacity to know those risks are constructed by the cultures themselves.

21. Hochschild, 2006.

22. Friedland and Thomas, 1974.

23. Friedman, 1996.

24. Jasper, 1997, 264.

25. Guthman, 2011; Besky, 2014; Bowen, 2015.

26. Gusfield, 1981; Baumgartner and Morris, 2008.

27. Laudan, 2013.

28. Kamp, 2006; Pearlman, 2013.

29. Aronczyk, 2013.

30. In May 2014, elections were held across Europe for seats in the European Parliament. France, like many other countries, saw an unexpectedly large turnout for the Front Nationale, the right-wing political group led by Marine Le Pen, daughter of Jean-Marie Le Pen. This election's relationship to foie gras production and contestation is indirect at best, but it suggests that any attempt by European politicians to forbid

the production of foie gras in France is not going to succeed without a major fight.

31. Reported in Kcrana Todorov, "Judge Rejects Request to Dismiss Foie Gras Lawsuit," *Napa Valley Register*, July 10, 2013.

32. If anti–foie gras activism is ultimately legally successful at shutting down the few producers in the United States, distributors will get foie gras from Canadian producers (several of which are subsidiaries of French companies), which use individual cages for *gavage*, or from China, which is quickly becoming a large foie gras supplier for the growing Asian market. Consequently, removing foie gras producers from the US market may negatively affect the overall welfare of foie gras ducks raised for American consumption.

BIBLIOGRAPHY

Agnew, Robert. 1998. "The Causes of Animal Abuse: A Social-Psychological Analysis." *Theoretical Criminology* 2 (2): 177–209.

Almeling, Rene. 2011. *Sex Cells: The Medical Market for Eggs and Sperm.* Berkeley: University of California Press.

Anderson, Benedict. 1991. *Imagined Communities: Reflections on the Origin and Spread of Nationalism.* New York: Verso.

Appadurai, Arjun. 1981. "Gastro-Politics in Hindu South Asia." *American Ethnologist* 8 (3): 494–511.

———. 1986. *The Social Life of Things: Commodities in Cultural Perspective.* Cambridge, UK: Cambridge University Press.

Arluke, Arnold, and Clinton Sanders. 1996. *Regarding Animals.* Philadelphia: Temple University Press.

Aronczyk, Melissa. 2013. *Branding the Nation: The Global Business of National Identity.* New York: Oxford University Press.

Ascione, Frank R. 1993. "Children Who Are Cruel to Animals: A Review of Research and Implications for Developmental Psychopathology." *Anthrozoös* 6 (4): 226–47.

Aurier, P., F. Fort, and L. Sirieux. 2005. "Exploring Terroir Product Meanings for the Consumer." Anthropology of Food. http://aof.revues.org /index187.html.

Bandelj, Nina, and Frederick F. Wherry, eds. 2011. *The Cultural Wealth of Nations.* Palo Alto, CA: Stanford University Press.

Barham, Elizabeth. 2003. "Translating Terroir: The Global Challenge of French AOC Labeling." *Journal of Rural Studies* 19 (1): 127–38.

Barr, Ann, and Paul Levy. 1984. *The Official Foodie Handbook.* New York: Timbre Books.

Baumgartner, Frank R., and Bryan D. Jones. (1993) 2009. *Agendas and Instability in American Politics.* 2nd ed. Chicago: University of Chicago Press.

Baumgartner, Jody C., and Jonathan S. Morris, eds. 2008. *Laughing Matters: Humor and American Politics in the Media Age.* New York: Routledge.

Bearman, Peter, and Paolo Parigi. 2004. "Cloning Headless Frogs and Other Important Matters: Conversation Topics and Network Structure." *Social Forces* 83 (2): 535–57.

Beisel, Nicola. 1992. "Constructing a Shifting Moral Boundary: Literature and Obscenity in Nineteenth-Century America." In Lamont and Fournier 1992, 104–28.

———. 1993. "Morals versus Art: Censorship, the Politics of Interpretation, and the Victorian Nude." *American Sociological Review* 58 (2): 145–62.

———. 1997. *Imperiled Innocents: Anthony Comstock and Family Reproduction in Victorian America.* Princeton, NJ: Princeton University Press.

Belasco, Warren, and Philip Scranton, eds. 2002. *Food Nations: Selling Taste in Consumer Societies.* New York: Routledge.

Bell, David. 2003. *The Cult of the Nation in France: Inventing Nationalism, 1680–1800.* Cambridge, MA: Harvard University Press.

Bendix, Regina. 1997. *In Search of Authenticity: The Formation of Folklore Studies.* Madison, WI: University of Wisconsin Press.

Benedict XVI, Pope, and Peter Seewald. 2002. *God and the World: Believing and Living in Our Time.* San Francisco: Ignatius Press.

Bennett, Richard M., Johann Anderson, and Ralph J.P. Blaney. 2002. "Moral Intensity and Willingness to Pay Concerning Farm Animal Welfare Issues and the Implications for Agricultural Policy." *Journal of Agricultural and Environmental Ethics* 15 (2): 187–202.

Benzecry, Claudio E. 2011. *The Opera Fanatic: Ethnography of an Obsession.* Chicago: University of Chicago Press.

Berezin, Mabel. 2007. "Revisiting the French National Front." *Journal of Contemporary Ethnography* 36 (2): 129–46.

———. 2009. *Illiberal Politics in Neoliberal Times: Culture, Security and Populism in the New Europe.* Cambridge, UK: Cambridge University Press.

Berezin, Mabel, and Martin Schain, eds. 2003. *Europe without Borders: Remapping Territory, Citizenship, and Identity in a Transnational Age.* Baltimore: Johns Hopkins University Press.

Beriss, David, and David E. Sutton, eds. 2007. *The Restaurants Book: Ethnographies of Where We Eat.* New York: Berg.

Berry, Jeffrey M., and Sarah Sobieraj. 2013. *The Outrage Industry: Political*

Opinion Media and the New Incivility. New York: Oxford University Press.

Besky, Sarah. 2014. *The Darjeeling Distinction: Labor and Justice on Fair-trade Tea Plantations in India*. Berkeley: University of California Press.

Bessière, Jacinthe. 1996. *Patrimoine culinaire et tourisme rural*. Paris: Tourisme en Espace Rural.

Billig, Michael. 1995. *Banal Nationalism*. London: Sage.

Biltekoff, Charlotte. 2013. *Eating Right in America: The Cultural Politics of Food and Health*. Durham, NC: Duke University Press.

Bishop, Thomas. 1996. "France and the Need for Cultural Exception." *New York University Journal of International Law and Politics* 29 (1–2): 187–92.

Bob, Clifford. 2002. "Merchants of Morality." *Foreign Policy* 129: 36–45.

Boisard, Pierre. 2003. *Camembert: A National Myth*. Translated by R. Miller. Berkeley: University of California Press.

Boltanski, Luc, and Laurent Thévenot. 2006. *On Justification: Economies of Worth*. Princeton, NJ: Princeton University Press.

Bourdieu, Pierre. 1984. *Distinction: A Social Critique of the Judgment of Taste*. Translated by R. Nice. Cambridge, MA: Harvard University Press.

Bourdieu, Pierre, and John B. Thompson. 1991. *Language and Symbolic Power*. Cambridge, MA: Harvard University Press.

Bowen, Sarah. 2015. *Divided Spirits: Tequila, Mezcal, and the Politics of Production*. Berkeley: University of California Press.

Bowen, Sarah, and Kathryn De Master. 2011. "New Rural Livelihoods or Museums of Production? Quality Food Initiatives in Practice." *Journal of Rural Studies* 27: 73–82.

Bronner, Simon J. 2008. *Killing Tradition: Inside Hunting and Animal Rights Controversies*. Lexington, KY: University Press of Kentucky.

Brown, Linda K., and Kay Mussell. 1984. *Ethnic and Regional Foodways in the United States: The Performance of Group Identity*. Knoxville, TN: University of Tennessee Press.

Brubaker, Rogers. 1996. *Nationalism Reframed: Nationhood and the National Question in the New Europe*. Cambridge, UK: Cambridge University Press.

Calhoun, Craig J. 2007. *Nations Matter: Culture, History, and the Cosmopolitan Dream*. New York: Routledge.

Callero, Peter L. 2009. *The Myth of Individualism: How Social Forces Shape Our Lives*. Lanham, MD: Rowman & Littlefield.

Caro, Mark. 2009. *The Foie Gras Wars*. New York: Simon & Schuster.

Cavanaugh, Jillian R., and Shalini Shankar. 2014. "Producing Authenticity in

Global Capitalism: Language, Materiality, and Value." *American Anthropologist* 116 (1): 51–64.

Cerulo, Karen A. 1995. *Identity Designs: The Sights and Sounds of a Nation.* New Brunswick, NJ: Rutgers University Press.

Chan, Cheris. 2012. *Marketing Death: Culture and the Making of a Life Insurance Market in China.* New York: Oxford University Press.

Cohen, Lizabeth. 2003. *A Consumers' Republic: The Politics of Mass Consumption in Postwar America.* New York: Alfred A. Knopf.

Combret, Henri. 2004. *Foie gras tentations.* Escout, France: Osolasba.

Coquart, Dominique, and Jean Pilleboue. 2000. "Le foie gras: Un patrimoine régional?" In *Campagnes de tous nos désirs: Patrimoines et nouveaux usages sociaux,* edited by M. Rautenberg, A. Micoud, L. Bérard and P. Marchenay. Paris: Éditions de la Maison des Sciences de l'Homme.

Counihan, Carole, and Penny Van Esterik. (1997) 2013. *Food and Culture: A Reader.* 2nd ed. New York: Routledge.

Croucher, Sheila. 2003. "Perpetual Imagining: Nationhood in a Global Era." *International Studies Review* 5 (1): 1–24.

Curtis, Valerie. 2013. *Don't Look, Don't Touch: The Science behind Revulsion.* New York: Oxford University Press.

Daguin, André, and Anne de Ravel. 1988. *Foie Gras, Magret, and Other Good Food from Gascony.* New York: Random House.

Davidson, Alan. 1999. *The Oxford Companion to Food.* Oxford, UK: Oxford University Press.

DeSoucey, Michaela. 2010. "Gastronationalism: Food Traditions and Authenticity Politics in the European Union." *American Sociological Review* 75 (3): 432–55.

Di Leonardo, Micaela. 1984. *The Varieties of Ethnic Experience: Kinship, Class, and Gender among California Italian-Americans.* Ithaca, NY: Cornell University Press.

DiMaggio, Paul. 1987. "Classification in Art." *American Sociological Review* 52 (4): 440–55.

———. 1988. "Interest and Agency in Institutional Theory." In *Institutional Patterns and Organizations,* edited by L. Zucker. Cambridge, MA: Ballinger.

———. 1997. "Culture and Cognition." *Annual Review of Sociology* 23: 263–87.

Dobransky, Kerry, and Gary Alan Fine. 2006. "The Native in the Garden: Floral Politics and Cultural Entrepreneurs." *Sociological Forum* 21 (4): 559–85.

Douglas, Mary. 1966. *Purity and Danger: An Analysis of the Concepts of Pollution and Taboo.* London: Routledge.

———, ed. 1984. *Food in the Social Order: Studies of Food and Festivities in Three American Communities.* New York: Russell Sage Foundation.

Douglas, Mary, and Baron C. Isherwood. 1979. *The World of Goods: Towards an Anthropology of Consumption.* New York: Basic Books.

Douglas, Mary, and Aaron Wildavsky. 1982. *Risk and Culture: An Essay on the Selection of Technical and Environmental Dangers.* Berkeley: University of California Press.

Dubarry, Pierre. 2004. *Petit traité gourmand de l'oie & du foie gras.* Saint-Remy-de-Provence, France: Equinoxe.

Dubuisson-Quellier, Sophie. 2009. *La consommation engagée.* Paris: Les Presses de Sciences Po.

———. 2013. "A Market Mediation Strategy: How Social Movements Seek to Change Firms' Practices by Promoting New Principles of Product Valuation." *Organization Studies* 34 (5–6): 683–703.

DuPuis, E. Melanie. 2002. *Nature's Perfect Food: How Milk Became America's Drink.* New York: New York University Press.

Elder, Charles D., and Roger W. Cobb. 1983. *The Political Uses of Symbols.* New York: Longman.

Elias, Megan. 2011. "The Meaning of Gourmet." Gourmet Magazine Online. Accessed September 21, 2011.

Emirbayer, Mustafa. 1997. "Manifesto for a Relational Sociology." *American Journal of Sociology* 103 (2): 281–317.

Ferguson, Priscilla Parkhurst. 1998. "A Cultural Field in the Making: Gastronomy in 19th-Century France." *American Journal of Sociology* 104 (3): 597–641.

———. 2004. *Accounting for Taste: The Triumph of French Cuisine.* Chicago: University of Chicago Press.

———. 2014. *Word of Mouth: What We Talk About When We Talk About Food.* Berkeley: University of California Press.

Fine, Gary Alan. 1996. *Kitchens: The Culture of Restaurant Work.* Berkeley: University of California Press.

———. 2001. *Difficult Reputations: Collective Memories of the Evil, Inept, and Controversial.* Chicago: University of Chicago Press.

———. 2003. "Crafting Authenticity: The Validation of Identity in Self-Taught Art." *Theory and Society* 32 (2): 153–81.

———. 2004. *Everyday Genius: Self-Taught Art and the Culture of Authenticity.* Chicago: University of Chicago Press.

Fletcher, Nichola. 2010. *Caviar: A Global History.* Chicago: Reaktion Books.

Foer, Jonathan Safran. 2009. *Eating Animals*. New York: Little, Brown and Co.

Fourcade, Marion, and Kieran Healy. 2007. "Moral Views of Market Society." *Annual Review of Sociology* 33: 285–311.

Fourcade-Gourinchas, Marion, and Sarah Babb. 2002. "The Rebirth of the Liberal Creed: Paths to Neoliberalism in Four Countries." *American Journal of Sociology* 108 (3): 533–73.

Francione, Gary L., and Robert Garner. 2010. *The Animal Rights Debate: Abolition or Regulation?* New York: Columbia University Press.

Franklin, Adrian, Bruce Tranter, and Robert White. 2001. "Explaining Support for Animal Rights: A Comparison of Two Recent Approaches to Humans, Nonhuman Animals, and Postmodernity." *Society & Animals* 9 (2): 127–44.

Friedland, William H, and Robert J. Thomas. 1974. "Paradoxes of Agricultural Unionism in California." *Society* 11 (4): 54–62.

Friedman, Monroe. 1996. "A Positive Approach to Organized Consumer Action: The 'Buycott' as an Alternative to the Boycott." *Journal of Consumer Policy* 19 (4): 439–51.

Furlough, Ellen. 1998. "Making Mass Vacations: Tourism and Consumer Culture in France, 1930s to 1970s." *Comparative Studies in Society and History* 40 (2): 247–86.

Gabaccia, Donna R. 1998. *We Are What We Eat: Ethnic Food and the Making of Americans*. Cambridge, MA: Harvard University Press.

Gamson, William, and David S. Meyer. 1996. "The Framing of Political Opportunity." In *Comparative Perspectives on Social Movements*, edited by D. McAdam, J. D. McCarthy, and M. N. Zald. Cambridge, UK: Cambridge University Press.

Garner, Robert. 2005. *Animal Ethics*. Cambridge, MA: Polity.

Giacosa, Ilaria G. 1992. *A Taste of Ancient Rome*. Chicago: University of Chicago Press.

Gille, Zsuzsa. 2011. "The Hungarian Foie Gras Boycott." *East European Politics & Societies* 25 (1): 114–28.

Ginor, Michael A., Mitchell Davis, Andrew Coe, and Jane Ziegelman. 1999. *Foie Gras: A Passion*. New York: Wiley.

Goodman, David. 2002. "Rethinking Food Production-Consumption: Integrative Perspectives." *Sociologia Ruralis* 42 (4): 271–80.

Goody, Jack. 1982. *Cooking, Cuisine, and Class: A Study in Comparative Sociology*. New York: Cambridge University Press.

Gopnik, Adam. 2011. *The Table Comes First: Family, France, and the Meaning of Food*. New York: Knopf.

Gordon, Philip H., and Sophie Meunier. 2001. *The French Challenge: Adapting to Globalization*. Washington, DC: Brookings Institution Press.

Grant, Joshua I. 2009. "Hell to the Sound of Trumpets: Why Chicago's Ban on Foie Gras Was Constitutional and What It Means for the Future of Animal Welfare Laws." *Stanford Journal of Animal & Law Policy* 2: 53–112.

Gray, Margaret. 2014. *Labor and the Locavore: The Making of a Comprehensive Food Ethic*. Berkeley: University of California Press.

Grazian, David. 2003. *Blue Chicago: The Search for Authenticity in Urban Blues Clubs*. Chicago: University of Chicago Press.

Greene, Joshua. 2013. *Moral Tribes: Emotion, Reason, and the Gap between Us and Them*. New York: Penguin Press.

Griswold, Wendy. 1987. "A Methodological Framework for the Sociology of Culture." *Sociological Methodology* 17: 1–35.

———. (1994) 2013. *Cultures and Societies in a Changing World*. Thousand Oaks, CA: Sage.

Guémené, Daniel, and Gérard Guy. 2004. "The Past, Present and Future of Force-Feeding and 'Foie Gras' Production." *World's Poultry Science Journal* 60 (2): 210–22.

Guémené, Daniel, Gérard Guy, J. Noirault, M. Garreau-Mills, P. Gouraud, and Jean-Michel Faure. 2001. "Force-Feeding Procedure and Physiological Indicators of Stress in Male Mule Ducks." *British Poultry Science* 42 (5): 650–57.

Guérard, Michel. 1998. *Le jeu de l'oie et du canard*. France: Cairn.

Gusfield, Joseph R. 1981. *The Culture of Public Problems: Drinking-Driving and the Symbolic Order*. Chicago: University of Chicago Press.

———. (1963) 1986. *Symbolic Crusade: Status Politics and the American Temperance Movement*. 2nd ed. Urbana, IL: University of Illinois Press.

———. 1996. *Contested Meanings: The Construction of Alcohol Problems*. Madison, WI: University of Wisconsin Press.

Guthman, Julie. 2007. "Can't Stomach It: How Michael Pollan et al. Made Me Want to Eat Cheetos." *Gastronomica* 7 (3): 75–79.

———. 2011. *Weighing In: Obesity, Food Justice, and the Limits of Capitalism*. Berkeley: University of California Press.

Guy, Kolleen M. 2003. *When Champagne Became French: Wine and the Making of a National Identity*. Baltimore: Johns Hopkins University Press.

Haidt, Jonathan. 2001. "The Emotional Dog and Its Rational Tail: A Social

Intuitionist Approach to Moral Judgment." *Psychological Review* 108 (4): 814.

Hall, Stuart. 1992. "Questions of Cultural Identity." In *Modernity and Its Futures*, edited by S. Hall, D. Held, and A. McGrew. London: Polity Press.

Haraway, Donna. 1988. "Situated Knowledges: The Science Question in Feminism and the Privilege of Partial Perspective." *Feminist Studies* 14 (3): 575–99.

Harper, Gemma C., and Aikaterini Makatouni. 2002. "Consumer Perception of Organic Food Production and Farm Animal Welfare." *British Food Journal* 104: 287–99.

Harrington, Alexandra R. 2007. "Not All It's Quacked Up to Be: Why State and Local Efforts to Ban Foie Gras Violate Constitutional Law." *Drake Journal of Agricultural Law* 12: 303–24.

Healy, Kieran. 2006. *Last Best Gifts: Altruism and the Market for Human Blood and Organs*. Chicago: University of Chicago Press.

Heath, Deborah, and Anne Meneley. 2007. "Techne, Technoscience, and the Circulation of Comestible Commodities: An Introduction." *American Anthropologist* 109 (4): 593–602.

———. 2010. "The Naturecultures of Foie Gras: Techniques of the Body and a Contested Ethics of Care." *Food, Culture and Society* 13 (3): 421–52.

Held, David, and Anthony G. McGrew. 2007. *Globalization/Anti-Globalization: Beyond the Great Divide*. 2nd ed. Cambridge, UK: Polity.

Held, David, Anthony McGrew, David Goldblatt, and Jonathan Perraton. 1999. *Global Transformations: Politics, Economics and Culture*. Palo Alto, CA: Stanford University Press.

Heldke, Lisa. 2003. *Exotic Appetites: Ruminations of a Food Adventurer*. New York: Routledge.

Heller, Chaia. 1999. *Ecology of Everyday Life: Rethinking the Desire for Nature*. Montreal: Black Rose Books.

———. 2013. *Food, Farms, and Solidarity: French Farmers Challenge Industrial Agriculture and Genetically Modified Crops*. Durham, NC: Duke University Press.

Herzfeld, Michael. 2004. *The Body Impolitic: Artisans and Artifice in the Global Hierarchy of Value*. Chicago: University of Chicago Press.

Herzog, Hal. 2010. *Some We Love, Some We Hate, Some We Eat: Why It's So Hard to Think Straight about Animals*. New York: Harper.

Hewison, Robert. 1987. *The Heritage Industry: Britain in a Climate of Decline*. London: Methuen.

Hobsbawm, Eric, and Terence Ranger, eds. 1983. *The Invention of Tradition.* Cambridge, UK: Cambridge University Press.

Hochschild, Adam. 2006. *Bury the Chains: Prophets and Rebels in the Fight to Free an Empire's Slaves.* Boston: Houghton Mifflin.

Hoffman, Barbara T., ed. 2006. *Art and Cultural Heritage: Law, Policy, and Practice.* New York: Cambridge University Press.

Hollows, Joanne, and Steve Jones. 2010. "'At Least He's Doing Something': Moral Entrepreneurship and Individual Responsibility in Jamie's Ministry of Food." *European Journal of Cultural Studies* 13 (3): 307–22.

Holt, Douglas B. 2004. *How Brands Become Icons: The Principles of Cultural Branding.* Boston: Harvard Business School Press.

Hugues, Robert. 1982. *Le grand livre du foie gras.* Toulouse, France: Éditions Daniel Briand.

Inglis, David. 2005. *Culture and Everyday Life.* Abingdon, UK: Routledge.

Inglis, David, and Debra L. Gimlin, eds. 2009. *The Globalization of Food.* New York: Berg.

Inglis, David, and John Hughson. 2003. *Confronting Culture: Sociological Vistas.* Malden, MA: Polity Press.

Jacobs, Meg. 2005. *Pocketbook Politics: Economic Citizenship in Twentieth-Century America.* Princeton, NJ: Princeton University Press.

Jasper, James M. 1992. "The Politics of Abstractions: Instrumental and Moralist Rhetorics in Public Debate." *Social Research* 59 (2): 315–44.

———. 1997. *The Art of Moral Protest: Culture, Biography, and Creativity in Social Movements.* Chicago: University of Chicago Press.

———. 1999. "Recruiting Intimates, Recruiting Strangers: Building the Contemporary Animal Rights Movement." In *Waves of Protest: Social Movements Since the Sixties,* edited by J. Freeman and V. Johnson. Lanham, MD: Rowman & Littlefield.

Jasper, James M., and Dorothy Nelkin. 1992. *The Animal Rights Crusade: The Growth of a Moral Protest.* New York: Free Press.

Johnston, Josée. 2008. "The Citizen-Consumer Hybrid: Ideological Tensions and the Case of Whole Foods Market." *Theory and Society* 37 (3): 229–70.

Johnston, Josée, and Shyon Baumann. 2010. *Foodies: Democracy and Distinction in the Gourmet Foodscape.* New York: Taylor & Francis.

Johnston, Josée, and Michael K. Goodman. 2015. "Spectacular Foodscapes: Food Celebrities and the Politics of Lifestyle Mediation in an Age of Inequality." *Food, Culture & Society* 18 (2): 205–22.

Jullien, Bernard, and Andy Smith, eds. 2008. *Industries and Globalization: The*

Political Causality of Difference, Globalization and Governance. New York: Palgrave Macmillan.

Kahler, Susan C. 2005. "Farm Visits Influence Foie Gras Vote." *Journal of the American Veterinary Medical Association* 227 (5): 688–89.

Kahneman, Daniel. 2011. *Thinking, Fast and Slow.* New York: Farrar, Straus and Giroux.

Kamp, David. 2006. *The United States of Arugula: How We Became a Gourmet Nation.* New York: Broadway Books.

Kingsolver, Barbara, Steven L. Hopp, and Camille Kingsolver. 2007. *Animal, Vegetable, Miracle: A Year of Food Life.* New York: HarperCollins.

Kirshenblatt-Gimblett, Barbara. 1998. *Destination Culture: Tourism, Museums, and Heritage.* Berkeley: University of California Press.

Koopmans, Ruud. 2004. "Movements and Media: Selection Processes and Evolutionary Dynamics in the Public Sphere." *Theory and Society* 33 (3/4): 367–91.

Korsmeyer, Carolyn, ed. 2005. *The Taste Culture Reader: Experiencing Food and Drink.* New York: Berg.

Kowalski, Alexandra. 2011. "When Cultural Capitalization Became Global Practice: The 1972 World Heritage Convention." In Bandelj and Wherry 2011, 73–89.

Kuh, Patric. 2001. *The Last Days of Haute Cuisine.* New York: Viking.

Laachir, Karima. 2007. "France's 'Ethnic' Minorities and the Question of Exclusion." *Mediterranean Politics* 12 (1): 99–105.

Lakoff, George. 2006. *Whose Freedom?: The Battle over America's Most Important Idea.* New York: Farrar, Straus and Giroux.

Lamont, Michèle. 1992. *Money, Morals, and Manners: The Culture of the French and American Upper-Middle Class.* Chicago: University of Chicago Press.

Lamont, Michèle, and Marcel Fournier, eds. 1992. *Cultivating Differences: Symbolic Boundaries and the Making of Inequality.* Chicago: University of Chicago Press.

Lamont, Michèle, and Virag Molnar. 2002. "The Study of Boundaries in the Social Sciences." *Annual Review of Sociology* 28 (1): 167–95.

Lamont, Michèle, and Laurent Thévenot, eds. 2000. *Rethinking Comparative Cultural Sociology: Repertoires of Evaluation in France and the United States.* Cambridge, UK: Cambridge University Press.

La Pradelle, Michèle de. 2006. *Market Day in Provence.* Chicago: University of Chicago Press.

Laudan, Rachel. 2013. *Cuisine and Empire: Cooking in World History.* Berkeley: University of California Press.

Lavin, Chad. 2013. *Eating Anxiety: The Perils of Food Politics.* Minneapolis: University of Minnesota Press.

Lazareff, Alexandre. 1998. *L'exception culinaire française: Un patrimoine gastronomique en péril?* Paris: Éditions Albin Michel.

Leitch, Alison. 2003. "Slow Food and the Politics of Pork Fat: Italian Food and European Identity." *Ethnos: Journal of Anthropology* 68 (4): 437–62.

Lévi-Strauss, Claude. 1966. *The Savage Mind.* Chicago: University of Chicago Press.

Long, Lucy, ed. 2003. *Culinary Tourism.* Lexington, KY: University Press of Kentucky.

Lowe, Brian M. 2006. *Emerging Moral Vocabularies: The Creation and Establishment of New Forms of Moral and Ethical Meanings.* Lanham, MD: Lexington Books.

MacCannell, Dean. 1973. "Staged Authenticity: Arrangements of Social Space in Tourist Settings." *American Journal of Sociology* 79 (3): 589–603.

Mannheim, Karl. 1985. *Ideology and Utopia: An Introduction to the Sociology of Knowledge.* Edited by L. Wirth and E. Shils. San Diego, CA: Harcourt Brace.

Matza, David, and Gresham M. Sykes. 1961. "Juvenile Delinquency and Subterranean Values." *American Sociological Review* 26 (5): 712–19.

McCombs, Maxwell E., and Donald L. Shaw. 1993. "The Evolution of Agenda-Setting Research: Twenty-Five Years in the Marketplace of Ideas." *Journal of Communication* 43 (2): 58–67.

McMichael, Philip. 2012. *Development and Social Change: A Global Perspective.* 5th ed. Los Angeles: Sage.

Mennell, Stephen. 1985. *All Manners of Food: Eating and Taste in England and France from the Middle Ages to the Present.* New York: Basil Blackwell.

Merry, Sally Engle. 1998. "The Criminalization of Everyday Life." In Sarat, Constable, Engel, Hans, and Lawrence 1998, 14–39.

Meskell, Lynn. 2004. *Object Worlds in Ancient Egypt: Material Biographies Past and Present.* New York: Berg.

Meunier, Sophie. 2000. "The French Exception." *Foreign Affairs* 79 (4): 104–16.

———. 2005. "Anti-Americanisms in France." *French Politics, Culture & Society* 23 (2): 126–42.

Meunier, Sophie, and Kalypso Nicolaidis. 2006. "The European Union as a Conflicted Trade Power." *Journal of European Public Policy* 13 (6): 906–25.

Miller, Laura J. 2006. *Reluctant Capitalists: Bookselling and the Culture of Consumption*. Chicago: University of Chicago Press.

Mintz, Sidney W. 1985. *Sweetness and Power: The Place of Sugar in Modern History*. New York: Viking.

———. 2003. "Eating Communities: The Mixed Appeals of Sodality." In *Eating Culture: The Poetics and Politics of Food*, edited by T. Döring, M. Heide and S. Mühleisen. Heidelberg, Germany: Winter.

Myers, B. R. 2011. "The Moral Crusade against Foodies." *The Atlantic*, March.

Naccarato, Peter, and Kathleen LeBesco. 2012. *Culinary Capital*. New York: Berg.

Nagel, Thomas. 1974. "What Is It Like to Be a Bat?" *The Philosophical Review* 83 (4): 435–50.

Nelson, Barbara J. 1984. *Making an Issue of Child Abuse: Political Agenda Setting for Social Problems*. Chicago: University of Chicago Press.

Nestle, Marion. (2003) 2010. *Safe Food: The Politics of Food Safety*. 2nd ed. Berkeley: University of California Press.

Nora, Pierre. 1996. *Realms of Memory: Rethinking the French Past*. Translated by L. D. Kritzman. New York: Columbia University Press.

Nyhan, Brendan, and Jason Reifler. 2010. "When Corrections Fail: The Persistence of Political Misperceptions." *Political Behavior* 32 (2): 303–30.

Nyhan, Brendan, Jason Reifler, Sean Richey, and Gary L. Freed. 2014. "Effective Messages in Vaccine Promotion: A Randomized Trial." *Pediatrics* 133 (4): e835–42.

Ohnuki-Tierney, Emiko. 1993. *Rice as Self: Japanese Identities through Time*. Princeton, NJ: Princeton University Press.

Ollinger, Michael, James M. MacDonald, and Milton Madison. 2000. *Structural Change in U.S. Chicken and Turkey Slaughter*. Washington, DC: U.S. Department of Agriculture Economic Research Service.

Paxson, Heather. 2012. *The Life of Cheese: Crafting Food and Value in America*. Berkeley: University of California Press.

Pearlman, Alison. 2013. *Smart Casual: The Transformation of Gourmet Restaurant Style in America*. Chicago: University of Chicago Press.

Perrier-Robert, Annie. 2007. *Foie gras, patrimoine*. Ingersheim-Colmar, France: Dormonval.

Peterson, Richard A. 1997. *Creating Country Music: Fabricating Authenticity*. Chicago: University of Chicago Press.

———. 2005. "In Search of Authenticity." *Journal of Management Studies* 42 (5): 1083–98.

Pilcher, Jeffrey M. 1998. *¡Que Vivan los Tamales!: Food and the Making of Mexican Identity*. Albuquerque, NM: University of New Mexico Press.

Pollan, Michael. 2006. *The Omnivore's Dilemma*. New York: Penguin Press.

Potter, Andrew. 2010. *The Authenticity Hoax: How We Get Lost Finding Ourselves*. Toronto: McClelland & Stewart.

Prasad, Monica. 2005. "Why Is France So French? Culture, Institutions, and Neoliberalism, 1974–1981." *American Journal of Sociology* 111 (2): 357–407.

Prasad, Monica, Andrew J. Perrin, Kieran Bezila, Steve G. Hoffman, Kate Kindleberger, Kim Manturuk, and Ashleigh Smith Powers. 2009. "'There Must Be a Reason': Osama, Saddam, and Inferred Justification." *Sociological Inquiry* 79 (2): 142–62.

Rao, Hayagreeva, Philippe Monin, and Rodolphe Durand. 2005. "Border Crossing: Bricolage and the Erosion of Categorical Boundaries in French Gastronomy." *American Sociological Review* 70 (6): 968–91.

Regan, Tom. 1985. *The Case for Animal Rights*. Berkeley: University of California Press.

Rohlinger, Deana A. 2002. "Framing the Abortion Debate: Organizational Resources, Media Strategies, and Movement-Countermovement Dynamics." *The Sociological Quarterly* 43 (4): 479–507.

———. 2006. "Friends and Foes: Media, Politics, and Tactics in the Abortion War." *Social Problems* 53 (4): 537–61.

Rollin, Bernard E. 1981. *Animal Rights and Human Morality*. Buffalo, NY: Prometheus Books.

———. 1990. "Animal Welfare, Animal Rights and Agriculture." *Journal of Animal Science* 68 (10): 3456–61.

Rousseau, Signe. 2012. *Food Media: Celebrity Chefs and the Politics of Everyday Interference*. New York: Berg.

Ruhlman, Michael. 2007. *The Reach of a Chef: Professional Cooks in the Age of Celebrity*. Berkeley: University of California Press.

Saguy, Abigail. 2013. *What's Wrong with Fat?* New York: Oxford University Press.

Saguy, Abigail, and Forrest Stuart. 2008. "Culture and Law: Beyond a Paradigm of Cause and Effect." *The Annals of the American Academy of Political and Social Science* 619 (1): 149–64.

Sahlins, Peter. 1989. *Boundaries: The Making of France and Spain in the Pyrenees*. Berkeley: University of California Press.

Sarat, Austin, Marianne Constable, David Engel, Valerie Hans, and Susan Lawrence, eds. 1998. *Everyday Practices and Trouble Cases*. Vol. 2, *Funda-*

mental Issues in Law and Society Research. Evanston, IL: American Bar Foundation and Northwestern University Press.

Savage, William W. 1979. *The Cowboy Hero: His Image in American History & Culture*. Norman, OK: University of Oklahoma Press.

Schapiro, Randall. 2011. "A Shmuz about Schmalz—A Case Study: Jewish Law and Foie Gras." *Journal of Animal Law* 7: 119–45.

Schlosser, Eric. 2001. *Fast Food Nation: The Dark Side of the All-American Meal*. Boston: Houghton Mifflin.

Schmidt, Vivien Ann. 1996. *From State to Market? : The Transformation of French Business and Government*. New York: Cambridge University Press.

Scholliers, Peter, ed. 2001. *Food, Drink and Identity: Cooking, Eating and Drinking in Europe since the Middle Ages*. Oxford, UK: Berg.

Schor, Juliet. 1998. *The Overspent American: Upscaling, Downshifting, and the New Consumer*. New York: Basic Books.

Schudson, Michael. 1989. "How Culture Works: Perspectives from Media Studies on the Efficacy of Symbols." *Theory and Society* 18 (2): 153–80.

Schwalbe, Michael, Daphne Holden, Douglas Schrock, Sandra Godwin, Shealy Thompson, and Michele Wolkomir. 2000. "Generic Processes in the Reproduction of Inequality: An Interactionist Analysis." *Social Forces* 79 (2): 419–52.

Serventi, Silvano. 1993. *La grande histoire du foie gras*. Paris: Flammarion.

———. 2005. *Le foie gras*. Paris: Flammarion.

Shields-Argelès, Christy. 2004. "Imagining the Self and the Other: Food and Identity in France and the United States." *Food, Culture and Society* 7 (2): 14–28.

Singer, Peter. (1975) 2002. *Animal Liberation*. New York: Ecco.

Sklair, Leslie. 2002. *Globalization: Capitalism and Its Alternatives*. Oxford, UK: Oxford University Press.

Smith, Laurajane. 2006. *Uses of Heritage*. New York: Routledge.

Sohn, Doug, Graham Elliot, and Kate DeVivo. 2013. *Hot Doug's: The Book*. Chicago: Agate Midway.

Somers, Margaret R. 1994. "The Narrative Constitution of Identity: A Relational and Network Approach." *Theory and Society* 23 (5): 605–49.

Spang, Rebecca L. 2000. *The Invention of the Restaurant: Paris and Modern Gastronomic Culture*. Cambridge, MA: Harvard University Press.

Standage, Tom. 2006. *A History of the World in 6 Glasses*. New York: Walker & Company.

Steinberger, Michael. 2009. *Au Revoir to All That: Food, Wine, and the End of France*. New York: Bloomsbury.

Steinmetz, George, ed. 1999. *State/Culture: State-Formation after the Cultural Turn*. Ithaca, NY: Cornell University Press.

Stiglitz, Joseph E. 2002. *Globalization and Its Discontents*. New York: W. W. Norton.

Sutton, Michael. 2007. *France and the Construction of Europe, 1944–2007: The Geopolitical Imperative*. New York: Berghahn Books.

Tarrow, Sidney G. 1998. *Power in Movement: Social Movements and Contentious Politics*. 2nd ed. Cambridge, UK: Cambridge University Press.

Téchoueyres, Isabelle. 2001. "Terroir and Cultural Patrimony: Reflections on Regional Cuisines in Aquitaine." Anthropology of Food. http://aof.revues.org/1531.

———. 2007. "Development, Terroir and Welfare: A Case Study of Farm-Produced Foie Gras in Southwest France." Anthropology of Food. http://aof.revues.org/510.

Tepper, Steven J. 2011. *Not Here, Not Now, Not That!: Protest Over Art and Culture in America*. Chicago: University of Chicago Press.

Terrio, Susan J. 2000. *Crafting the Culture and History of French Chocolate*. Berkeley: University of California Press.

Toussaint-Samat, Maguelonne. 1992. *A History of Food*. Translated by A. Bell. Cambridge, MA: Blackwell.

———. 1994. "Foie Gras." In *A History of Food*, 2nd ed., edited by M. Toussaint-Samat. New York: Blackwell.

Trubek, Amy B. 2000. *Haute Cuisine: How the French Invented the Culinary Profession*. Philadelphia: University of Pennsylvania Press.

———. 2007. "Place Matters." In Korsmeyer 2007, 260–71.

———. 2008. *The Taste of Place: A Cultural Journey into Terroir*. Berkeley: University of California Press.

Vannier, Paul. 2002. *L'ABCdaire du foie gras*. Paris: Flammarion.

Veblen, Thorstein. (1899) 2007. *The Theory of the Leisure Class*. New York: Oxford University Press.

Wagner-Pacifici, Robin, and Barry Schwartz. 1991. "The Vietnam Veterans Memorial: Commemorating a Difficult Past." *American Journal of Sociology* 97 (2): 376–420.

Wallach, Jennifer Jensen. 2013. *How America Eats: A Social History of U.S. Food and Culture*. Lanham, MD: Rowman & Littlefield.

Warde, Alan. 1997. *Consumption, Food and Taste: Culinary Antinomies and Commodity Culture*. London: Sage.

Waters, Mary C. 1990. *Ethnic Options: Choosing Identities in America.* Berkeley: University of California Press.

Weber, Klaus, Kathryn Heinze, and Michaela DeSoucey. 2008. "Forage for Thought: Mobilizing Codes in the Movement for Grass-Fed Meat and Dairy Products." *Administrative Science Quarterly* 53 (3): 529–67.

Wechsberg, Joseph. 1972. "Foie Gras: La Vie en Rose." *Gourmet*, November.

Weiss, Allen S. 2012. "Authenticity." *Gastronomica: The Journal of Food and Culture* 11 (4): 74–77.

Wherry, Frederick F. 2006. "The Social Sources of Authenticity in Global Handicraft Markets: Evidence from Northern Thailand." *Journal of Consumer Culture* 6 (1): 5–32.

———. 2008. *Global Markets and Local Crafts: Thailand and Costa Rica Compared.* Baltimore: Johns Hopkins University Press.

———. 2012. *The Culture of Markets.* Malden, MA: Polity.

Wilde, Melissa J. 2004. "How Culture Mattered at Vatican II: Collegiality Trumps Authority in the Council's Social Movement Organizations." *American Sociological Review* 69 (4): 576–602.

Wilk, Richard R. 1999. "'Real Belizean Food': Building Local Identity in the Transnational Caribbean." *American Anthropologist* 101 (2): 244–55.

———, ed. 2006. *Fast Food/Slow Food: The Cultural Economy of the Global Food System.* Lanham, MD: Altamira Press.

Winter, Bronwyn. 2008. *Hijab and the Republic: Uncovering the French Headscarf Debate.* Syracuse, NY: Syracuse University Press.

Wolfert, Paula. (1983) 2005. *The Cuisine of Southwest France.* New York: Wiley.

Wuthnow, Robert. 1987. *Meaning and Moral Order: Explorations in Cultural Analysis.* Berkeley: University of California Press.

Youatt, Rafi. 2012. "Power, Pain, and the Interspecies Politics of Foie Gras." *Political Research Quarterly* 65 (2): 346–58.

Zelizer, Viviana. 1983. *Morals and Markets: The Development of Life Insurance in the United States.* New Brunswick, NJ: Transaction Books.

———. 1985. *Pricing the Priceless Child: The Changing Social Value of Children.* New York: Basic Books.

———. 2005. "Culture and Consumption." In *Handbook of Economic Sociology,* edited by N. J. Smelser and R. Swedberg. Princeton, NJ: Princeton University Press.

———. 2011. *Economic Lives: How Culture Shapes the Economy.* Princeton, NJ: Princeton University Press.

Zukin, Sharon. 1995. *The Cultures of Cities.* Cambridge, MA: Blackwell.

INDEX

Note: Page numbers followed by *f* indicate a figure.

PRINCETON STUDIES IN
CULTURAL SOCIOLOGY

Paul J. DiMaggio, Michèle Lamont,
Robert J. Wuthnow, and Viviana A. Zelizer,
Series Editors